VIOLENCE
AND PEACE

From the Atomic Bomb to
Ethnic Cleansing

PIERRE HASSNER

Translation by Jane Brenton

CENTRAL EUROPEAN UNIVERSITY PRESS

Budapest   London   New York

Published by
Central European University Press
1051 Budapest, Nádor utca 9, Hungary

Distributed by
Oxford University Press, Walton Street, Oxford OX2 6DP
Oxford New York Athens Auckland Bangkok Bombay
Calcutta Cape Town Dar es Salaam Delhi Florence Hong Kong
Istanbul Karachi Kuala Lumpur Madras Madrid Melbourne
Mexico City Nairobi Paris Singapore Taipei Tokyo Toronto
and associated companies in Berlin Ibadan
Distributed in the United States
by Oxford University Press Inc., New York

First published as *La Violence et la paix: De la bombe atomique au nettoyage ethnique*,
© 1995 Éditions Esprit

English translation copyright © CEU Press 1997

British Library Cataloguing in Publication Data
A CIP catalogue record for this book is available from the British Library

ISBN 1-85866-075-0 Hardback
ISBN 1-85866-076-9 Paperback

Library of Congress Cataloging in Publication Data
A CIP catalog record for this book is available from the Library of Congress

Typeset by Mayhew Typesetting, Rhayader, Powys, UK
Printed and bound in Great Britain by Biddles of Guildford, UK

Contents

Contents

Acknowledgments

A T THE RISK of taking this pile of yellowing papers altogether too seriously, I would like to dedicate their contents to seven people no longer among us. To my parents, victims more than I of the hardships inflicted by our century, who did everything they could to protect me from them. To Titu Devechi, my first political mentor, in Bucharest. To Raymond Aron, my master in international relations and in intellectual hygiene. To Richard Löwenthal and Jean Laloy who, the one by his generosity and passion and inexhaustible dialectic, and the other by his elevated insights and mental rigour, encouraged me to look beyond interstate relations. Finally, Allan Bloom, whose explosions of enthusiasm and indignation were a regular feature of my life over three decades, whose transatlantic roars of laughter helped me to a different view of politics as being somewhere between dirty jokes and philosophy.

Nor can I end without expressing warm thanks to my friends Joël Roman and Olivier Mongin, who succeeded in getting this volume off the ground and wringing the introduction from me, thus completing a task embarked on several times previously, notably by Janine Mossuz-Lavau and by Nicolas Baverez and Denis Olivennes. If I alone am responsible for the contents (although many of the ideas and expressions emerged from contact with them) they cannot avoid their share of the blame if the reader judges that these pages would have been better left to what Marx called the criticism of rats.

Finally, the English translation of these essays calls for a new series of thanks: to my dear friend Pauline Wickham, who was the driving force behind this enterprise, and to Jane Brenton, the translator, and Judith Ravenscroft, the editor, whose exceptional competence and devotion went beyond anything I could have hoped for.

The following acknowledgments must also be made:

Chapter 1 was first published in *International Affairs* (London), 70: 4 (October 1994), and is reproduced with permission.

Chapter 2 was first published as 'Force et Politique aujourd'hui', in *revue Défense Nationale* (December 1971).

Chapter 3 was first published as 'Violence, rationalité, incertitude: tendances apocalyptiques et iréniques dans l'étude des conflits internationaux', in *Revue française de science politique*, no. 6 (1964).

Chapter 4 was first published in *Survey*, 67 (April 1968).

Chapter 5 was first published as 'Nukleare Abschreckung in der Kontroverse: Die vier nationalen Debatten in den Vereinigten Staaten, der Bundesrepublik Deutschland, Grossbritannien und Frankreich', in Uwe Nerlich and Trutz Rendtorff (eds), *Nukleare Abschreckung – Politische und ethische Interpretation einer neuen Realität* (Baden-Baden: Nomos, 1989), pp. 57–101.

Chapter 6 is adapted from 'Le totalitarisme vue de l'Ouest', chapter 1 in *Totalitarismes*, ed. Guy Hermet, Pierre Hassner and Jacques Rupnik (Paris: Economica, 1984): published with the gracious authorization of the author and the publisher.

Chapter 7 was first published as 'Une notion insaisissable mais irremplaçable', in *Révision de l'histoire: totalitarismes, crimes et génocide nazi*, ed. Yannis Thanassekos et Heinz Wismann (Paris: Le Cerf, 1990); based on an address to a symposium on 'Communist totalitarianism and Nazi genocide', organized by the Auschwitz Foundation, Brussels, 3–5 November 1988.

Chapter 8 was first published as 'Nationalisme et relations internationales', in *Revue française de science politique*, no. 3 (1965).

Chapter 9 was first published as 'Culture and Society', in *The International Spectator* (Rome), 26: 1 (January–March 1991).

Chapter 10 was first published as 'Par delà le national et l'international: la dérision et l'espoir', in *Universalia 1993* (Paris: Encyclopædia Universalis).

Chapter 11 was first published as 'Vers un universalisme pluriel', in *Esprit* (December 1992).

Chapter 12 was first published as 'Le XXe siècle, la guerre et la paix', in *Pensée Politique*, 2 (Paris: Le Seuil/Gallimard, 1994).

Introduction

I T IS A STRANGE experience to reread texts written over a period of some thirty years, especially since, in the absence of a coherent body of published work, they constitute the sole written record of a lifetime's experiences and reflections.

First it is necessary to overcome once again a reluctance (diminishing, admittedly, as the moment for testaments and reckonings approaches) to tear oneself away from the Pascalian diversions of daily life in order to rake over the past and talk about oneself.[1] Next, one experiences a variety of reactions, all no doubt equally justified: a text is too diffuse, too repetitive, its argument is circular or, more accurately, describes a loop on the point of completion as it returns to its original starting point. It is that last impression I should like to develop a little further, derived as it may be in part from making this retrospective reconstruction, collecting texts inspired often by stray speculations, commissions or chance encounters. Such an impression would have been even more pronounced had we extended the span of this volume to include my earliest essays from the 1950s, examining Kant's views on war and peace, and those on Kant and Hegel written in 1963 for the *History of Political Philosophy* edited by Leo Strauss and Joseph Cropsey;[2] also, at the other end, an article on Rousseau and international relations to be published in 1996, and a text on the theory and practice of international relations with particular reference to the refugee problem, published in February 1995 in the periodical *Esprit*. There is a sense in which all those decades largely devoted to international relations appear to me now like a vast digression, taking me back not only to my early works on the history of political philosophy but also to the more fundamental experience in my youth of rootlessness, persecution and exile.

My oscillations between philosophy, the object of my university studies, and the analysis of international events, which has dominated my professional activity, between the East, where my childhood spanned one war and two totalitarian regimes, and the West which received and raised me, are of no conceivable interest except in so far as they occur within a dual dialectic, both historical and eternal, that links together the themes of this book: war, totalitarianism and nationalism, as well as, more generally, the search for identity and for the universal, the experience of violence and of peace.

The key to this volume lies in the parallels between the disillusionments experienced after 1945 and again after 1989, when, on the one hand, the collapse of Nazism and the end of the Second World War were followed by the emergence of communism and the flight to the West, and, on the other hand, the collapse of communism and the end of the Cold War were followed by the return of war and the horrors of ethnic cleansing in Yugoslavia; the return too of a sense of powerlessness, to halt the crime, to aid the victims or to shake the ignorance and indifference of a complacent West.

At the beginning of *Native Realm*, Czeslaw Milosz eloquently described the feelings of insecurity and fundamental vulnerability of which no Central/Eastern European can rid himself, and the difficulty of putting this across to a Westerner who has never known more than one national identity and one political regime. A bitter consolation, to belong for ever to the category described by Hannah Arendt as the most representative of the twentieth century, that of displaced persons. It can hardly be by chance that the great historical tragedies are mirrored in the minor vicissitudes of an individual life. A Romanian educated in France, a Frenchman of Romanian origin, a Jew educated in the Catholic religion, teacher at an American university in Italy twice a month for twenty years, interpreter of the East to the West, and of the West to the East in numerous international colloquia, torn since my Balkan childhood between a passion for current affairs and a longing for a truth that would transcend them again and again, disillusioned with metaphysical abstractions yet not tempted to replace them with those of sociology, neither a philosopher nor a journalist, eternally the author of texts somewhere between articles and books, incapable of immersing myself totally either in thought or action, I have always seen myself in some degree as displaced. I have always looked with envy at those whose origins or vocation had supplied them with a feeling of identity, of community or belonging, which I grievously lacked. At the same time, perhaps, my only vocation, my only form of belonging, was to remain faithful to those 'fallen angels' of the communist paradise described by Koestler and, more generally, to that 'community of the disturbed' referred to by Patocka, and to make my small personal disturbances echo the great disturbances of Europe itself and of the century.

If, in 1955, I deserted philosophy for international relations, it was also, and perhaps chiefly, because I wanted desperately to find out which would be the victor, totalitarianism or freedom, and because, following in the steps of Raymond Aron, I knew that at the time of the great schism this conflict could not be viewed apart from the confrontation between East and West. If the disturbances in Paris and Prague in 1968 woke me from my diplomatic/strategic sleep, certainly it is true that I wanted to make sense of events I had failed to predict, but it is also true that I was prepared for the unpredictable. In 'Violence, Rationality and Unpredictability' (1964), included here as chapter 3, I held out against a too calculated or static view of conflicts, arguing for the dynamic of the passions, the uncertainty that results from their confrontation with the efforts of political rationality to control them. In 'Nationalism and International Relations', written in 1965 (chapter 8), I foresaw the resurgence of nationalism. In that article, and also one written in 1967 on 'The Nation-State in the Nuclear Age' (chapter 4), from which I quote here, I made the point that the most striking characteristic of the present situation was

> a particular type of multidimensionality, or a particular combination of independence and interdependence, of separation and interaction. Dimensions that could be considered as indicators of each other because they used to be roughly inseparable in fact, or confused in analysis, must today be distinguished in a more systematic way because their discrepancy raises all kinds of paradoxes: this goes for deterrence and defence, for military force and diplomatic influence, for flexibility and security, etc. But, next to confusing them, the most dangerous error is to think that because they must be distinguished they are not related, or that because they do not automatically reinforce each other they are automatically contradictory.[3]

In 1965–7 I pursued this idea by devising an elementary grid applicable to the European situation. Notably in my two Adelphi Papers, *Change and Security in Europe*,[4] I proposed distinguishing three levels: that of the *system*, corresponding both to the bipolar equilibrium of deterrence and, in Europe, to the territorial division into two blocs; that of *states* searching for an independent foreign policy, following the French and Romanian initiatives of 1965; and that of *societies*, domestic and transnational, viewed either as structures or in terms of dynamics. I brought out the contrast between the tendency of the system towards rigidity, the states' quest for diplomatic flexibility, and, crucially but elusively, the evolution of societies, sometimes gradual and hidden, sometimes occurring in explosive outbursts (as was to be the case in 1968, in 1981 and again in 1989), as well as their reciprocal influences on one another. And I predicted that the major upheaval would not come about either as the result of the military superiority of one or other camp, or through negotiated disarmament, but at this third level.

From 1968 to 1989, my fundamental preocupation was with how long the waves of evolution and revolution in societies would be contained or repulsed by the system, and when they would finally begin to erode it or blow it apart. I was not so much interested in the diplomatic/strategic level (except when, as with Willy Brandt's *Ostpolitik*, it was based on the intuition that acceptance of the status quo would liberate forces more likely to challenge it than all the interstate posturings) as in these forces and the movements in which they were embodied: Eastern dissidence and the whole human-rights movement that culminated in Solzhenitsyn and Solidarity, the Portuguese revolution, Eurocommunism, pacifism.[5]

Almost invariably, I was critical of these movements for taking insufficient account either of the differences between political regimes or of the constraints of the strategic balance of power. But I almost always sympathized with the aspirations to which they gave voice, and the questions they asked I adopted as my own.

My attentiveness to these expressions of views from within society goes a long way towards explaining my participation in collective enterprises. These include the working group on relations between societies in Europe, set up in collaboration with Pierre Grémion within the framework of the Centre d'Etudes et de Recherche Internationales (CERI) as the Helsinki process was getting under way (resulting in the volume *Vents d'Est: vers l'Europe des etats de droit?*[6]); my work for organizations such as the Helsinki Federation for Human Rights and the Helsinki Citizens' Assembly and currently the committees on Vukovar–Sarajevo[7] and Kosovo; there is also my sympathy for the political circles usually called in France 'the second Left', my increasingly close association with the periodicals *Intervention* and *Esprit*, and finally my political position overall, which I have often defined as being against the bobos (the Bonapartists and the Bolsheviks) and for the lilis (the liberals[8] and the libertarians). For much those reasons, I have also concentrated increasingly on the eternal questions of political philosophy, as my writings during the mid-1980s on totalitarianism and the ethics of deterrence attest to.

At last came 1989, blowing away the totalitarian Soviet empire, and along with it the Cold War and a divided Europe – not only the straitjacket that restricted the continent's development but also the conceptual framework within which development could be measured. It was the victory of processes over structures, but hence also the triumph of uncertainty as to the respective power and possible combinations of the forces analysed in this volume, violence and rationality, totalitarianism and nationalism, liberty and peace. The uncertainties surrounding that conjunction of forces make us aware also of uncertainties, eternal but previously hidden or suppressed, surrounding our own fundamental conceptions of politics and history. At each step, the observer finds himself confronted with fresh paradoxes: the precariousness of totalitarian power and the persistence of its effects on the societies of the East; the decline of the nation-state and the rise of nationalism; the fact that peace is less impossible than during the Cold War and war less unlikely; that apparently intractable conflicts are in the course of being resolved or at least contained, in Africa or the Middle East, while war and genocide are returning to the European continent; that the West is victorious but paralysed, fixated on an imaginary enemy yet inactive in the face of real horrors, the media promoting solidarity while manipulating events, civic life and democracy, the nation and Europe, prey both to globalization and internal crises of identity, confrontation and the combined power of money and violence, in a situation of political disorientation and incoherence.

My interventions in the past five years are marked by two things, a certain confidence that simplifications are inappropriate, whether euphoric or catastrophic in nature, and also a considerable uncertainty about the answers to the really decisive questions. On the one hand, in the winter of 1989–90, I expressed fears that the coming together of the two Germanys and the two Europes would end in mutual disappointment, and I suggested that in the East enthusiasm for Western capitalism as the successor to communism would be followed by a third phase, which might lead, variously, to a sort of primitive fascism, xenophobic and populist, a return to the communists, if not communism as such, or to social democracy doing its best to reconcile the market with social protection, openness to Europe and the rediscovery of the state.[9] In the same way, when asked by the European Strategy Group, of which I have been a member for the past ten years, to apply to the post-Cold-War period the sort of predictive analysis of change and security in Europe which I undertook in the 1960s, I could only declare my inability to do so – although with a tinge of irony directed at premature initiatives to construct an 'architecture of European unity' – mere castles in the air built, like the various subsequent diplomatic initiatives for settling the Yugoslav conflict, on the shifting sands of an anarchic or revolutionary reality.[10]

I went on to criticize Francis Fukuyama's unilateral projections of the end of history[11] and those of Samuel Huntington on the conflict between civilizations.[12] But all these critical articles ended in question marks. In the same way, when I invented the slogan, 'We are moving towards a new middle ages', in *Le Monde* (27 October 1992), my point was precisely to underline the ambiguities inherent in the proliferation of allegiances and tendencies towards refeudalization, to refuse to make a choice between idyllic or apocalyptic simplifications. Finally and most importantly, articles like 'Beyond the Three Traditions' and 'Beyond Nationalism and Internationalism', included here (chapters 1 and 10), are attempts at synthesis that end in doubts and objections, so bringing us back to the very tensions that inspired the structure and development of this book.

First, the current manifestations of war and peace bring us back to the eternal problem of violence. The grip – in Europe especially – of the Cold War, often summed up in the expression 'neither peace nor war', has been succeeded by a no less paradoxical situation in which, in the developed Western world, traditional war over territory has become absolutely unthinkable, and societies are dominated by individualism and the economy, but where, on the same continent, actual war rages, in the name of territorial claims based on history or ethnicity. That latter variety of warfare may be seen as a return to the tradition of national conflicts or imperial wars of succession, but the former represents something entirely new in the history of the planet. The temptation is to look for the explanation in the separation that exists between two polarized worlds: for some, that opposition would lie between 'the empire and the new barbarians',[13] the centre and the periphery; others see it as between states that have achieved prosperity and stability, that have gone beyond history, and those that have not yet come to the end of the painful road towards a time when conflict has been rendered superfluous. But that is to forget that conflict and its concomitant violence are also attached to immigration, drugs, social disintegration, the gratuitous violence that lies at the very heart of the 'pacified' world, to the extent indeed that Enzensberger has talked of a civil war that exists at both the global and molecular levels,[14] and Robert Kaplan has drawn the parallel with the African model of states and frontiers withering away under the combined effect of epidemics and ethnic confrontations.[15] A synthesis of the two views might

6

consist in observing that a 'secession of the privileged' is taking place within developed societies and towns as well as in the international sphere, with a growing polarity between pleasant areas guarded by the police or private militias and no-go areas. The contrast of 'walled city' and 'borderless world'[16] would appear to be the most universally valid, a fact that should make us examine the reciprocal relationship between violence and social marginalization.

In any case, it becomes increasingly clear that if we are to understand the relationship between war and politics, we need to expand our idea of both of these. Not so much nuclear war as violence, not diplomacy but the crisis of democratic society — that should be our general drift.

The first stage is to make the point that the post-Cold-War, although it does not, as some have suggested, automatically usher in the 'post-nuclear age', does put into question the idea that the strategic significance of nuclear weapons is exhausted by the concept of deterrence, and especially the idea that enjoys widespread support in France, that the very notion of deterrence spells the end of the possibility of war. Today, when we think of nuclear weapons, we think of proliferation rather than deterrence, we refer at least as often to the dangers of terrorism or accident as to the abstract logic, or theology, of strategy. At the very least, the latter loses its pre-eminent position and becomes one factor among many, alongside arms or drugs trafficking, the disintegration of the Soviet Union and the confrontation with mafias and fanatical groupings.

The second stage follows: not only should the theory of nuclear war (or non-war) be reintegrated with that of war as such, but interstate war itself should be seen — at least during this time of disintegration and disputes over the reconstitution of territorial units — as a particular, or perhaps exceptional, case of armed conflicts as a whole. In a recent article, Gareth Evans, Australian Minister of Foreign Affairs and a member of the Carnegie Commission on the Prevention of Deadly Conflict, noted that the majority of today's conflicts take place within state boundaries, and he quoted the astonishing figure of 29 out of 32 in 1992.[17] One may dispute the actual figures, as many conflicts are civil wars for one of the parties and interstate wars for the other, and the category they belong to may change because of the outcome of the confrontation and the verdict of the 'international community'; the general trend, however, is not in doubt.

Another piece of data from the same source is yet more striking and significant, and could indeed serve as the epigraph for this collection of essays. From the beginning of the twentieth century to 1987, according to Rudolph Rummel's estimate in the *Journal of Peace Research*, some 151 million people have been killed by governments, and that is over and beyond the victims of war and civil war (almost 39 million). An overwhelming majority of these killings were perpetrated by governments against their own citizens. Totalitarian states were responsible for at least 84 per cent of these deaths, authoritarian states for most of the remainder. The democracies are answerable for no more than a relatively small proportion (although the absolute figures are high).[18]

Here again, let us not rely too much on figures and classifications, which are always debatable. Nor should we embark on a discussion (tackled at some length in chapter 1) of the peaceful nature of democracies or the hidden institutional or structural violence on which the liberal societies are based.[19] Let us instead stress one crucial fact: neither wars, nor injustice and inequality, are twentieth-century inventions; what is new is, on the one hand, the way war has lost its significance for the liberal societies and, on the other hand, the over- whelming reality of the Shoah, the Gulag, Auschwitz, the Moscow show trials, the systematic killing frenzy that erupts at the heart of modernity to seek the root-and-branch elimination of what is alien: in other words, genocide and totalitarianism. This leads us inevitably to the third stage in the expansion of our ideas of war and politics, and also to the third section of this volume.

Where totalitarianism is concerned, the current state of affairs presents us with the old familiar themes, while raising the question whether new variations are likely. Does the crumbling of the Soviet Union, accomplished more or less peacefully, invalidate or confirm the notion of totalitarianism? Did it perish along with the other great all- inclusive ideologies or might it be reborn in other forms, as for example a media-based pluto-populism? Declining communist regimes, ex-communist regimes converted to nationalism, Islamic fundamentalism, can all these be called totalitarian? These are problems I hope to address at a later date,[20] but the two essays in this book dealing with totalitarianism contain the outlines of a debate that seems to me highly topical, and also supplies the necessary transition to the final sections of this book. It concerns the relations of the universal and the particular.

The immediate relevance of this debate centres on the question whether communist totalitarianism was defeated by the universal attraction of democratic ideas or, more prosaically, the attractions of the modern consumer society, or, on the other hand, because of the enduring nature of national cultures or identities. But that question is inseparable from two others, one relating to the past – does not the concept of totalitarianism mask the fundamental opposition between the universalist inspiration of Marxism and the racist inspiration of Nazism? – and the other relating to the future, which inquires into the nature of future forms of combination or polarity as between *Gesellschaft* (competitive, rationalized universal society) and *Gemeinschaft* (particularist, affective community).

I am careful to make no claim to resolving any of these three questions. I wish merely to point out the dangers of making too simplistic an opposition between universality and identity. As long ago as 1965, in an article entitled 'Nationalism and international relations' (chapter 8), I pointed out the convergence between universalist (and militant) nationalism, of which Nazism is an extreme example, and nationalist universalism, as represented by revolution adopted or enacted by a single country. More recently, in a brilliant piece of argument, a much more detailed case has been made by K. Minogue and B. Williams that

> nationalism, as an ideology, is ultimately no less universalistic than communism itself. It is basically the doctrine that all conflict comes from imperialism, that is, the dominance of one nation over another, and that the condition of universal peace would be the establishment of entirely homogeneous nation-states. Such a conception is no less visionary than that of the ultimate communist unity of mankind; nor is it in actuality more particularist than communism, since what communists seek must be achieved through the victory of a highly particularist proletariat, led by a particular avant-garde. More fully understood, then, *both* these doctrines (like all ideologies) will be found to be compositions of both universal and particular.[21]

That should not dissuade us – indeed rather the contrary – from seeking to establish the different proportions that exist in each, from distinguishing like P.-A. Taguieff, for example, between forms of racism (and antiracism) that are universalist and those that are differentialist, and between civic and ethnic concepts of nationhood. But it should prevent us from positing a radical opposition between defensive nationalism as a good, and offensive nationalism as an evil, between the good civic nation and the evil ethnic nation. Offensive and defensive, civic and ethnic, come together in a variety of complex dialectical relations; civic purification by ideological terror may precede ethnic purification, or the two may exist in combination, as with the Khmer Rouge. The crucial factor, it would seem, is to avoid both arbitrary exclusions and destructive combinations, not to let the demands of the universal, and the reality of interpenetration, cloud the need for respect of particular communities; and equally, not to let these latter become immured in their selfish isolation, forgetting that openness and solidarity can be the condition of identity, and shared risk the condition of peace. For the rest, modern man as a political being is condemned to steer his course between the acceptance of a heterogeneity and complexity he finds intolerable and the search for a simplicity and stability that are unattainable.[22] Nor, as a philosophical being, can he either divest himself of his particularity or renounce the quest for a universal that will remain for ever out of reach.

PART ONE

VIOLENCE AND RATIONALITY

1

Beyond the Three Traditions: The Philosophy of War and Peace in Historical Perspective

'Why is there no international relations theory?'

I T IS TO Martin Wight's everlasting credit that the question he asked several decades ago is still with us. Yet a fresh look at it is made all the more necessary by the puzzling and paradoxical turn that the question of war and peace has taken in our time, particularly in the years since the fall of the Berlin Wall. In concluding his review of the three traditions – the realists, the rationalists and the revolutionists – Martin Wight discerns a dominant trend: the erosion of rationalism and the triumph of realism.[1] Yet, in the world of nuclear deterrence and of social and economic interdependence, one may well argue that, on the one hand, new restraints such as those favoured by the rationalist or Grotian school are imposed, at least upon nuclear power, by the necessity of survival; and that, on the other hand, the power of nation-states to control their societies and to pursue their foreign interests is being hampered by transnational trends which they find more and more difficult to manage, or even to understand. More than a world community, as aimed at by revolutionists, we have a world of rival nation-states; but more than an old-fashioned game of power politics, as described by the realist school, we have a world of turbulence where mass communication, financial networks, popular explosions constantly interfere with the calculations of diplomats and soldiers, a world where ambiguity and unpredictability seem to reign supreme.

What, then, have the three traditions of thought about the relations between states to tell us about such a world? Perhaps their respective teachings are more relevant today, after the end of the Cold War,

13

in the sense that peace and war may be resuming their historical meaning. The formula for the Cold War was 'neither war nor peace'; or, to use Raymond Aron's well-known formulation, dating from 1947 and reconfirmed on the eve of his death in 1983, 'peace impossible, war unlikely'.[2] Real peace was impossible, because of the bipolar ideological antagonism; actual war was unlikely because of the risk of escalation and of mutual nuclear destruction.

Today, peace has become less impossible, since the disappearance of the Soviet empire and of the global East–West confrontation, but war has become rather less improbable. To put it another way, a third world war may have become even less likely, but local wars have become not only more likely but more prevalent. The formula for the post-Cold-War world may, instead of 'neither war not peace', rather be 'both war and peace'. Indeed, this formula is illustrated on the European continent itself, where, in the West, people have eliminated the very possibility of war from their daily concerns and yet where, a few hundred miles to the southeast, a genuine bloody war with 200,000 casualties is raging, But this is only one – if perhaps the most significant – of the paradoxical combinations made possible by the end of the Cold War.

On paper, one could distinguish six possible successors to the situation of 'neither war nor peace'. First, there was the hope that the Cold War would be followed by a real peace. It would be based, in one version, upon a change in the structure of the international system: this would be the long-awaited coming of 'collective security' under the label of 'the new international order' or of cooperative security based on the Conference on Security and Cooperation in Europe (CSCE) or on a revival of the United Nations. At about the same time, that is between 1989 and 1991, another version of the advent of peace arose in the form of Fukuyama's 'end of history' based less on any international mechanism than on the fundamental ideological, social and economic transformation represented by the victory of the market and of liberal democracy.[3]

Fairly soon, international events shifted the trend in thinking in two other directions, having more to do with war, or at least with conflict, than with peace. One was the return to the old world of interstate rivalries, to the collapse and re-emergence of empires and of nations: from Sarajevo to Sarajevo. The other was a new bipolarity, North against South instead of East against West, or 'the West against the rest'. It could be seen, in Samuel Huntington's terms, as the clash of civilizations.[4] According to him, the nineteenth century witnessed the conflict of nations, the twentieth the conflict of ideologies; the twenty-first will bear the mark of the conflict of civilizations or of religions (the two notions being somehow treated as synonymous).

Nobody could deny that each of these four visions contains some element of truth. But nobody could claim that any one of them is true to the complexity of the present situation. This is why the two most plausible versions, in my view, return to the mixture of war and peace which characterized the Cold War, but in different combinations.

The first, well expressed in the book by Max Singer and Aaron Wildavsky, *The Real World Order*, generalizes or extrapolates from the situation I described above for Europe.[5] The world is divided into two parts: one, that of the comparatively free, comparatively prosperous and comparatively peaceful democracies, has become a 'security community' or a 'peace zone', where war is no longer an instrument of politics; the other, consisting of the rest of the world, is hopelessly entangled in war, poverty and disorder resulting either in anarchy or in local or regional hegemonies. This stark opposition has much in common both with Fukuyama's vision (he would say that the first group is experiencing the end of history while the second is still in the midst of it) and with Huntington's (since the 'peace zone' corresponds, roughly, to the West). But Fukuyama would maintain that the rest of the world will eventually follow the lead of the West out of history, and Huntington would stress the conflict between the two worlds and, in particular, the threat that the second, essentially represented by Islamic fundamentalism, raises for the first. By contrast, the point of the Singer–Wildavsky thesis is the relative separation of the two worlds, and the fact that the first should neither feel too threatened by the second nor harbour too many illusions about solving its problems through aid, intervention or peacekeeping. But it is precisely this isolation which seems very hard to maintain in an age of mass communications, of mass migrations, of the free movement of capital, of drugs and of weapons, when the Third World and its rootless, its homeless and its lawless are present in the heart of the cities of the developed world.

It is only natural, then, that besides the two-worlds model the opposite one should have emerged: that of universal interpenetration, universal anarchy and universal hostility; or, to quote the German writer Hans Magnus Enzensberger, a civil war which is both global and molecular.[6] Enzensberger brings together Los Angeles and Sarajevo, xenophobic violence and organized crime, tribal warfare and uncontrolled urban strife. To him, the diffusion of violence may be the price we pay for the decline of interstate war; conflicts may no longer be ideological, but nationalism and ethnicity, racism and fanaticism are only very thin rationalizations for a raw hatred and violence which is directed against oneself as much as against the foreigner or 'the other' as such. Its ultimate source may have to be sought in the nature of modern society or in that of humankind itself.

What, then, are we to do with these partly conflicting and partly complementary interpretations? Or, to come back to Martin Wight, where are the three traditions now that we need them? It appears that the exit from the Cold War has made them even harder to apply but that we need even more to look at the prospects for war and peace in the light of reflections about the nature and history of man and society.

To find a guiding thread in this enquiry, we may do worse than use a classification which complements that of the three traditions: I refer to the 'three images' introduced in the literature around the same time by Kenneth Waltz in *Man, the State and War*.[7] Waltz distinguishes, among philosophers, those from St Augustine to Freud who see the causes of war in the nature of man; those who see them in the nature of the political or of the social and economic regime, for whom war comes from monarchic or military rule or from capitalism, and for whom peace will be brought about by democracy, or by modern commercial or industrial society, or by the end of class struggle; and those for whom the ultimate cause of war lies in the anarchic structure of the international system, in the absence of a world government and the plurality of states which makes war possible even between perfectly peaceful people and societies. I shall start from Waltz's third image, from the plurality of states, and examine the interplay between their mutual relations and the evolution of domestic and transnational societies. Indeed, it would be hard to do otherwise, for, it seems to me, it is precisely this phenomenon of the plurality of states which constitutes a deeply disturbing puzzle for political philosophers and social reformers alike.

It is probably not by chance that, in the history of philosophy as well as of ideologies, international relations occupies an embarrassingly discreet and modest place. Somehow it always seems to be sacrificed, or a victim of a hostile fate. Perhaps one would be closer to answering Martin Wight's question 'Why is there no international relations theory?' if one knew why Jean-Jacques Rousseau never wrote the second part of the *Contrat social*, which was supposed to deal with international relations and to contain the key to his whole enterprise; or why Marx never finished *Das Kapital*, whose last book was also supposed to contain the international dimension. In the works of Hobbes and Locke as well as Plato and Aristotle, international relations figures almost like a postscript or an afterthought, but one which, according to the author himself, is liable to put his whole project into question. For the thinker, the legislator or the statesman who is trying to promote the virtue or the freedom of citizens, the justice or harmony of the city, the external environment raises an ever recurrent and never quite soluble problem. Whether through the corrupting influences of commerce and immigration, or through the risk of military invasion and the necessity of defence, the problem is the same for the Platonic republic or for the Stalinist 'socialism in one country': ties with foreign lands trouble the unity of the body politic and the exclusive loyalty of its citizens; the needs of defence force a change of priorities concerning not only budgets but also political and social structures, as well as moral and legal rules. The imperatives of survival tend to replace those of the good life; the city risks being dominated by those who defend it, or having to imitate those who threaten it and whom it would like to avoid. This is Machiavelli's problem: can one be good in a world where everyone else is bad? In another way, it is the problem Rousseau raises for his Polish friends: should we accept conquest rather than risk losing our identity in the process of defending it? It is the problem of the sizes of states, raised, after the Greeks, by Montesquieu and, in a more acute from still, by Rousseau: if it is small, a republic risks losing its existence; if it is big, it risks losing its reasons for existing. In one case, it risks becoming the victim of external war; in the other, it risks becoming the victim of domestic discord.

The pursuit of loneliness

There are two solutions, then, if one wants to be left alone (and virtuous) in peace: either to withdraw from the world or, conversely, to absorb it. These correspond to the isolated community on the one hand and to the universal empire on the other. One may be tempted, in Hegelian fashion, to read into their succession a coincidence of the logical and the chronological order: the Greek city-state would be the thesis, the Roman and medieval empire would be the antithesis and the modern nation-state would be the synthesis. Let us not forget, however, that the temptation of withdrawing into isolation and that of launching a crusade or seeking world domination exist in every period including our own; that American policy has traditionally swung between the wish to escape the rivalries and compromises of the old continent and the wish to 'make the world safe for democracy'; and that twentieth-century totalitarianism has as often taken the shape of small states seized by a passion for unity and purity, which leads them to withdraw from the world and to turn their frenzy inward (in the Cambodian or Albanian style), as it has that of expansionist empires. The fact remains that, on the level of political philosophy, it is in the dialogue of Plato, Aristotle and Thucydides that the ideal of peace through the closed community has been developed both for their time and for ever. The same goes for Dante and the struggle between Pope and Emperor over the idea of peace through universal order, and for Montesquieu and Rousseau and for the American dialogue between Federalists and anti-Federalists over the dilemmas and compromises of the big modern republics.

In the first book of the *Laws*, Plato considers the notion that all cities are by nature in a state of mutual war, and he extends it to the notion that every man may be an enemy for every other man and that, in private life, every individual man would be one unto himself. But this threefold parallelism contains a fundamental duality. The correspondence between the parts of the soul and the parts of the city is the guiding thought of *The Republic*. For Plato, like, later, for Rousseau, discord within each of them is the greatest evil; conversely, the aim of politics is to establish a peace which can be found only in a harmony based on justice, the latter being essentially hierarchical. But this unity and this hierarchy cannot be found in relations among cities. Between them, peace can only be negative, it consists in avoiding not only war but interpenetration which would disturb interior unity. This is why the platonic city will cultivate, through a 'noble lie', the myth of autochthony, or of a difference in nature between its citizens and other men, it will be far from the sea, and will discourage travel and contacts with foreigners, which will be reserved for ambassadors and philosophers.

Aristotle criticizes Plato's excessive insistence upon domestic unity and external isolation; but the basic idea that the end of the city is virtue and that what makes it a city, beyond the reciprocity of interests, is *philia*, friendship or trust among citizens, still points to a city of reduced size which should live for peace but give a central, though not supreme, place in the education of its citizens to the preparation for war.

Hence there is a double-sided problem, which will reappear with Rousseau. On the one hand, in terms of political education, the dream of philosophers, from the *Republic* to *The Government of Poland*, seems to be to create a kind of chauvinistic Robinson Crusoe: citizens should live in isolated cities, should have no external ambitions and should not have to fight, but their sense of citizenship and their patriotic virtue, which are indispensable for their individual perfection and for the interior order of the city, should imply a belief in the latter's superiority and some hostility towards foreigners, even though this hostility and these martial virtues would not in fact find occasion to be applied. The superiority of peace would find its expression in philosophic life, but political life would be that of warriors without war.

The other side of the coin is that precisely these warlike virtues always end up by finding a role in spite of themselves, for the isolation of the city can never be either total or perpetual. Whether through communications or commerce, through migrations or through war, it will always tend to be reabsorbed by the environment from which it has tried to get away. Of course, this absorption, in turn, is not necessarily complete or final. The example of Poland and, more generally, the perpetual rebirth of ethnic or national identities despite the weakness both of their material and of their historical bases, show that the need for affirming their continuity and their difference can enable communities to survive against all odds. Besides, there is a principle (invoked ever since the Greeks and emphasized by Montesquieu and Rousseau as much as by today's federalists) that would enable city-states to resist empires or small states to defend their existence before big ones: this is the notion of federations or confederations, which would combine the inner cohesion of small communities and the external (at least defensive) power of big states. But there is always the danger of sliding either into anarchy or into centralization. Federations and confederations can survive only within an unstable and shifting equilibrium which is constantly faced with the problems of plurality, with its conflicts and compromises, which the separate community was precisely supposed to avoid.

There are analogous difficulties in the opposite direction, that of universal empire. For Augustine, it is the city of God, as the city of real peace, based on order and justice. The earthly city is that of passions and discord, hence of war. The world of states seems to alternate between the two; but its justice is relative and formal, its peace is inseparable from war and from sin. The just wars of which St Augustine is the first theoretician, the human peaces he envisages, are based on the multiplicity of political units. The separation of the spiritual and the secular realms, even though attenuated by later Christian thinkers, dominates the middle ages with the conflict of Pope and Emperor. But it is combined, within the secular realm itself, with the separation of nations or states. Even Dante's *imperium mundi* is a *communitas communitatum*: the emperor would exercise his authority over principalities and republics, not upon their subjects directly. Even more clearly, later legal and theological constructions, such as those of Vittoria and Suarez, combine the idea of the community of all people, of *civitas maxima* or *societas humana*, with a plurality of states, which have to be regulated and brought together in exceptional cases.

Neither the unity of Christendom not the appeal to natural law as a basis for *jus gentium* can ignore multiplicity: there is no cosmopolitanism without interstate relations, hence without rivalry or conflict. With the Reformation, secession is introduced within the spiritual realm itself and it is, on the contrary, the secular realm, with the emergence of the secular and sovereign state, which appears as *defensor pacis*, to use Marsilius of Padua's expression, and puts an end to religious wars. But the sovereign state, while a defender of domestic peace, is at the same time an international warmonger, since the appeasement of civil strife through state sovereignty and territorial division legitimizes, by the same token, external rivalries and interstate conflicts.

We are back, then, with this 'mixed state' which was to be denounced by Rousseau and from which the dreams of community, whether isolated or universal, had vainly tried to escape. The period between the end of the seventeenth century and the beginning of the nineteenth, between Hobbes and Hegel, is the one when it was made a central theme of political thought through the opposition between the civil, or legal, state within states and the state of nature among them.

The author who has expressed most eloquently the central consequence for human life and for political philosophy of this opposition is Rousseau:

> The first thing I notice, in considering the condition of the human species, is an open contradiction in its constitution, which causes it to vacillate incessantly. As individual men, we live in a civil state subject to law, as people we each enjoy a natural liberty; this makes our position fundamentally worse than if these distinctions were unknown. For living simultaneously in the social order and in the state of nature, we are subjected to the inconvenience of both, without finding security in either: in the mixed condition in which we find ourselves, whichever system we prefer, making too much or too little of it, we have achieved nothing and are in the worst state of all. That, it seems to me, is the true origin of public disasters.[8]

How, asks Rousseau, can the philosopher or the citizen rest satisfied with the peace and justice established by the civil order, when, lifting his eyes, he sees 'everywhere the face of death and agony. So this is the fruit of these peaceful institutions. Pity and indignation rise from the bottom of my heart. Barbarous philosopher! Come and read us your book on the field of battle!'[9]

What, then, should the philosopher do, as he is caught in the middle of this virtual or real battlefield of the international environment? Three directions are possible. The first consists in, so to speak, settling down on the battlefield and basing his thinking not on peace but on war, not on the idea of the good society but on the reality of the struggle for power. The second consists in trying to beautify the battlefield, to transform the battle into a rite, a game or a sport, by submitting it to rules and to limits through law and through voluntary and reciprocal cooperation between states. The third consists in hoping that the 'old mole' of history will dig a tunnel under the battlefield. It tries to overcome the conflicts of states neither by suppressing their plurality nor by trying to convince them to adopt other rules of behaviour, but by shifting the ground of their rivalry through social, technological, cultural or even anthropological change, uncovered by the philosophy of history.

From war to international politics

The first direction is illustrated by the three greatest thinkers on war, none of whom is a philosopher in the technical or classical sense: Thucydides, Machiavelli and Clausewitz. All three start not from the problem of order but from that of action.

Thucydides' narration is based on the polarity of movement and rest: it is centred on the former but its melancholic tone indicates a preference for moderation, always in danger of being overwhelmed by passions or by chance. By contrast, Machiavelli delights in emphasizing the primacy of movement over rest, of the extreme case over the normal one, of daring over prudence, or virtue over *fortuna*. By showing the violent origins hidden behind peaceful laws and orders, he does not praise violence and war as such but he delegitimizes all the barriers which might disqualify them as paths towards the most powerful and noble passion: the desire for individual or collective domination and glory.

Clausewitz's thought is dominated more by the tension between violence and reason, between war and politics, both in theory and in practice. Two things are certain. First, as Raymond Aron has forcefully demonstrated, Clausewitzian thought is the opposite of militarism and bellicism, since it emphasizes the primacy of politics over war. But, on the other hand, his definition of politics itself does not go beyond 'the intelligence of the personified state' and the importance of 'moral forces'. It is set within the framework of the competition (whether peaceful or violent) between states; it does not go beyond it to raise the question of the legitimate domestic or international order, or to question the institution of war itself.

This same ambiguity and this same prudence are to be found in the European tradition of reason of state, or *Realpolitik*, or in the American realist school. They disappear when the Clausewitzian formula is turned on its head, and politics becomes the continuation of war by other means, when, with Treitschke and the German nineteenth-century tradition, one proclaims the primacy of foreign policy, or, with the American Social Darwinists, the primacy of the struggle for life and the 'survival of the fittest'. But even then the idea of regulating the struggle through balance and reciprocity is not necessarily thrown overboard.

From power politics to international society

This regulation is, by contrast, at the centre of the second way out of the battle, what Martin Wight called the rationalist school, which emphasizes the notion of international society. Of course, this points not to a world community but to a society of states, which accept a number of rules in their mutual relations and collaborate in the functioning of a number of institutions aimed, in particular, at the limitation of war. The sources of the conventions aiming at limiting war are manifold. One could mention the Christian doctrine of the 'just war', with its imperatives of discrimination and proportionality. Its trace is still present in Grotius, as well as in that other aspect of traditional doctrine, that of 'just cause'; war may be aimed at punishing the guilty party in a conflict, in the name of a universal duty of solidarity. But with Pufendorf, Wolff or Vattel, the centre of conceptions such as international society and the limitation of war moves from the idea of justice towards the notions of balance and reciprocity, from the Christian or human community towards the sovereignty of states, from the cause towards the means, from the *jus ad bellum* towards the *jus in bello*. War becomes a juridical state which occupies a place in the international system symbolized by the Treaty of

Westphalia and based on the territoriality and sovereignty of states. Order becomes synonymous with equilibrium; the codification and limitation of war are based on its legitimation.

But this order and equilibrium are precisely what is being derided by philosophers like Rousseau, Kant and Hegel. In spite of their differences, they are united in their ironical stance towards the theorists of international law and diplomacy. In addition, Rousseau and Kant, as distinct from Hegel, are indignant about the legitimation bestowed by international law on an immoral institution like war. If, on the other hand, as Hegel admits, international law is based only on the will of states whose nature and duty command them to respect their commitments only as far as they correspond to their interests, if there is no universal law and no umpire who can guarantee it by sanctioning its violators, what is the function of international lawyers besides offering legal alibis for the calculations of the powerful and for a situation which is the very negation of law? Of course, Kant himself delineates the principle of a law of war; but for him it is based precisely on the obligation of abandoning the state of war in order to institute the state of peace.

In reality, for Rousseau, Kant and Hegel, international law, and in particular the law of war, is problematical in both its basis and its application. Rousseau and Kant accuse the jurists of infering from the 'is' to the 'ought'; Hegel, conversely, accuses international law of remaining 'on the mode of the "ought"'.[10] All three appeal to a tribunal which they see as more fundamental or more far-reaching than law, namely their philosophy of man, society and history.

From balance to history

The eighteenth-century philosophers who were, implicitly or explicitly, pinning their hopes on the pacification of international society were not relying primarily either on international equilibrium or international law. For Locke and Montesquieu, the obstacle to the spirit of domination and of conquest, among states as well as among individuals, was the spirit of acquisition and of commerce.

Interests were supposed to replace passions, economics to replace politics; the social ties of mutual sympathy, stressed by the Scottish Enlightenment, and of mutual advantage between individuals, were supposed to replace the glory of princes and of states. For Rousseau, on the other hand, the main sources of war and oppression are precisely luxury and civilization, because acquisition breeds competition, because it creates the opposition between the poor and the rich which law serves to sanctify, and because it encourages *amour-propre*, this 'urge for self-comparison' which is the source of all evils. Only an unlikely return to the simplicity and unity of small, austere and homogeneous units, perhaps protected by their alliance into federations, can bring back domestic peace and push back external war.

The decisive transformation brought about by the philosophy of history with Kant and, each in his own way, by Hegel and Marx, consists in accepting the Rousseauist reversal but reversing it in turn. Passions and vices, discord and war are indeed the stuff out of which culture and history are made; but it is also these things which, in the long run, are opening the road to morality, to concord and to peace.

> Thanks are due to nature for man's quarrelsomeness, his enviously competitive vanity and for his insatiable desire to possess and to rule; without them all the excellent natural faculties of mankind would forever remain underdeveloped. Man wants concord but nature knows better what is good for his kind, nature wants discord . . . All wars are therefore so many attempts (not in the intention of men but in the intention of nature) to bring about new relations among the states and to form new bodies by the break-up of the old states to the point where they no longer maintain themselves alongside each other and must therefore suffer revolutions until finally, partly through the best arrangement of the civic constitution internally, and partly through the common agreement and legislation externally, there is created a state which, like a civic Commonwealth, can maintain itself automatically.[11]

For the time being, 'at the degree of education reached by the human race, war is an indispensable means to better it further; and it is only after the completion (God knows when) of this education that an eternal peace would be beneficial for us and peace would become possible'.[12] Now, if it is possible, peace is necessary; or, rather, it is possible because it is morally necessary: 'Morally practical reason proclaims in us its irresistible veto: there should be no war. We must act as if the thing which perhaps will never be were to come about and establish the constitution (perhaps the republicanism of each and all states) which seems most capable of leading us there.'[13]

Kant's political doctrine is above all a philosophy of war and peace because it is a juridical philosophy based on a philosophy of morality and supported by a philosophy of history. But the articulation of these three dimensions raises serious difficulties.

24

The treaty on eternal peace consists of three articles: (1) the civil constitution in each state should be republican; (2) the law of nations should be based upon a federation of free states; (3) the cosmopolitan or world law shall be limited to conditions of universal hospitality.[14]

Each of these raises a difficult problem concerning the nature of the change from the present situation. In particular, Kant falls short of advocating not only a world state, which would risk being tyrannical and ineffective, but even a federation which risks being resisted by the existing sovereign states. He seems to be content, as a lesser evil, with a very loose alliance of states against war. This alliance would lack coercive power: would it suffice, then, to bring states from the state of nature to the civil state? Cosmopolitan law, based on the fact that 'more or less close relations between all peoples of earth have spread universally to such an extent that a violation of right on one point of the planet is being felt everywhere', contains the promise, beyond civil and international law, of a 'public law of men in general' (third definitive article) thanks to which no individual would any longer be in the state of nature, or, as Hannah Arendt was to say, deprived of 'the right to have rights'. But in practice it does not go beyond the right to communication and to hospitality.

Indeed, one does not know whether what Kant envisages in order to go beyond, both at interstate and at the cosmopolitan level, is an asymptotic progress from war to peace or a brutal reversal due to the costs and horrors of war and to the loss of its unifying function. Above all, if peace is possible 'even for a people of devils provided it has a good constitution', this organization does not yet amount to genuine peace. That can come only from a moral revolution which can be prepared only by culture and law and whose idea can be suggested by history only in certain circumstances, when the signs of a moral disposition of humanity are being shown, as for instance in the enthusiasm with which the French Revolution was greeted. 'An agreement which has been extracted pathologically for the purpose of establishing a society can be converted into a moral whole';[15] but it is, precisely, a conversion. The most essential step still has to be taken.

Hegel's approach is both parallel to and sharply contrasting with Kant's. For him, as for Kant, history is being made by its negative side, which, even more than for Kant, must lead to reconciliation. Even more than for Kant, war fulfils an essential mission, that of unifying the human race, but, as for Kant, it tends to lose this historical function. For him too, as for Rousseau and for Kant, war tends to become impossible in Europe, because of the great cultural commonality and of the interdependence of interests. It still has a role in relations with non-civilized peoples, or in regions like America, where the rational bureaucratic and prosaic state is not yet fully developed. Like Kant, Hegel seems, in the *Phenomenology of Spirit*, to be attracted by the idea of a world state; but, more than Kant, whose pacifist and universalist illusions he derides, he rallies to the necessary plurality of states, since an alliance or a confederation of states must necessarily be provisional and give birth to disagreements which can be solved only by war.[16]

More important still, war is not only made possible by the plurality of states, it fulfils a much more central and permanent positive function than for Kant. On the one hand, it alone can, much better than any moralizing sermon, remind man of the vanity of earthly possessions and make him face the risk of violent death which constitutes his humanity and which, through the struggle of the master and the slave, is the source of society. On the other hand, only war can restore the unity of the state, by allowing its individuality to manifest itself in opposition to other states and, above all, by shaking the inertia into which individuals are sinking through the primacy of private or economic life. Much more than Kant, Hegel reacts negatively to the selfishness and prosaic heartlessness of modern society and tries, without abandoning it, to recover the sense of community, authority and action which lay at the heart of politics as lived by the ancients. But at the same time, he does not hide his pessimism as to the result: the modern individual's only relation to the state is through taxes and military service; virtue is reduced to the work ethic and to the chastity of women; war itself, since the invention of firearms, has become impersonal and abstract.[17]

Modern society is indeed dominated by prose. Heroic individuals and the literary form dedicated to singing their praises, the epic, can only, according to Hegel, find a provisional haven in America.

The synthesis of the ancient and the modern world, of the public and the private dimension, thanks to the Napoleonic or Prussian citizen–soldier, looks as distant and exceptional as Kant's moral conversion. In the last analysis, war, in Hegel's perspective, was supposed to fulfil the same task as morality for Kant, the philosopher of peace: to lift man above himself, i.e. above the primacy of needs and of calculations. And yet, it is still the society of political economy, it is still the world of commerce and industry, defended by the English thinkers of the seventeenth and eighteenth centuries and by French liberals from Montesquieu to Constant and Guizot; it is the primacy of the private over the public, of the individual over the state, of security over glory, which progresses through the imposing constructions of German idealism, in spite of the latter's appeals to moral or political heroism.

From universal history to modern society

The outcome of the philosophy of history, then, brings us back to the dimension that Raymond Aron had chosen as being the most significant for analysing the phenomenon of war: that of industrial society and of its great nineteenth–century interpreters. One can, indeed, agree with his statement:

> Humanity has experienced, during the last century, a kind of revolution, perhaps one should say a mutation, whose first phases predate the nineteenth century and whose pace has quickened during the last decades. Every generation, every thinker since the beginning of the last century has tried to define this historical innovation. Saint-Simon and Auguste Comte have spoken of an industrial society, Alexis de Tocqueville of democratic society, Karl Marx of capitalist society.[18]

Aron stresses above all the replacement of military society by industrial society thanks to science and technology, but he consciously adopts Tocqueville's tone when he speaks of the 'intellectual, technical, economic revolution which, like a cosmic force, carries humanity towards an unknown future'. He wonders, however, why, contrary to the predictions of Saint-Simon and Auguste Comte (to whom one could add Herbert Spencer), this future was not peaceful. There are four possible answers to this question.

The first answer is Marx's: industrial society leads to contradictions and crises which in turn produce revolutions and wars, as long as society is based on exploitation. This interpretation has seemed to be confirmed in the short term but long-term events have disproved it. At any rate, it is a more complicated version of Saint-Simonian optimism.

The second answer, that of Schumpeter and Vebben, which Aron has examined in *War and Industrial Society*,[19] attributes the wars of the twentieth century less to capitalism, whose spirit, according to them, is essentially peaceful, than to its fusion with precapitalist values and groups, particularly in the case of Germany and Japan.

Aron himself proposes a third answer which can be seen as a version of the second. It is based upon the duality of the process and the drama: 'on the one hand the necessity of progress, on the other history as usual, and the drama of empires, of armies and of heroes'.[20] Aron recognizes that one cannot leave the matter at this point, with the juxtaposition of technological progress and the permanence of politics: all the more so if, at the philosophical level, one adds the opposition between the

Kantian perspective of human reconciliation and the Thucydidian vision of history as tragedy. He knows that politics and technology are bound to meet one way or the other. 'In a sense, this is where "history as usual" and historical necessity meet: are knowledge and power the tools of power politics or are they, as Auguste Comte thought, the harbingers of the end of power politics, so that a unified humanity may pursue the only valid struggle for mastery over nature and the well-being of all men?'[21] He points out that Germany and Japan have responded by putting technology in the service of power; he proclaims his ignorance of the future but he also confesses a kind of timid optimism based on the nature of modern armaments and economy and on the improved awareness of these realities in our societies.

There is a fourth answer, however: this is Nietzsche's. For him, the result of modern society, of the movement towards equality and peace, is the decadence of man. It is the victory of the slave over the master, the advent of a humanity whose reconciliation is that of Zarathustra's 'last man' for whom fighting is bad for the stomach: 'One herd and no shepherd'.[22] This perspective is implicit in Hegel's idea of the end of history as the victory of prosaic, individualistic rationality. But Nietzche's point is that history does not stop there. The peace of decadence can bring about in return the revolt of the masters, of the superior, creative human beings, who would attempt to revive war and, through it, to impose a planetary aristocracy. As opposed to the predictions of peace we have mentioned, Nietzsche prophesies that the twentieth century will be the century of war, of a struggle for world domination waged in the name of philosophic principles. According to the German philosophic historian Ernst Nolte, fascism is, precisely, the expression of the revolt of the hierarchical and warlike community against the modern movement of universalization and against the transcending of differences which, as Nietzsche saw, was common to Christianity and democracy, to capitalism and socialism.[23]

It should be obvious that the twentieth century, with its two world wars and its two totalitarian imperialisms, has amply confirmed Nietzsche's prophecy. But the successive crumbling of the two total ideologies and of their conquering empires; the resulting victory of liberal democracy, left alone on a battlefield deserted by its opponents; the replacement of the threat of a third world war by the balance of deterrence and then by dialogue and cooperation among adversaries; and finally, and perhaps most importantly, the fact that not only war but the use of its threat has become totally inconceivable in the mutual relations of Western countries, brings the idea of peace through inter-dependence and democracy back into fashion. Certainly an extremely important development has taken place in the West, a development whose source is as debatable as that of the nineteenth-century revolution mentioned by Aron (industrial society? democracy? capitalism? individualism? economic and demographic evolution?), but whose reality is not: relations between liberal developed countries can no longer be understood in the light of the definition of international relations as a state of nature, characterized by the possibility of resorting to force. Neither the constraints nor the priorities of the modern state can be thought through satisfactorily on the basis of its classical attributes such as sovereignty and territoriality; even less, on the basis of the extreme case, that of war.

But where does the 'unknown future' towards which the 'cosmic force' invoked by Tocqueville and Aron is dragging us lie? It is to be found 'beyond the nation-state' or in a return to an earlier reality? In the direction of 'cosmopolitan law' or in that of the state of nature of individuals and of sub- and trans-state groups? And will this new state of nature be made more moderate by its complexity or more unmanageable by its turbulence?

From modern society to human nature

These questions agitate, nowadays, a public opinion disoriented by the novelty of the situation and the collapse of the century's ideological answers. The trend is towards rediscovering older answers, by going back to Kant and Hegel or even, to some extent, to Grotius or to medieval law in order to understand our own time.

Two young American scholars have tried, in the 1980s, to show that history had proved either Kant or Hegel right.

For Michael Doyle, the three articles of *Perpetual Peace* either have become reality or are about to do so.[24] First, republican states do not wage war on each other. According to Doyle's empirical inquiry, in essence confirmed by others, no real armed conflict has placed two modern democracies in opposition since the nineteenth century. Second, their mutual relations within Western organizations correspond to this 'alliance of free peoples who have decided not to wage war on each other' which was foreseen by Kant's second article. The Group of 7 and the UN Security Council can be seen as a potentially universal concert of powers. The idea of international organization itself, based on Kantian principles, has been given a new lease of life by the hopes associated with the United Nations and CSCE.

Finally, the aspect of the Kantian project which appears as the most prophetic today is the cosmopolitan dimension. The revolution of communications lends a concrete reality to the idea that 'a violation of right on one point of the planet is being felt everywhere'; a planetary consciousness of sorts is expressed on issues such as human rights and the environment, and gives birth to transnational movements and non-governmental organizations. This common responsibility is given a partial reality by what could be called the triad of 'conscience, experts, concert'. It does coexist, however, as Kant acknowledged, with the multiplicity of states. Power still lies mainly with the latter, but its meaning and scope are submitted to increasingly stringent constraints.

What about the sources of this situation? Here too the Kantian analysis seems to be confirmed in some unexpected ways. Nuclear deterrence and the abandonment of the strategic arms race by an exhausted Soviet Union seem to illustrate two major sources of peace: the unbearable cost of the preparation for war and the suicidal character of war itself. Beyond this negative peace, the transition from deterrence to detente and cooperation through the institutionalization of dialogue and negotiation seem to illustrate the Kantian notion of a 'pathologically extracted agreement' which may lead to a 'moral whole'.

Besides nuclear deterrence, the other great force for peace, manifested in the breakdown of the Soviet Union, seems indeed to be the one indicated by Kant's eighth proposition of the *Idea for a universal history with cosmopolitan intent*: violations of the citizens' freedom harm the economic power of the state and its foreign relations; on the other hand, 'the effect of each impact of a government upon other governments in our continent, where the states have become so very much linked through commerce, will become so noticeable that the other states, compelled by their own danger, even when lacking a legal basis, will offer themselves as arbiters'.

For Francis Fukuyama, the victory of liberal democracy and the elimination of the threat of a world war represent the fulfilment of the Hegelian 'end of history'.[25] He stresses more particularly the influence of the ideas of universality and equality, thereby identifying the generalization of liberal democracy with the coming of the 'universal and homogeneous state' which, according to Alexandre Kojève's interpretation, represents the final goal of history in Hegel's perspective. But the main point is the end of negativity and hence of wars and revolutions, or at least of their meaningful historical role.

Finally, in a more diffuse way, the theme of the 'new middle ages' or, more modestly, of the return to *jus gentium* as opposed to international law, has emerged as a consequence of a number of developments: the decline of territoriality; the re-emergence, both in political discourse and in common consciousness, of the idea of humanity which brings back the notion of world (and not only international) society, the idea of a duty to intervene (*droit d'ingérence*) in favour of human rights which recalls the *jus gentium intra se* of the Spanish theologians and law teachers; the multiplication of types of actor and legitimacy, the growing importance of European law which takes precedence over the domestic law of states without being rooted in popular sovereignty. All this points not to the return of the spiritual unity of Christendom or the secular unity of empire, but, as indicated by Ole Wæver, to a hybrid phase which would combine a universal natural right, a multiplicity of levels and, nevertheless, a political primacy of states and state-based organizations.[26] But this is precisely what makes a thinker like Grotius relevant today, since his doctrine is essentially linked to a period of transition.

But transition towards what? Towards a return to the premodern situation or towards a new world order? For each of the considerations above, which motivated a return to the great doctrines of the past, there is an alternative view.

Let us look first at the Kantian legacy. Michael Doyle himself points out that while Western democracies have managed their mutual relations in a peaceful and, on balance, positive manner, they have signally failed to do so in their relations with totalitarian as well as with colonial and formerly colonial countries. Of course, one may argue that both will, in the long run, be included in the liberal 'peace zone'; but this assumes that the many objective economic, demographic and cultural difficulties which stand in the way of this harmonious outcome will be overcome. Even in that case, there inevitably remains a period of transition which has to deal with a fundamentally heterogeneous world, as far as attitudes towards war and peace are concerned.

Far from overcoming this heterogeneity, the collapse of communism has rather increased it. Hence arises a fundamental and unsolved problem: upon what common code or what means of pressure and defence can an essentially modern, civilian, secular, economic and peaceful national or international society rely when faced with a minority of citizens or countries which remain faithful to the old code and attached to territory or to glory?

A second reason for scepticism lies in the fact that the emerging elements of international organization and world solidarity are devoid of constraining power, and are likely to remain so unless they slide into a return to empire which seems to go against the grain of our societies. This explains the acute embarrassment of the European Union and the United Nations in the face of conflicts which they cannot ignore but which they cannot solve by force as they might have attempted to do in other times.

The third point concerns nuclear weapons. They play a positive, stabilizing role as long as deterrence works. Indeed, mutual deterrence, whether bipolar or multilateral, is an extreme illustration of the rationalist idea of the interstate balance or of international society. Already during the Cold War, however, one could speculate whether the possible failure of deterrence, and hence the possibility of nuclear war and of the self-destruction of the human race, were not raising fundamental problems about the meaning of history and about man's position in the world which would challenge the very basis of any philosophical optimism. But today, the problem has taken a new turn. Nuclear weapons are seen less from the point of view of deterrence than from that of proliferation, which is inextricably linked to the arms trade, to the disintegration of empires, to the world economic crisis, to the role of private mafias and terrorist states, to the joint dangers of anarchy and fanaticism. They become, then, the most extreme example not of order but of the gap between the global and diffuse character of problems and the partial and specialized character of the institutions which are supposed to manage or to control them.

Finally, social and economic interdependence cuts both ways. It threatens the autarky desired by totalitarian regimes, but also the comfortable stability of democratic societies, if only because of the fear provoked by migrations and of the resulting reactions of self-closure and rejection. The common fate, in the short term, of all modern societies, is destabilization through opening.

The return to Hegel is fraught with similar ambiguities. Francis Fukuyama recognizes that the Hegelian/Kojèvian 'end of history' is not so distant from the Nietzschean 'last man'. The possibility therefore arises that the undifferentiated boredom of universal society will lead to a revolt of *thymos*, of that part of the soul which, according to Plato, has to do with courage and pride, with power and glory. But it is clear that the modern state is not able to satisfy it while also controlling it, as Hegel had wished. Hence the danger of a nihilistic, unpredictable and explosive violence.

This same danger of violent anarchy may also be the darker face of 'neo-medievalism'. Among its defenders, some look forward to a plurality of communities and allegiances, whose partial and multiple character would make for balance and tolerance. But others, particularly Italian authors such as Umberto Eco, see, in this 'return to the middle ages', rather a world of feudal hierarchies without a central power or common rules, which would be plagued by the very arbitrariness, private violence and civil or religious wars to which the institution of the modern state aimed to put an end. The clear and distinct divisions of the classical age are gone; but the fluid and shifting world which seems to be rising, a world of new wandering crowds, new pirates, new sects, would, in this view, be a world of fragmentation and insecurity rather than of order and peace.

We have reached, then, the ultimate dimension of our subject, a dimension that goes beyond interstate war. As long as there are several states, war among them will be possible; but, as we have seen, it has already lost its justification, or its meaning, and it may become less and less frequent and less and less central to political life. But could it be that the decline of war will have to be paid for with an increase of private, individual or civil violence? We live in a period of permanent destructuring; but can the individual, the city and humanity build themselves without referring to stable structures and institutions against which action and change can be measured? Can one eliminate the Platonic question of the relation of the structure of the soul with those of the city and of the world?

Never before has this relationship appeared so problematic. In all other civilizations or periods some kind of religious understanding of the world shed light as well as imposing constraints upon the relationship of men and cities with each other. In our situation, which Hannah Arendt characterizes as 'worldlessness', the question is whether men can organize their coexistence in a peaceful and rational manner or whether they are the slaves of needs and passions which may reassert themselves all the more violently for having been ignored or repressed. The post-Cold-War horrors of the former Yugoslavia shock us to a greater extent than the even more gruesome ones of Rwanda because they are happening in a country which seemed more familiar and to be penetrated by modern individualistic culture. One cannot help thinking, then, of Freud's remarks in his letter to Einstein about war: civilization leads to the aggressive or destructive instinct's being turned inwards, and transformed into guilt or self-hatred; but since this development does not take place everywhere at the same time and at the same pace, those who have experienced it are horrified and helpless before those whose aggressivity is still following its spontaneous, brutal and cruel course against external enemies. On the other hand, once rediscovered, destructive violence, among the civilized, can be even more cruel and limitless than among the non-civilized. The Freudian notion of the 'return of the repressed' seems to shed important light on totalitarianism, just as that of the 'narcissism of small differences' (recently put to good use by Michael Ignatieff in his *Blood and Belonging*) helps to explain why the increase in homogenization which goes with modernity seems to encourage the revival of national or ethnic rivalries.[27] Freud used to say that men can substitute love for aggression within a community, as long as there remains another one on which they can vent their need to hate.

If there is some truth in this view of human nature, the issue is raised of its compatibility with democracy and with peace. For Bergson, democracy is the least natural political regime: the society according to nature is the closed, warlike one; openness and peace have always to be conquered by the vision (whether religious or intellectual) of universal brotherhood and the will to act upon it. The question remains of what beliefs and institutions are able to consolidate this victory over aggressive parochialism. Liberal democracy is the regime which tries, unlike all other societies, not to embody the unity of the community in a sacred leader and not to embody evil and violence in a scapegoat, domestic or external. Precisely because of that, it is always in danger of being challenged by the thirst for absolutes, or by the need to find an enemy. The totalitarian temptation is the ever recurring companion of individualistic democracy, just as the risk of blind self-destruction is the ever recurring consequence of the declining relevance of war.

Our time has taught us that we live in one world, and that peace is possible. But it has also shown us the frailty of humanity, in both meanings of the term: humankind can be destroyed by atomic weapons; and our respect and pity for our fellow human beings can fall prey to the return of archaic myths, to the emergence of new fanaticisms, or to the permanence of basic instincts, if education, institutions and forceful resistance do not stand in their way.

Is this view a rationalist, a realist or a revolutionary one? Probably a combination of all three. Martin Wight himself pointed out that while his division into three schools had much pedagogic value, most serious thinkers were necessarily overcoming it in order to attempt some particular synthesis. The same goes for Waltz's three images. My purpose has been only to follow in the footsteps of these two authors, while stressing even more that we cannot pass judgment on the anarchic structure of the international system or the attempt to build an international society without reflecting on the recurring paradoxes of history, the unprecedented opportunities and dangers of our society, and the permanent nature of man.

2

Force and Politics Today

C LAUSEWITZ: THE LAST DAYS?', or *Still going strong after all these years*. That title would more or less sum up the scenario played out in certain aspects of strategic, political and philosophical thinking on the role of violence in interstate relations, certainly since 1918, if not since the industrial revolution. For the Clausewitzian notion, that force is the instrument of politics and war the continuation of politics by other means, has in the modern era been subject to a more or less continuous sequence of confirmations and rebuttals.

The eighteenth-century utopias of peace achieved through trade were followed by the Napoleonic wars, and the utopias of the nineteenth century, of peace achieved through science, industry or democracy, by the 1914–18 war. Then, with the advent of propaganda warfare, the Soviet revolution, the birth of totalitarian states, we seemed to have entered an era in which Clausewitz was superseded not only by Lenin but also by Ludendorff, both of whom saw politics as the continuation of war by other means: neither the politics of the 1930s nor the catastrophe of the Second World War appeared to prove them wrong.

After 1945, a new turn of events: optimism for a peace sustained by international organizations, typical of postwar periods, a peace achieved through the primacy of the peaceful values of common interest and cooperation, experienced an initial setback, and then renewed support, because of the nuclear factor: while this at first appeared to spell doom, it was subsequently seen as the guarantee of equilibrium. Between the great powers in Europe, the combination of 'peace through terror' and the 'peace of contentment', to borrow terms used by Raymond Aron, appeared to have eliminated the use of force from international politics.

35

Yet the efforts of the great powers to maintain or increase their nuclear potential were fair indication that, in their eyes at least, nuclear capacity was not without political significance, even if, mercifully, it was not put to the classical test of armed conflict. In Korea and Vietnam, Hungary and Czechoslovakia, in the Middle East or between India and Pakistan, there was no lack of examples of wars involving, not the two superpowers, but the intervention of one or the other, or of confrontations between other powers. Finally, and perhaps most significantly, another incarnation of Clausewitz appeared in the shape of Mao, whose 'power comes from the barrel of a gun' may be seen either as a reaffirmation of the primacy of politics, or equally as its militarization: doubtless both are true of the Chinese example and of revolutionary or subversive war in general. That form of struggle, whether in the Chinese revolution or during decolonization, represents one of the most significant phenomena of the twentieth century, most particularly in the underdeveloped countries.

But here again, it would be too simplistic to regard it purely as a newly discovered instrument or means of serving fixed political and ideological ends or purposes. The more widespread revolutionary war becomes, the more it seems to be diluted, increasingly full of ambiguities as to its origins, conduct and consequences. For a long time it was possible to regard it essentially as an indirect form of strategy, a subversive manoeuvre on a global scale. Today in the Third World there is a proliferation of civil wars, *coups d'états*, ethnic conflicts ranging from guerrilla warfare to genocide, but the most striking thing about them is their diversity, and the difference in the roles played by the outside powers, who sometimes provoke them and sometimes exploit them, but just as frequently help to put them down or remain hovering permanently on the brink, even when they pretend to revolutionary ideals. This is even more true in the developed West, where the decline of institutions and the resurgence of violence from within seems to mark a sort of 'Third-Worldization', and unrest and conflict are inspired by groups dedicated to terrorism and urban guerrilla warfare. Sometimes these are directly exploited by organized national or international forces, such as communist parties or the Soviet Union, but it remains very frequently the case that those who cause the disturbances are not the same as those who exploit them or profit by them: some dream of social unrest, others have it thrust upon them. The disparity that exists between political calculations and actual outbreaks or campaigns of violence suggests that the more violence penetrates to the heart of societies, the harder it appears to be to predict, influence or control.

But, from a different perspective and in an entirely different way, can the same not be said of nuclear power? Perhaps – and that is the thesis of this chapter – the element of Clausewitz's proposition that is challenged by contemporary developments is not whether force is present, or its importance for politics, but rather the nature of the relationship between the two elements; perhaps that relationship, far from ceasing to exist, has in some ways become so close that there is no longer any clear distinction or fixed hierachy as between force that is essentially politicized and politics that is essentially conflictual. The Clausewitzian relationship would then become a particular case, applicable only to a certain type of politics where a clear distinction can be made between interstate diplomacy and internal politics, and to a certain type of force which we would tend to describe today as classical or conventional. What we have today is, on the one hand, the interpenetration of external and internal phenomena in our societies, with alongside it the establishment of a genuinely transnational politics, and on the other hand, the emergence and growing role of force at the nuclear and revolutionary levels. The effect is to shuffle the pack entirely, for these changes challenge not merely Clausewitz's proposition but the entire basis of the classical analysis of the respective roles of force and politics in intrastate and interstate relations, according to which it is precisely in respect of violence that the fundamental distinction is drawn between the two. Intrastate relations are characterized by the civil state, in other words the relinquishing of the natural state in which each man makes his own justice, in favour of a legitimate authority which has the power to arbitrate in disagreements between citizens and to organize their security. States, on the other hand, remain in a state of nature in their dealings with one another, they are not subject to a higher authority capable of implementing its decisions and are therefore in a state of virtual war, permanent vigilance and insecurity. We find this idea expressed with perfect clarity in the philosophical sphere by Hobbes (his definition of the state of nature as a state of war of all against all) and in the sociological sphere by Max Weber (who defined the modern state as holding the monopoly of legitimate violence), as well as, in the contemporary analysis of international relations, by Raymond Aron: what, for him, characterizes interstate relations is, precisely, that each state reserves the right to resort to force; hence the specificity of 'diplomatic/strategic conduct' (in which the Clausewitzian duality recurs) and the definition of international relations as a theory of war and peace.[1]

It is this straightforward polarity that seems to have collapsed today, and in the most paradoxical manner. To all appearances, the state finds it harder both to uphold its monopoly of legitimate violence internally, and to exercise its capacity to resort to force externally.

If it is that latter capacity that defines diplomatic/strategic conduct, is one not justified then in saying that relations between developed Western states, for example, whether negotiations, pressures, crises or conflicts, actually now bear a closer resemblance to internal politics? Whatever tensions or ruptures in relations may arise, can we really say that they are characterized by the ultimate possibility of a recourse to force, that the extreme case of a war between France and Holland or between the United States and the Common Market countries actually lurks somewhere on the horizon?

To take another example, of the major nuclear powers. Here the possibility of war is very much at the forefront of relations between them, but rather in terms of the absolute necessity of avoiding it; and the effort to put this negative response on a permanent footing begins to acquire the nature of cooperation, via the institutions of the nuclear-test-ban and non-proliferation treaties and the Salt negotiations. Certainly the danger of nuclear war exists, but we cannot say that the threat of resorting to it forms part of the diplomatic arsenal.

Conversely, if the relations between states sometimes take on the character of 'worldwide internal politics', relations within certain states sometimes take on the character classically attributed to international politics, peace depending not so much on the authority of a central power, or the law or a sense of community, but rather on an unstable balance of power between groups prepared to use force. In many underdeveloped or multinational countries, peace is in fact a state of virtual war, either of all and against all, or between two polarized communities in a state of 'cold civil war', to use the expression of André Fontaine. This in fact degenerates into full-blown war more often than 'international Cold War'. If there is an apparent diminution of violence in interstate relations, there is also an apparent increase of violence within states: social unrest, civil war, revolution, wars of subversion. Since the Second World War, the vast majority of violent conflicts have taken place in the Third World, and within the frontiers of one state at a time.[2] Today, in the developed countries, individual social and political violence is perhaps statistically no greater than in any other age, but we are more aware of it. This is not only because it is reflected, amplified, indeed often provoked by the mass media, and particularly television, but because of the contrast it presents with our hopes of progress and social harmony in an age of plenty, the fact that, as wars between states have become less frequent, we have less need to fear them. If Belgium or Canada experience violence, it is much more likely to be between Belgians or between Canadians than directed against other states. It is also the case that the greatest violence arises out of conflicts involving minorities or nationalities, or in other words conflicts that (potentially at least, and in the eyes of at least one of the parties) take place between nations or states. But it seems beyond argument that even social conflicts, and even those that do not extend to guerrilla warfare or civil war, are once again becoming marked by a potential for violence that had seemed to be a thing of the past. Certainly, in much the same way as the accepted mechanisms for change and the establishment of a new equilibrium in the international sphere (negotiations, wars, annexations of territory) appear very often to be skewed towards peace, so the mechanisms for achieving internal equilibrium and peaceful change, through parliamentary institutions or official bargaining processes, seem frequently to have seized up altogether, opening the way for violence to break out – spontaneous, diffuse, anarchic, explosive or anti-authoritarian – in the various categories of society.

On closer examination, these two opposite cases prove to have common roots. Force is not stopped, neutralized or contained, except by an equivalent or superior force that has managed both to win acceptance (transforming itself into law) and to reserve a number of issues for peaceful change. There are two power structures that can achieve this, internally as well as externally: either a superior authority exercising rights of sanction and arbitration, or a state of balance between comparable powers. The modern European system was based on the fulfilment of the first condition internally (the authority of the state tempered by the separation, and therefore balance, of the powers within constitutional states), and of the second condition externally, in the form of the international balance of power. Might the current crisis not arise from the fact that the authority of national states (internally) and the calculations of diplomatic and strategic equilibrium (internationally) are being put under pressure by new circumstances?

Don't authority and equilibrium imply respect for certain rules that are founded in a mixture of community and competition (competition *within* the community at the internal level, competition *between* communities at the international level), and would not these rules therefore be challenged by the violence of these new conflicts and the emergence of these new allegiances?

Equally, don't the intrinsic characteristics of modern technology make national societies doubly vulnerable, in a way that if not entirely new is at least on a new scale? For they are vulnerable both to being totally destroyed from the outside, through nuclear weapons, and to disintegration from within, because of the penetration of transnational tendencies that is the inevitable result of modern communications and their potential for being manipulated.

The two crucial factors in both strategic and political development are material and mental resources, that is, technology (in the narrow sense of military technology and the wider sense of the technological society) and social psychology (in the narrow sense of ideological attitudes and the wider sense of aspirations to higher values and standards). At present, they would seem to conspire towards the destruction, or at least the separation, of politics and strategy, opting instead for the coexistence of nuclear peace, founded on a new technical stability, and social anarchy, founded on a state of permanent psychological instability.

We are back to Clausewitz again, the limitations of diplomatic/strategic conduct and the forms of balance it can engender. Perhaps 'diplomatic/strategic conduct' presupposes freedom of action on the part of states, and that in turn requires a unity of the body politic and flexibility or adaptability of its military instrument – things that are difficult to achieve when the levels proliferate, with their different structures and dynamics: the nuclear balance of power, guerrilla or revolutionary war, transnational politics, where trends and influences pass across frontiers, either in their original form, or by imitation or contagion or as the result of the political or military reaction of one state to internal developments in the society of another.

To understand the current relationship between politics and force, we must first distinguish these various levels and analyse the relationships among them, how they operate in different parts of the world and within the global international system.

Most striking and most relevant is the fact that, although a relatively clear relationship exists between the classical political and military levels, expressed in Clausewitz's proposition, that is not true of the other levels. At the upper level, it is hugely difficult to translate the phenomenon of the nuclear balance of power into politics, and so it tends to become fixed as an unchanging, autonomous equilibrium. Conversely, at the levels of subconventional war and transnational politics, the tendency is for the two to become confused in a shared reality of conflict and transformation, fluctuating between violent and peaceful, slow and explosive; collective and unstructured in form and rhythm, they do not readily lend themselves to clear-cut definitions and distinctions, still less to the rules and mechanisms of official intstitutions, diplomacy or strategy.

40

Between the tendency of the nuclear equilibrium to be frozen and unchanging, the classical diplomatic/military tendency towards flexibility of action tempered by prudent calculation, and the transnational revolutionary tendency to change punctuated by explosive action, links are established, the nature of which determines the precise situation in all the different regions and within the system as a whole.

Thus in Europe, where up to the time of writing classical or guerrilla war remains unlikely because of the direct nuclear involvement of the great powers and the nature of the societies concerned, the dialogue that takes place in the shadow of the rockets is essentially between the diplomatic and socio-ideological levels. In the Middle East, diplomacy and of course conventional war play a much greater role, while the nuclear level and two substate levels are far less important. In Africa, it is essentially within states that new dawns and revolutions occur, be they peaceful or violent. In Asia, all the levels are in play although the nuclear level has a less decisive role to play than in Europe.

Broadly speaking, there has up to now been a certain approximate coincidence of the balance of nuclear power, the industrialized world and peace. More specifically, it is possible to classify regions in terms of their relationship to the global balance of strategic power between the great powers and the likelihood of the escalation of local conflicts, based on the degree of great-power involvement or presence on the ground. At one extreme there is Europe where, because of the presence both of nuclear arms and of US and Soviet troops, the link between local equilibrium and the global strategic balance is strong, and East–West conflict could not break out because it would lead to escalation and widespread war. That is why war between the two Germanys has never happened, while it did between the two Vietnams and the two Koreas. Intervention to stop a German war would have been inevitable, but the character of the two societies and regimes rendered such intervention unnecessary. On the other hand, sticking with the same example, what the two Germanys gained in security they lost in terms of freedom of action compared with other regions, as the presence of the two superpowers implied not only protection but control.

At the other extreme are regions like Africa, where societies are highly unstable but the great powers are not directly involved on the ground. Interstate wars are rare, for the governments' weakness precludes them from embarking on military adventures and imposes a degree of active or passive soldidarity against attempted subversion or secession. Violent conflicts ranging from *coups d'état* to genocide take place within states, and can run their bloody course without leading to escalation or massive interventions and without significantly affecting the balance of power.

Lastly, there are regions such as Asia or the Middle East, which are sufficiently important for the superpowers to be involved. However, their presence is ambiguous, to the point that no one, not even themselves, can say in advance how much control they have over their allies, the extent of their involvement or what risks they are ready to take with each other in order to protect their friends. Patently, these are the most dangerous regions, for social instability and the existence of territorial disputes coincide with strategic importance and the involvement of the great powers. In areas such as Latin America or Eastern Europe where, effectively, only one of the big powers has a presence, then the risks of escalation to the level of world war are not so great, for either of the great powers can go ahead and intervene as much as it likes without automatically provoking a reaction from the other, even though there may be a risk of escalation because of ideological solidarity (Cuba) or geographical proximity (Berlin, East Germany, Yugoslavia).

Even in the predominantly bipolar system we have experienced hitherto, the diversity of different regions and the ambiguous nature of many situations have tended already to cast doubt on the idea that force – whether controlled or not – no longer has a role to play. But the system is changing. Its territorial and political basis (a strict control of the communist world by the Soviet Union, coupled with a more flexible and subtle domination of the rest of the world by the United States) is under threat on all sides. There are changes in the balance that exists between the two superpowers, there is a proliferation of power centres outside their sphere of influence, and there are internal crises within their empires and their own societies.

In this changing world, the two main factors we have identified as challenging the classical relationship between diplomacy and force – the nuclear balance of power and social and ideological change – begin to operate in an even more complex manner than before, and one that, in my view, is even more likely to justify the diagnosis that the role of force, far from being eliminated or even necessarily reduced, simply becomes more indirect, more roundabout, and less easy to predict or calculate.

The nuclear factor has always had the dual characteristic that it not only hinders interstate war but also the political solution of problems. The zones protected by the nuclear umbrella have undoubtedly been less exposed to war, but their problems have had less chance of amelioration. The logic of the nuclear reality is that of the status quo, of petrification. Existing positions are frozen, towns, countries and continents maintained in a divided state or under a domination that might otherwise have given way to war, but might equally have resulted in freedom or reunification. One day, the frustrations contained by this nuclear cap may boil over, especially if it is lifted even very slightly.

The efficacy of the nuclear stalemate may indeed already be under threat. It depends on equilibrium (or slight superiority for the party defending the status quo) at the nuclear level, and also the existence of a clear link or connection of the nuclear level with the other levels to which it is supposed to communicate something of its own stability. The global balance of power has not prevented wars outside Europe because events elsewhere did not pose a direct threat, and the presence of troops and tactical atomic weapons did not act as a link in the chain of escalation.

Moreover, on every front, the changes that are taking place bring with them as many hidden dangers for security as they do promises of flexibility. The nuclear balance of power between the two super-powers, if current tendencies prevail, looks as if it will be threatened by the astonishing progress made by the Soviets in the past few years. At the very least, a parity recognized and put on a formal basis by the Salt negotiations records a reduced level of US protection, which owed part of its credibility to US superiority.

It will be objected that notions of superiority and protection have long since lost all meaning, and that what guarantees the balance of power, and also renders protection impossible, is rather the impossibility of a counterforce strategy. That is probably true militarily, and in the middle term. It is probably not true psychologically in the short term or perhaps even militarily in the long term.

What is true of the vagaries of indirect rivalry in the Third World is also true of the vagaries of the nuclear arms race. It would be wrong in both these cases to see the situation in terms of a fight to the death, leading inexorably to the victory of one camp and the achievement of world domination, and it would be equally wrong to see it as something unimportant that has no effect at all on the relations of military strength between the great powers. What is affected, in both cases, is their sense of confidence or uncertainty, their desire for involvement or restraint, their willingness to take risks. And it is here that the other factor, of presence on the ground, becomes even more crucial. If, at the same time as the global balance of power shifts to its disadvantage, the United States slackens the ties which link it to the

European equilibrium, if the withdrawals of troops and tactical atomic weapons, the negotiations on strategic arms and the reduction of forces in Europe end up 'uncoupling' or separating the European theatre from the nuclear equilbrium of the two superpowers, while the Soviet Union strengthens its military power and diplomatic effectiveness, then Europe risks experiencing the problems and dangers that already afflict the other continents.

The states of Western Europe would gain in freedom of action but lose in security. They would find themselves facing the problems of independence, allegiance or protection. Germany, notably, would see new opportunities and new dangers: if Europe offers no security or community of interest, no specifically European balance of power or framework, Germany will be tempted to cling to the last tatters and illusions of US protection, and at the same time to seek assurances of security or promises of influence in an unconditional detente or special relationship with Moscow; unless the Germans seek to embark on a national nuclear programme, which would not be looked on kindly or without considerable anxiety by those same outside countries unable to conceive of nuclear arms as having any other function today than as a national weapon of deterrence. Europe risks experiencing not only the same uncertainty as other continents, but a vulnerability and paralysis born of mutual suspicion that would effectively make it a neutralized zone: it would renounce force, but would as a result be even more susceptible to pressure, usually implicit, indirect or negative, applied by the nearer or more determined of the great powers.

Elsewhere, the uncertainties of political development might encourage nuclear proliferation in the two main danger zones – Asia and the Middle East. If Japan, India or Israel became nuclear powers, who could guarantee that the outcome would be like the European model, a stable balance of power precluding the use of atomic weapons and making the use of other weapons less probable? Of course, there is no reason not to hope this would be the case, but the essential point is that the change in the international system would have different consequences in respect of the part played by the nuclear factor in different regions; it could lead to a balance of power, but it could also lead to the opposite, an erosion of power structures or an explosion of violence.

The second factor, which we will call social modernization, has even more complex and contradictory effects. Take for example the case most often cited to prove the ineffectiveness of the use of force today, that of the United States in Vietnam. If the USA failed to

achieve its objectives by force, it was partly because of the resistance
put up by North Vietnam and partly because of the way internal US
opinion reacted. The first of these causes may be accounted for, in the
context of decolonization, by the desire for independence and the
willingness of an underdeveloped people to accept sacrifices, or, in an
ideological and strategic context, by the organization and discipline of
a state run by a communist movement born out of a revolutionary
war. Similarly, the second cause can be explained either as the effect
of television, the primacy of civil values and the decline of the desire
for power in a society of plenty, or by the difficulty (analysed long ago
by Montesquieu and Tocqueville) for a liberal democracy of conducting a war of conquest, or limited war, or even having a foreign policy
at all.

Commentators may look at it from the point of view of the
Vietnamese or the Americans; they may lay the stress on stages of
economic and social development or types of political organization.
Nevertheless, the mere fact of creating these distinctions allows us to
be more discriminating and subtle in our judgment of the role of
force, and permits us to ask a number of questions, to which for the
time being no answer is possible.

First, what makes colonial wars more difficult today is the
undisputed fact of a higher level of sociopolitical mobilization in the
underdeveloped countries (where a growing proportion of the
population is brought into contact by some means or other with
national or international politics). Conversely, much has been said
about the depoliticization of the developed countries, for in the West
as well as the East, it seems that the role of private, individual, family
and professional life is growing (as was noted long ago by Benjamin
Constant in contrasting the respective freedoms of modern and ancient
peoples) at the expense of the collective life (at least when the times
are not exceptional). It also seems that a certain violent form of
nationalism is on the increase in the newly independent countries, and
on the decline in developed countries, at least in the West. Hence the
problem: is it more difficult to conquer or occupy militarily an
underdeveloped country such as Vietnam, than a developed country
such as Czechoslovakia? The gut opposition of the Czech people to
the Soviet occupation was certainly no less heartfelt than that of the
North Vietnamese to the Americans. If there was no comparable
military resistance, was that due solely to the nature of the terrain or
also to the fact that a Western people – urbanized and converted to
bourgeois values – does not fight unless there is a prospect of victory
(something which, turning the argument upside down, would explain

why Bosnian or Montenegran peasants possess a superior power of deterrence)?

But there is also a second angle, that of which great power is involved, and here the question of political regime becomes a factor: a liberal democracy has difficulty in using force, since it is apparently a violation of its principles and flies in the face of internal public opinion. The Soviet Union does not have these problems: neither its electorate nor its universities protested against the Prague invasion in the way the US electorate did following the Tet offensive and the invasion of Cambodia. Are we not therefore bound to conclude that the role of force is fundamentally different, depending on whether the adversaries are an overdeveloped liberal democracy facing an underdeveloped people under a communist regime, or a (partially) underdeveloped communist power confronting a developed European country under a liberal (or even communist) regime?

It would be wrong to conclude from this that primacy of civilian values necessarily results in a lack of desire to defend oneself, or that the tendency of certain groups to adopt a viewpoint based on generational affinity rather than the broader political community necessarily leads to reduced identification with one's country or the West in general. Faced with the direct threat of force or oppression, past experience shows that the spontaneous responses of democracies are often more effective than the discipline of dictatorships. But the danger is not so much of invasion or the brutal, direct threat of force, rather the gradual erosion (whether inspired or imported or arising spontaneously) in times of peace of a concern for solidarity in pluralist societies, a concern for defence in societies at peace, and a concern to maintain an external balance of power on the part of the liberal democracies.

All of us are affected by this crisis of relationship between states and societies, and in the international sphere between the relatively stable state system and the haphazardly evolving transnational society. There are several possible outcomes. A state, or states overall, may choose repression rather than social disorder, and take advantage of this to increase its authority internally or its sphere of action externally, even at the risk of provoking an explosive reaction in the future. On the other hand, the crisis may lead to a slow decline or a slow absorption of authority by society. This would cause the systems to be eroded: the state continues to exist through its institutions, the alliance through its military apparatus, but as they confine themselves to a narrow technical definition of their function, concerns and values, they have increasingly little to do with the way society evolves. The concerns of the *part* (the nation within the alliance, groups or individuals within the nation) will prevail over those of the *whole*, with no more than a few specialists left in overall charge. Hence the risk of a state that has no citizens and no statesmen, the war with no soldiers.

In an international system that is at stalemate, or in a bureaucratized society, one could imagine an almost permanent state of virtual internal anarchy, kept within certain bounds by structures that continue to exist. Yet the long-term dangers of loss of legitimacy, or collapse or violent reaction, are still very real. Furthermore, they may be sparked from outside if the effects of explosions of violence within another subsystem spread to the subsystem that is already weakened, or if the latter arouses the other's expansionist appetite.

Between societies that have grown up more or less under the protection of the nuclear umbrella, the probability is that the ideas of equilibrium, power, influence and conquest would take on new meaning. In this scenario, the system continues to hold, but internal developments, from one subsystem to another, are subject to a negative race towards erosion or decline, and represents in fact the modern equivalent of the race for power. No one conquers anyone, no one persuades anyone to abandon his alliance with the enemy; externally, as far as territorial divisions or the dangers of aggression go, absolutely nothing happens. Everything that happens goes on internally, in terms of the way the people of these nations or alliances perceive their relative stability, unity or dynamism. In this situation, political aggression does not consist in trying to destroy one's adversary, or the system of which he is part, but in attempting to sap the sources of his unity and strength, and promote, not revolution, but a mixture of paralysis and anarchy. Perhaps, in the nuclear age, that is the substitute for conquest, for the overthrow of alliances, and it is also a way of insuring against the total collapse of the system or any radical transformation of it.

Be that as it may, it is principally in this complex, indirect dialectic of erosion and contraction, expansion and explosion, that the problem of the relations between force and politics manifests itself today.

In general, the forces that encourage expression, erosion and contraction seem more apparent in the West, while those that encourage repression and expansion, and carry the risk of subsequent explosion, are more usual in the East. For the time being, it is the Soviet Union and, since the end of the Cultural Revolution, China, that enjoy the greatest freedom of action concerning external politics, military intervention and their ability to keep order in their respective states and spheres of influence. The signs of erosion and contraction in the West are more apparent than the prospects of overextension or future explosions in the East.

However, if we bring the Third World into the picture, we see that the communist countries occupy an ambivalent and provisional position as far as internal violence is concerned. If one wanted to sum up simply the relative positions of the 'three worlds', one might say that there are internal conflicts of considerable extent and violence in the developing countries, which are also characterized by insecure and unstable state organizations and power structures. In the West, there are growing internal conflicts of relatively modest intensity, within relatively flexible organizations and power structures. In the communist world, repression is structural but open internal violence is very rare because of the rigid organizational and power structure. But the great question is whether the communist world will evolve (by erosion or regeneration?) towards a flexible disorder of the Western sort, or if it will explode in praetorian conflicts, clashes between nations and wars of liberation like those experienced in the Third World.

As for the interstate violence that was the initial subject of our speculations, it seems to us a function above all else of just such internal developments as these. What has declined is the deliberate use of direct force between developed states, particularly in a nuclear context. There is an emphasis on rational calculation (economic and strategic) which should tend to rule out adventures. And yet sometimes, where the two sides are not equal, just such calculation may lead more readily to the use of force between states, as with Czechoslovakia. Above all, on top of the continuing or even growing propensity to violence of states in the process of modernization (often restrained by internal weakness), interstate violence is finding other more subtle ways to manifest itself.

First of all, if as war becomes less frequent there is a resurgence of conflict and violence at the internal level, the latter may in turn have an effect on interstate relations because of the dangers of escalation and the opportunities for intervention they present. Granted, the great powers try not to go down that path and sometimes, as happened recently in Ceylon, go so far as to set up a sort of universal Holy Alliance to maintain the status quo. But one has merely to recall Poland's troubles or observe the situation in Latin America to realize that there is room for other Czechoslovakias, even other Vietnams, to see that sometimes the dangers of internal instability and external intervention threaten regions such as Yugoslavia, the Middle ·East or India, which belong to the ambiguous, hence dangerous zone.

Second, the possibility remains of the indirect use of military force as a form of subtle but firm diplomatic pressure, as is illustrated by the situation of many small states, neutral or allies, that are either geographically close to a major power or under its protection. This is the danger that threatens Europe if we are not careful.

Most important, finally, are the even more indirect effects of force related to those above, on the strategic balance, the balance of hopes and fears, the balance of wills. This is the element that is hardest to quantify, or even identify, but it may be the most decisive for the international world of tomorrow. In that world, the direct offensive use of force will almost always be disastrous — and we must therefore hope it will be increasingly rare. However, the indirect and defensive potential of force, as an element of balance and stability, if not a means of subtle influence, will be the inevitable and indispensable reverse side of the reduction in offensive force. Between states and within societies, the advancement of civilization does not consist in suppressing force but in domesticating it, so that it can be used against itself.

3

Violence, Rationality and Unpredictability: Apocalyptic and Pacific Tendencies in Studies of International Conflict

I
T ALL GOES back to Unesco. Of course, there have been wars and
conflicts since time immemorial, and for almost that long there
have been people trying to give an account and explanation of
them. There was one historian who wanted his meticulous and
stylized study of a very particular conflict to stand as a model for all
time – and anyone who wishes to understand such sophisticated
modern ideas as 'international system', 'bipolarity' or 'cumulative
interactive decisions', or just appreciate the interplay of calculation and
passion, necessity and chance, need look no further than Thucydides.
But the idea of sending all the historians, diplomats and soldiers
packing, dismissing all the experts on war and politics and instead
looking for the key to these things within broader and at the same time
more familiar disciplines, the idea of summoning the social scientists,
psychologists and sociologists, better still the social psychologists, letting
them arrive at a scientific understanding of international violence that
would enable it to be eliminated or prevented, the idea of studying the
contrast between cities and the countryside or the tensions between
fathers and sons as a way of arriving at an understanding of the Cold
War, the idea, in short, of trying to interpret conflict between states by
looking at conflict between groups and individuals (or within individuals), in terms, therefore, of the prejudices and misunderstandings
between protagonists or, by extension, the deficiencies of their psychic
wellbeing, that whole approach dates back essentially to the last war: it
represents the decisive contribution of the Unesco project on social
tension to the history of the study of conflict. Whatever term is used,
whether 'tension' or the later 'conflict', the intention was the same:

using new techniques, to discover a general theory that would at once explain what conflict was, prove the concept was not founded in a valid opposition and suggest the remedy that would eliminate it once and for all.[1]

We changed all that. In the work cited above, which covers all the research on conflicts up to 1955, Jessie Bernard distinguished two broad lines of approach: the sociopsychological interpretation, which underlies the study of tension, and what she called the sociological interpretation, which treats conflicts as interactions of systems caused by genuine incompatibilities and permitting of rational strategies, based on the calculation of costs, stakes and risks.[2] She severely castigated the first approach for its unjustified extrapolation from the individual to the collective, accusing it of ignoring conflict as such, because its optimistic premises forced it to look for the source of conflict in the agents, to regard it as necessarily pathological, and to relinquish thereby any opportunity of understanding its rational aspects or social function. Bernard hailed the first tentative steps of the second school, mentioning the work on social mathematics by Rashewski, Richardson, etc., and in particular early game theory, in which by 1950 she discerned the seeds of what she rather surprisingly called the 'modern sociology of conflict'. She deplored the fact that the, in her opinion, sterile investigations of the first school were so dominant and widespread, and that sociologists and mathematicians had not yet got together to provide the second with the tools it required.

The years passed, and in March 1962, the American political scientist Charles McClelland contributed to the *Journal of Conflict Resolution*, published by the Center for Research on Conflict Resolution, a review of two books entitled *The Strategy of Conflict* and *Conflict and Defense*. He was by then able to respond to Bernard's plaintive rhetorical question 'Where is the modern sociology of conflict?' by entitling his own article 'The reorientation of the sociology of conflict' and to assert triumphantly: 'The study of conflict, particularly of the special case, international conflict, is not simply expanding; it is doing something not vastly short of bursting or exploding.'[3] He also noted a quite abrupt change of direction, as the intellectual methods, general theories and specific studies of the first school, as defined by Bernard, were transferred over to the second. Indeed McClelland comments that the whole 'tensions' approach, using the concepts of frustration/aggression, etc., was in eclipse, and the emphasis was placed increasingly on interaction, on social processes viewed as systems, their properties not reducible to the traits of participating actors. In the very first issue of the *Journal of Conflict Resolution* (1957), Mack and Snyder had already noted, somewhat optimistically, the existence of a vast literature on social conflict, with an impressive amount of data to show that a direct approach, geared to suppressing or modifying the sources of conflict, was not necessarily an efficient way to combat conflict itself.[4] The effort, therefore, should be directed to understanding and influencing the modalities of its development and outcome. Thus, the changed orientation that gave a new lease of life to the study of conflict may be defined as an emphasis on the *interaction* rather than the *nature* of the actors, and on the *resolution* of conflicts rather than their *causes*. Logically, one would imagine these two changes might be likely to suggest a third, an emphasis on decisions and their interdependence, hence on the *strategies* adopted by the actors, on the conscious and rational element of their actions rather than their unconscious and irrational underlying causes. In fact, it was specifically this area, the way the first two pairs of polarities related to the third, the role of rational strategy as it related to that of psychology or even pathology in interactive decision-making, that was to throw up new problems, new trends, procedures and processes.

What had happened? In the ten years that separated Bernard's *De Profundis* and McClelland's *Magnificat*, a series of revolutions had taken place, for better or worse, in the social sciences in general and the theory of international relations in particular. There was an awareness of new developments in mathematics, physics, biology and even the social sciences, of new directions and disciplines that broke down the traditional barriers and in so doing raised the prospect of a general operational and systems theory, that is, a general theory of complex organized wholes and the interactions between them – or in other words, of conflicts within and between systems. Game theory influenced economics, strategic planning, operational research, biology, mathematics, cybernetics; it inspired organization theory, communication theory, information theory, general systems theory, behavioural theory, the use of models in economics, of electronic machines for data analysis, etc.; and this raised the prospect of an integrated science of society and behaviour that combined a multiplicity of techniques and approaches within a formally established unifying general theory. Interdisciplinary collaboration and analogy would be practised under the aegis of a common science of international conflict, crisis and war, in the light of other more general phenomena, and thanks to the discovery of structures and processes capable of being precisely formulated rather than by the use of set criteria. Thus the two or three years from 1955 to 1957 saw the sudden flowering of a series of convergent intellectual endeavours with the common aim of using the scientific insights of the past few years to understand and resolve international conflicts.

That concern informs the recommendations made by Quincy Wright and Karl Deutsch, in 1955, for the Carnegie Endowment's project on conflict.[5] Deutsch wanted 'a concerted research attack, combining the methods of several of the social sciences'.[6] The approach he suggested was based essentially on the study of mass communications and decision-making, including the interactive nature of the latter. Thomas Schelling, bemoaning 'the retarded science of international strategy', laid the foundations for a strategy of conflict defined as a 'theory of interdependent decision', which, he said, 'looks like a mixture of game theory, organization theory, communication theory, theory of evidence, theory of choice, and theory of collective decisions'.[7] This theory too concentrates on rational calculation, in the broader sense of the term. But the ambitions of most of those promoting the new approaches went even further. In the same period, the economist Kenneth Boulding was using data taken from anything ranging from cybernetics to management studies to lay the foundations of a new 'eiconic' science, a theory of the images organizations form of one another. In particular he attempted to generalize its validity by applying it, in Schelling's words, to 'virtually all social interaction processes – from war to courtship, from competitive advertising to the lynx and the rabbit – that lend themselves to a common style of systematic analysis',[8] and by using it as the basis for tackling the problem that interested him most, that of war and peace. Boulding believed that 'applied science cannot succeed unless it guides its empirical study by reins, however loose, of pure abstract theory'. Moreover, he explains in the preface to his book *Conflict and Defense*, in 1954–5 he acquired

> the conviction that, in order to develop a theoretical system adequate to deal with the problem of war and peace, it is necessary to cast the net wider and to study conflict as a general social process, of which war was a special case. Out of a small group of scholars who shared this conviction grew first the *Journal of Conflict Resolution*, beginning in 1957, and then the Center for Research in Conflict Resolution at the University of Michigan in 1959.[9]

The journal's manifesto (it has the subtitle 'A Quarterly for Research Related to War and Peace') explains that, although in the last analysis it is principally concerned with the problem of the prevention of global war, its method is that of interdisciplinary studies, with contributions invited from sociologists, psychologists, educationalists and pioneers of behavioural science rather than from the traditional disciplines, based on the belief that 'the behavior and interactions of nations are not an isolated and self-contained area of empirical material but part of a much wider field of behavior and interaction', and that the structures and processes found in industrial disputes or inter-personal quarrels are no less valuable in arriving at a general theory of conflict.[10] Hence the journal's very open policy, with studies of international conflict constituting no more than approximately one-third of the published articles, every other conceivable form of conflict (within the individual, between individuals or companies, etc.) occu-pying roughly the same proportion, and the remainder devoted to general studies on the theme of conflict, the only condition generally observed being that contributions should be oriented towards the human sciences rather than history or politics in the narrow sense.

Another major conflict-study project, also established in 1957, was closely associated with the *Journal of Conflict Resolution* and shared many of its aims, although it concentrated its imposing array of up-to-the-minute concepts and techniques on a specific study of the causes of the First World War; the project came under the umbrella of the programme, Stanford Studies in International Conflict and Integration, directed by Robert C. North. Here again, the principal concern was with interstate conflict and the problem of war and peace in particular, examining the difference between conflicts that led to violence and those that did not; here again, the method was 'interdisciplinary' and 'scientific', and based on a general, abstract theory. Contributions were invited from political scientists, historians, economists, psychologists, anthropologists and sociologists, the idea being to establish a highly abstract and complex conceptual framework focusing on the idea of integration (the hypotheses envisaged were, first, that conflicts could in some degree contribute to integration between systems or organiza-tions, and, second, that insufficiently integrated systems could in themselves be a cause of conflict or provoke their descent into violence). The other aim of the project was to determine how states behaved in times of crisis, using a sophisticated analysis of the data to study communication between states, the way it is disrupted or distorted, and the interaction of tensions, perceptions and decisions in statesmen. This sort of crisis analysis, in terms of systems and inter-active decision-making, nevertheless links up with some of the old themes dear to the hearts of the social psychologists – hostility, tension, the distortion of mutual perceptions through stereotyping. Up until now, it is on that latter type of interaction that the Stanford programme has tended to focus, rather than on an examination of rational strategies and calculations of force.[11]

And here we come to a parting of the ways. For if I am to ask the question, so excellently put by McClelland, as to what this movement has contributed since it started in 1955–7, I shall be rather less enthusiastic than he is about both its unanimity and its achievements.

For McClelland, the evidence of that unanimity and achievement resides largely in three great books with a common emphasis, shared also by many of the above-mentioned studies they inspired. These books are: Schelling's *The Strategy of Conflict*, Rapoport's *Fights, Games and Debates*,[12] and Boulding's *Conflict and Defense*. Their common emphasis is on interaction: the application of the principle 'To know your enemy, you must first know yourself'; the study of processes (negotiations, price wars, the arms race, escalation, wars) that consist in a succession of states resulting from the interaction of two or more systems; the idea too that this interaction is cumulative, it does not only produce reciprocity of viewpoint and interdependence of situation, but also the dynamic force of a common history. Yet it is precisely in respect of the interaction and dynamic of conflicts that such wide variations exist, both as to their nature and their consequences; and here the different orientations of the authors and schools of thought come very much into the equation.

Boulding and Rapoport, as founders and joint editors of the *Journal of Conflict Research*, have much more in common with each other, in terms of theoretical approach and practical options, than they do with Schelling, a major contributor to the journal in its early years. Where Schelling explicitly states that he is leaving aside the pathology of conflict and its irrational and unconscious motivations, to concentrate on the strategy of interdependent decisions made by agents seeking rationally to promote their own interests (including showing that this rationality may extend to apparently irrational acts), Boulding and Rapoport are concerned to construct a general theory and, while going further than Schelling in expressing it in mathematical form, attempt to introduce either concrete social and historical data or moral considerations. Rapoport establishes a hierarchy between fights (where the aim is to destroy your adversary), games (where it is a matter of being smarter than him), and debates (where the purpose is to win him over): moving from one level to the next constitutes an inevitable increase in humanity, subtlety and comprehension of one's opponent, as well as in the element of common interest. Boulding arrives at international conflict by studying conflict between individuals, groups and organizations, discussing economic and industrial conflict, and developing a theory of 'viability' which, since it has its source in the analysis of business rivalry, reaches the conclusion that the nation–state is obsolete because advances in weaponry mean it is unable to defend itself. Where Schelling is content to advocate an extension of game theory that emphasizes the contribution of intuition and cooperation, Rapoport and Boulding end up condemning it, even though they make more use of it than its supporters, or else they accuse it of having autodestructed and demand it be passed over in favour of psychology and ethics (the study of hostility, fear, suspicion, trust and altruism).[13] Where Schelling tries to reconcile strategy and cooperation as a means of achieving peace, Rapoport forcibly stresses their mutual incompatibility.[14] Given the situation of an arms race, one sees the possibility of controlling it, making it serve as a vehicle for messages or tacit bargaining,[15] the other two emphasize the 'Richardson process', an inevitable escalation of hostility, calculable by differential equations, leading to the outbreak of violence.[16] Where Schelling attempts to show that the system of mutual threat that constitutes deterrence also constitutes a communications system that may contain within it processes of accommodation, and that it may be relatively viable, Boulding believes it to be inherently unstable and doomed to end in disaster, unless it transforms itself into a system of contracts and exchanges.[17] The bias towards formalization and the bias towards disarmament come together in the condemnation of particular (i.e. political) points of view: looking at things as systems constitutes a 'Copernican revolution' that is also an ethical revolution. Schelling attempts to demonstrate the way in which the viewpoint of one of the adversaries in a conflict articulates with, and to an extent coincides with, the other's; Boulding and Rapoport consider that the very fact of looking at things from the point of view of one of the agents, rather than at the system as a whole, is proof of moral insensitivity or intellectual naiveté; Schelling attempts, in a series of cautious and paradoxical insights, to show that in a world where the worst is always possible, it will not necessarily happen, that the threat of force may lead to its use or may instead act as a substitute for it, that it may spark a process of escalation or of negotiation. Rapoport and Boulding announce in a flurry of indignant equations the near-certainty of catastrophe.

It will by now be clear that, interaction and mathematics notwithstanding, Boulding and Rapoport and their disciples at the *Journal of Conflict Resolution* are not as far away as we might have thought from what we have described as the Unesco approach. In contrast with the strategic school, which starts with games and ends with deterrence and arms control, we may note that the pacifist psychosociologists are back on the offensive, though armed this time with equations and experimental games as well as their indignation and plans for peace.

The position adopted by Thomas Schelling is central (and I would say pre-eminent). He has been hugely influential (all his critics use his concept of non-zero-sum games; his ideas are applied not only to strategy and diplomatic negotiation,[18] but to theological or ideological disputes[19]); indeed, so many are the attacks and exaggerations to which his approach has been subjected, one could practically construct a typology of possible attitudes to international conflict.

The tendency he represents has been attacked both as too rationalistic and too psychological, too competitive and too cooperative, as implying too much or too little symmetry between the parties to the conflict. One of the most eminent experts on game theory and bargaining, John Harsanyi, criticizes Schelling for stretching the idea of rationality too far; he favours a strictly defined rationality based on 'strong postulates', such as the individual maximization of utility, symmetry, the restriction of variables and the mutual expectation of rationality, since these represent the only means of attaining the point of equilibrium that constitutes the solution to the game;[20] this can then be compared with the state of the parties as it unfolds in the real world. He feels that Schelling, in wanting to make his models too close to actual psychological reality, risks losing the advantages that the use of models drawn from game theory was meant to bring to the analysis of bargaining in the first place.

Conversely, a number of critics believe that the Schelling school (its activity evident in the doctrine of arms control[21]) remains over-dependent on the concept of rational calculation.

Those from a political or historical background (Raymond Aron, Jean-Baptiste Duroselle, Stanley Hoffmann) insist that the issues at stake are indeterminate and undefined, that precise calculation is impossible, that symmetry between the two sides does not exist; they stress the role of the reasonable as against the rational (Aron), of prediction based on ideology not game theory (B. Brodie on the Cuban missile crisis), and are inclined to agree with Stanley Hoffmann (who does however note the advances made using the mixed theory of conflict, which moves away from the idea of game as an algebraic problem towards game as simulation) that 'in the scientific sphere, the idea of a theory of rational conduct in a competition with multiple dimensions and unrestricted stakes is in danger of remaining a delusion'.[22]

Others, looking to the precepts of psychology, sociology or decision-making or to the imperatives of absolute morality, believe that viewing the strategy of conflict as a theory of interdependent decisions is based on a fiction, the notion that purely rational decisions may be arrived at by individual nations, regarded for the purpose as being the same as individual persons. There are a number of things that approach fails to acknowledge. First, the multiplicity of international influences and compromises that go towards the making of diplomatic and strategic decisions. Second, the multiplicity of psychological influences, intellectual prejudices and emotions (feelings of threat or hostility, projected aggression, etc.) that act on the decision-maker and prevent his embarking on a rational examination of the messages sent by his adversary, and so arriving at a calculated choice of a well-considered strategy. Third, the irreducible character of certain moral choices (whether or not to use atomic weapons), where strategic or analytical arguments simply do not apply. (Rapoport holds the extreme view that the science of strategy and the technique of war are based, as they stand, on a response that is unthinkable, the absurdity and revolting nature of which would be revealed under psychological examination.) At one moment, strategy and rational conduct are accused of covertly suggesting answers to ethical questions that involve value judgments, at the next they are accused of refusing to take on board these very same value judgments, of ignoring the ethical problem altogether and being prepared to contemplate anything, so combining instrumental rationality with ethical ambivalence. Either way, they are said to contribute to the Cold War and hence to mutual hostility and the very risk of violence they claim to reduce.[23]

Thus the polarization of the rational and psychological becomes a polarization of conflict and cooperation. Certain commentators (John Harsanyi in the above-mentioned article, Duroselle[24]) accuse Schelling of overemphasizing tacit coordination or common interest, and neglecting the part played by the equilibrium of forces or by conflict. The leading lights of the *Journal of Conflict Resolution*, however, accuse him of being trapped in an overly conflictual or rivalrous point of view, of believing that peace and international order can be based on a system of mutual threat and suspicion, that there is no need for positive sentiments of cooperation and understanding and an organization in which these values may be enshrined. They accuse him, in short, of assuming either that the constant implied threat of force could never result in its use, whatever crises and conflicts might occur, or that it would be rational to use force, even if atomic weapons were involved, just as long as it was done in a calculated and considered manner and according to the rules, by conducting a dialogue of thermonuclear messages with the adversary.

Each of these contradictory criticisms seems to me to contain a degree of truth or at least some sort of salutary warning; but not only do they seem applicable more to certain tendencies or distortions of Schelling's ideas than to his own work, but that work – particularly certain recent articles – itself provides, in my opinion, the best possible rebuttal of them. What is more, it is not Schelling's supporters so much as his critics who are frequently far more guilty than Schelling himself of the faults of which they accuse him.

Perhaps the essence of his viewpoint (also that of Kahn or Wohlstetter, closely related on this point) is the way it avoids the wholesale espousal of the concepts of rationality or irrationality, trust or hostility, peace or apocalypse.

What one is dealing with is a dialectic of two opposing wills confronting and communicating with each other, in such a way that confrontation serves as a means of communication and communication as a form of confrontation. Ignorant of each other, the two guess what each other is like, and their principal means of exerting influence and communicating is by using threats and, potentially, force. The essence of such limited confrontation and restricted communication, the essence of the violence they attempt to tame and exploit, is to be never quite predictable or quite unpredictable. It is the old familiar interplay of chance and free will: it is impossible to have complete control, but it is possible to make use of that impossibility, to let oneself freely engage in a process one may not be able to stop, but which one must nevertheless try to control once embarked on that particular course. This represents one of the most important aspects of the theory and practice of conflict management and crisis control. The belief is that it is disastrous to decide in advance the rationality or irrationality of the actors' behaviour, the impossibility or inevitability of violence, whether conflict or cooperation will be uppermost, whether the dialectic of antagonism or of common interest will prevail. As the threat is always present, violence is always possible, and violence by its nature has threat implicit within it, at every stage, from the most passive or pacific or improbable of deterrents right up to the ultimate catastrophe. As Clausewitz was so well aware, violence always has two faces: the wild face of homicidal folly, prone to escalate to extremes, and the rational face, of the message it sends to sap an adversary's will, whether demanding an alliance or inviting surrender. Hence three equally serious errors: to believe violence is impossible because no one wants it, whereas the adversaries' agreement to avoid it is founded precisely on its omnipresent possibility; to believe it is uncontrollable and condemned to run its full course once unleashed, whereas, as long as two men exist, there remains a chance that out of the depths of their confrontation new and unexpected forms of communication will arise, a new rationality out of the depths of irrationality; and finally, to believe that because violence can also act as a sign or message it will in every respect function as such, or that communication in an atmosphere of panic and dread can ever remotely resemble a rational and relaxed dialogue.

That is why Herman Kahn, while rejecting the postulate that rationality ends where violence begins, nevertheless recognizes that there is an element of truth in the accusation of 'ritualized rationality' levelled at supporters of arms control; but, he insists, such rationality in deterrence, in crises and even in violent conflicts is not in itself good, merely a matter of making the best of a bad situation; nor is it automatic, and that is precisely the point of crisis management, to make it routine, to create a state of rational control.[25] Schelling, in commenting on a series of studies of limited strategic war, warns of two dangers. One consists in

thinking about strategies and situations as though they were predictable, artificially pure and simple, could be relied on to go off as expected, and recognizable at the time for what they were – without the fog of war, the passions and the uncertainties; the snafus, misunderstandings, missed cues, and compromises; and the inevitable lack of any detailed plan for the actual situation that arises.

The other danger, even more important is

thinking that to conduct war in the measured cadence of limited reprisal somehow rescues the whole business of war from impetuosity and gives it rational qualities that it would otherwise lack. . . . Even if this kind of warfare were irrational, it could still enjoy the benefits of slowness, of deliberateness, and of self-control. The situation is fundamentally indeterminate as far as logic goes. There is no logical reason why two adversaries will not bleed each other to death, drop by drop, each continually feeling that if he can only hold out a little longer, the other is bound to give in. . . . That is not to deprecate the value of cool, measured, deliberate action in contrast to spasmodic violence. It is simply to remind us that there is no way to convert war between major adversaries into a rational process that both sides will find satisfying. There are bound to be limits to the safety and security that can be achieved in any style of limited war. The reason is simple: limited war is to a large extent a competition in risk-taking.[26]

These remarks, addressed to the optimists who believe in the possibility of controlled war, have their exact counterpart in criticisms addressed both to the pessimists for whom the system of nation-states is on the verge of destroying itself and to the optimists who believe in generalized mutual deterrence. In his critique of Boulding's book, which regards national defence as obsolete because armed forces can no longer deny enemy forces access to their territory, Schelling accuses the author of having no theory of violence:

War is not just acquisition and loss; it is violent, coercive bargaining – bargaining with demonstrations and threats of further pain, privation, destruction and risk. And it is often inefficient, hotheaded, undisciplined bargaining – in danger of losing contact with policy.

War involves *intentions* as well as *capabilities*. It involves coercion, intimidation, and deterrence. If a model of warfare ignores the pain, the fear and the cost of war, it cannot encompass the bargaining procedure. It cannot recognize deterrence, intimidation, limited war or surrender. The economics of viability is a benchmark in the analysis of bargaining, but only a benchmark. Furthermore, without explicit uncertainty it is hard to generate the phenomenon of brinkmanship – of competitive risk-taking, of the game of 'chicken' . . . . Don't we need models that explicitly examine the motives and decisions to initiate war, to limit or expand it, and to terminate it, and not just examine the prerequisites for military victory?

But if Schelling accuses Boulding of failing to show how wars start, he also accuses him of being too sceptical about the prospect that, with deterrence acting as a substitute for defence, wars may be averted. 'Boulding's opinion is that deterrence depends on threats, threats induce desperation, and war is nearly inevitable. Whether deterrent threats lead to desperation, hostility and panic, or to quiescence, confidence, and security, probably depends on how the threats are arrived at and expressed, what demands accompany them, and the costs and risks of initiating violence and reacting to it.'

Schelling nevertheless ends on a note of caution: 'It takes more than just willingness on both sides to do this, though. It takes skill, and perhaps some luck; . . . My point is not that it is little white threats that make the world go round. It is that nations needn't give up just because military brute force may have to be replaced by threats as a means of protection.'[27]

I have quoted extensively from this article by Schelling because it seems to me to provide a useful corrective to work undertaken on both sides of the Atlantic, valuable in itself, inspired by the idea of non-zero-sum games or the dialectic of antagonism and communication. Several theoretical or experimental studies, notably in the *Journal of Conflict Resolution*, have tried to emphasize the psychological and ethical aspects of communication, and the old idea of the mirror-image and projection surfaces again every year.[28] The role of suspicion, fear, mistrust and mutual hostility leading to aggression is demonstrated in experimental games as well as international crises;[29] and, conversely, there are many other experiments examining and making claims for the reverse cumulative process, that is, the reduction in mistrust, the growth of a sense of collaboration, etc.[30] Schelling would not disown such notions, but issues an urgent reminder that, while we wait for these attempts to succeed, it is necessary, and perhaps not impossible, to go on living, for which purpose, any empirical recipe is welcome:

> We tend to identify peace, stability, and the quiescence of conflict with notions like trust, good faith, and mutual respect. To the extent that this point of view actually encourages trust and respect it is good. But where trust and good faith do not exist and cannot be made to by our acting as though they did, we may wish to solicit advice from the underworld, or from ancient despotisms, on how to make agreements work when trust and good faith are lacking and there is no legal recourse for breach of contract. The ancients exchanged hostages, drank wine from the same glass to demonstrate the absence of poison, met in public places to inhibit the massacre of one by the other and even deliberately exchanged spies to facilitate transmittal of authentic information. It seems likely that a well-developed theory of strategy could throw light on the efficacy of some of those old devices, suggest the circumstances to which they apply, and discover modern equivalents that, though offensive to our taste, may be desperately needed in the regulation of conflict.[31]

But does this not clearly show that, far from eradicating conflict, hostility, mistrust, bad faith, misunderstanding, bluff, the threat and possibility of the use of force, and escalation, tacit bargaining depends in fact on their existence?

That is the lesson that needs to be learned in France today. And one of the most recent and encouraging developments in the theory of international relations since Raymond Aron's *Paix et guerre*, is the publication of a certain number of studies on the theory of international conflict – I have in mind various pieces by J.-B Duroselle,[32] articles by J. Vernant in the *Revue de défense nationale*,[33] and a study of the Cuban crisis by Alain Joxe, part of which was published in the first issue of *Stratégie*.[34] Two of these articles are specifically concerned with bargaining, which I have considered with reference to Schelling, taking his position as central.

Curiously, the bias in the French articles is towards what Schelling would call 'war without pain' or 'crisis without danger'. True, Duroselle in his general theory of conflict lays very considerable emphasis on risk and violence and irrational factors. But in his pages on tacit bargaining, while careful to show he has taken into account the enduring nature of conflicting interests and the risk of accident, he nevertheless appears to see tacit bargaining as the opposite of brink-manship, and indeed also of conflict of interest. Vernant, describing situations in which force will be used, sees bargaining and war as clear alternatives, and points up the opposition between Schelling and Aron. Equally, Duroselle's account of the Cuban crisis regards it as a triumph of tacit bargaining, of playing the game according to the rules; in this respect it reaches conclusions not dissimilar to certain of those in Alain Joxe's study. Tacit bargaining seems such a collabor-ative, organized activity, atomic deterrence so positively reassuring, the diplomatic give-and-take so very much under control, that one could be forgiven for thinking: 'Oh, what a lovely little war!'

I have no wish at this point to embark on a discussion in which I have nothing better than personal impressions to counter interpret-ations I acknowledge as containing a large element of truth; as long as violence has not broken out, no one can show it was not impossible in the first place, that conflict and threats were not part of some elaborate hoax conducted by two accomplices bent on deceiving or educating their respective populations. Looking at it from the dual viewpoint of sociology of knowledge and Schelling's analysis, I would simply point out, on the one hand, the very different perspective of the majority of French writers as compared with the majority of American writers, and, on the other hand, that Schelling's concepts are used by the former in an interpretative framework more theirs than his.

On the first point, among the American writers, the optimists are those who consider it possible to avoid disaster in the long term. Pacifists and strategists alike, not one subscribes to the formula ruling out the use of atomic weapons altogether. Given the same situation, of an approximate equilibrium among the atomic powers or mutual deterrence, which makes deliberate, unpunished aggression supremely unlikely, writers such as P.-M. Gallois and J. Vernant treat the problem as though it is already solved, regarding conflict as restricted henceforth to the non-atomic nations, while the American commentators redouble their efforts and keep asking questions. If war is not going to break out as the result of a surprise attack, might it conceivably do so by accident, or through misunderstanding or escalation? And if it were ever to break out in this way, in a situation of equilibrium, how could one imagine it developing or ending? Hence the proliferation of studies of crises on the one hand and of limited war on the other, with the necessity for conflict management apparent at every level. In France, Vernant believes that 'all speculations on the diplomatic/strategic process as it should be conducted in the current situation start from the premise that the behaviour of states, or in other words the decisions of their statesmen, are rational, and will become more so as the states in question get rid of their weapons of massive deterrence and in so doing become subject to the law of mutual deterrence'.[35] At the same time, in the United States, Hermann Kahn declares:

> We do not assume the other side is rational. Where I work we fire people for assuming that. . . . I do want to make clear that we do not assume either the antagonist will be wildly irrational. That is quite different from assuming that he is going to be rational. There are many degrees of rationality. Nobody is completely rational. Very few people are completely irrational, and one wishes to be in a position to exploit and encourage certain kinds of rationality and discourage other kinds.[36]

That leads him to think that optimism based on deterrence is only fully justified in general terms or 'in normal times'.

> When the provocation is slight, a probability of reprisals or a level of weak reprisals will suffice. But acute crises and wars are not normal times. The stakes are raised very high, credibility and power of response are challenged, and the 'unacceptable' nature of the damage becomes an object of calculation rather than an *a priori* premise. Such circumstances may still arise, and when they do, the details of military policy may have consequences of the first magnitude.[37]

On the second point, both Schelling's recent work and his definitions in *The Strategy of Conflict* seem to place him as far away from the notion of the perfect idyll as from that of the inevitable apocalypse. Because one of his original contributions was to insist on the cooperation and common interest that exist between adversaries, we risk forgetting that he makes an explicit distinction between tacit coordination (where there are interests in common) and tacit bargaining (where both sides have different interests) and declares that coordination-game theory, while interesting in its own right, is interesting mainly for 'the light that it sheds on the nature of mixed-motive games'.[38] In his reclassification of games, he identifies the 'mixed game' (neither all-conflict nor all-cooperation) and the bargaining situation, and declares his interest in the 'distributional' aspect of bargaining rather than that of mutual advantage. Hence, the application of the theory not only does not assume common interest to be the only factor, it actually assumes the opposite; it does not even assume that common interest is more important than conflict: it does not pronounce on the proportions in which they should be combined, all it demands is that the two elements exist. As for bargaining, it is defined as the combination of promises and threats, and Schelling lays particular emphasis on the threats.[39] Where he quotes examples other than of international conflict, he does not appear either to deny or to minimize the importance of what Aron sees as the decisive characteristic of international conflict, namely, the risk of war. He mentions non-zero-sum games involved in wars and threats of war, strikes, negotiations, criminal deterrence, class war, race war, price war and blackmail, manoeuvring in a bureaucracy or in a traffic jam, and the coercion of one's own children.[40] Another list refers to 'threats and responses to threats, reprisals and counter-reprisals, limited war, arms races, brinkmanship, surprise attack, trusting and cheating'.[41] Far from defining bargaining as being the opposite of force, he describes his theory as the exploitation of potential force. Far from contrasting it with brinkmanship, on the contrary, he regards the latter as one of the most eloquent cases of tacit bargaining, one of the principal foundations on which his theory rests,[42] one of two subjects (the other being the role of military force in foreign politics) on which he was to concentrate in his subsequent research, awarding it a more prominent role than the majority of his colleagues in his policy recommendations.[43] If he introduces modifications in the concept of brinkmanship, it is, using his idea of the 'threat that leaves something to chance', in his insistence on accepting the risk of a result as disastrous for oneself as for one's adversary, rather than eliminating it altogether: 'I think we have got to learn, to believe in, and to accept the concept of partly controlled escalation – to utilize the *genuine* risk of the thing getting out of hand to make the Soviets unwilling to pursue advantages that otherwise they will have in many parts of the world'.[44]

This leads us on to the Cuban crisis, which provoked the following stimulating if ambiguous comment from Joxe: 'On the American as well as the Soviet side, the escalation of the crisis appears to be the result of a certain willingness on the part of both governments to let through plans of action by extremists in both camps, the result of very poor communications between the two goverments (at least in public), maintained right up to the brink and even in the heat of the crisis.'[45] This is the language of Schelling, which reappears, applied on a systematic basis, in Duroselle's short analysis of the crisis.[46] He offers a rather different interpretation from Joxe, believing that the Soviet Union hoped initially to improve its position by installing rockets, but subsequently, by not for a single instant offering resistance in the face of the US reaction, demonstrated its attachment to peace; and at a later stage, the United States, by tolerating the continuing existence of Soviet garrisons, demonstrated it was playing the game in a similar spirit, forbearing to take risks or make costly and dangerous attempts to gain ground, in the literal sense of the term. Joxe on the other hand seems to place a greater premium on motivations arising from internal relations from within the two camps and the two leading nations. But he sums it up as a 'highly educational demonstration of the virtues of peaceful coexistence'.

It is possible to agree with these two writers as to the final outcome of the crisis, and accept Duroselle's three propositions, yet still to think that Schelling would accuse them of the same things of which he accused his American colleagues: for you do not recognize in these descriptions the crisis as it was experienced by the protagonists (unless perhaps as some sort of gigantic hoax, if one could ignore all the evidence and indications of their state of mind). This is not the crisis, with all its surprises, misunderstandings, ambiguities, lies, resolutions, threats, risks, improvisations, accidents, anxieties, triumphs and reliefs, the crisis that was such a test of nerve and will. Can one really deny that the importation of Soviet missiles to Cuba came as a surprise to the Americans (particularly the theoreticians of tacit agreement)[47] or that the US reaction came as a surprise to the Soviets?[48] Can one ignore the developing rhythm of the crisis, the way the attitudes of the protagonists changed, their contradictory acts and statements? Can one regard the clandestine introduction of missiles into Cuba (as offensive or defensive weapons?) as a sign that the adversaries had reached 'in an almost unconsciously cooperative way . . . a mutually recognized definition of what constitutes an innovation, a challenging or assertive move, or a cooperative gesture', and developed 'some common norm regarding the kind of retaliation that fits the crime when a breach of the rules occurs'?[49] Did the importation of the missiles mean they were playing the game by the rules, 'forbearing to take risks or make costly and dangerous attempts to gain ground, in the literal sense of the term'? Perhaps this mutual understanding and this common norm have been achieved today, but that is after and because of the crisis, because the crisis demonstrated the need for these things; and it demonstrated that need precisely by showing the dangers of a situation where such agreement did not exist. The crisis *took place*, it was not the enactment of some preordained scenario. It is because it represented a monumental failure of communications between the two sides, because, with all the lies and misunderstandings, it was obliged to assume the guise of a test of willpower, a competition in risk-taking, that the urgent necessity for better communications, even an acceptance of the status quo, became apparent to both sides, and in particular the one that had hitherto rejected it. In that sense, we may perhaps talk of a 'test' or a 'highly educational demonstration', but only if we add that it was a negative one.

At the heart of the demonstration, the central feature of this tacit bargaining, was brinkmanship, the fact that, in Schelling's words, 'the United States has engaged in directly coercive military threats to deny the Soviets the military advantage of advance deployment of missiles',[50] the fact, above all, that they were in an escalating situation. President Kennedy had failed to show sufficient commitment to dissuade Mr Khrushchev from installing the missiles (possibly with a view to gaining for himself a psychological and symbolic advantage in the world order).[51] By his speech of 22 October, by preparations and indiscretions based on imminent action, he had created the type of situation described by Schelling, where one protagonist is too far committed to withdraw, he has burnt his bridges, and it is his adversary who, being less committed and freer to act, must withdraw, if he wants to stop the mechanism. Certain of Khrushchev's letters seem directly to betray this feeling of going right to the brink, of loss of control and spiralling risk.[52] If in the end there was a rational outcome to the crisis, and the transformation it wrought in the behaviour of the protagonists tended in the direction of increased security, all the indications are that such security and rationality were achieved through the experience of risk and irrationality, in a confrontation that at any moment could have got out of hand and taken a different turn, with a variety of possible consequences; and, as Duroselle has shrewdly pointed out, those consequences are still undetermined even today.

Here we touch on an important point, the relationship between rationality and predictability. The fact that adversaries try to act rationally, and that, retrospectively, the result of their confrontation also appears rational, does not, it seems to me, mean that it could be calculated in advance. The decision is an event, the interaction of decisions even more so, not to speak of the interaction of decisions and external circumstances, which multiplies the possibilities to infinity.

It is helpful to distinguish, in terms of our present concerns, between the *prospective* rationality of the theoretician, the *active* rationality of the player, and the *retrospective* rationality of the philosopher–historian.

In respect of the first of these, all serious theoreticians today recognize the impossibility of using game theory or any other mathematical tool to predict the conduct of the protagonists or the way conflicts will develop. They know that, when, in response to objections (by Aron and Duroselle, inter alia), they attempt to construct models of bargaining in which the utility function of the opponent is not known,[53] or where it is changed in the course of the negotiations, or where the negotiations themselves are undefined, etc., etc., then, in Raymond Aron's phrase, they move from the calculations of the mathematician to the intuitions of the psychologist. The object of their work is specifically to enlarge a field of possibilities, which they know to be inexhaustible.[54] But then we also know that it is precisely because of the fundamental unpredictability of the way conflicts develop that it is essential to preserve the opportunity for rational behaviour whatever the circumstances. The actual choices cannot be predicted, but the possibility of rational behaviour means one can conceive of certain alternatives that may or may not happen, among which the protagonist may decide as he chooses; at least the fact of having envisaged certain choices in advance may, if the need arises, help him to locate them when the storm is raging.

The principal error would be, in seeing the reasons for a choice, to believe it to be certain in advance or inevitable in retrospect. Nothing can replace the viewpoint of the protagonist who makes his choice in an atmosphere of uncertainty and risk. Or nothing, that is, unless it be the point of view of the person who knows the end of the story (if there is one) and the meaning men's acts acquire, unknown to themselves, when viewed in the perspective of historical reasoning. But, if this perspective exists, is it not then important to distinguish it from that of the protagonists? When we represent Khrushchev and Kennedy as simultaneously omniscient and yet incapable of controlling their respective extremists, trying to convince them with these 'highly educational demonstrations',[55] are we not confusing the role of these two men with the role of destiny? When we use terms like 'bringing about', 'leading towards', 'test destined to', 'means of achieving', are we not ascribing intentionality to what is merely an outcome?

Who knows, perhaps deterrence and peaceful coexistence will have the last word. Perhaps, through all the crises and conflicts, 'the cunning of reason' is at work. But that being the case, perhaps one may be allowed to paraphrase an illustrious expert on conflict, whose name belongs alongside Schelling's, and conclude by quoting Hegel. International relations and tacit bargaining may well be spoken of as a game of coexistence with itself – 'but this idea sinks into mere edification, and even insipidity, if it lacks the seriousness, the suffering, the patience, and the labour of the negative'.[56]

PART TWO

NUCLEAR DETERRENCE

4

The Nation-State in the Nuclear Age

NEVER HAVE theoretical concepts penetrated general discussion as widely as in contemporary international relations: bipolarity, balance of power, deterrence, nuclear age, polycentrism – this is the daily bread of editorials and speeches. But never have these concepts been so ambiguous, never has their use run such a risk of hiding certain aspects of a complex reality by the very process of stressing their equally valid counterparts.

To think about the fate of the nation-state today, even if one abstracts from its formation and its disintegration, from the numerous cases of nations in search of a state and of states devoid of a national basis, leads us immediately to a series of diverging trends and of contradictory conclusions: obviously in some respects the nation-state is flourishing and in others it is dying; it can no longer fulfil some of the most important of its traditional functions, yet it constantly assumes new ones which it alone seems able to fulfil. But what is significant is that the relative importance of these features and the balance between them varies from case to case. Although some features are declining and others growing in all nation-states, the fact is that some nation-states are more obsolete and others more obstinate than others. Indeed, the irony is that, as Horst Mendershausen has observed, 'the state that is eroded by ungovernable trans-national involvements is often not the dog-in-the-manger state, but the peaceful, civilized, orderly state, not East Germany but Belgium or Canada'.[1] The existence of contradictory trends towards integration and disintegration, independence and interdependence, paralysis and freedom of action, leads both to an increase in the number of possible distinctions and hierarchies between states, and to a change in the meaning of the existing ones. Not only is it difficult to talk about the nation-state as such, but any assessment based upon a strict definition of great, small and middle powers, of allied, neutral, and non-aligned, of nuclear, conventional, and potentially nuclear, not to speak of status quo and revisionist, or growing and declining powers, will be sometimes contradictory, often ambiguous and always provisional.

However, if nation-states have at least a superficially recognizable (even if ultimately deceptive) identity, can one say the same of the balance of power? One need not go into esoteric discussions about the nature of power and the mechanisms of the balance system to recognize that no obvious answer is available to the simple, immediate question: is there such a thing as *a* world balance of power, and if so, who balances whom, or what balances what, and how? The many dimensions of the states reflect the many dimensions of power; the existence of various types and hierarchies among both would seem to lead quite naturally to several balances, differing along both regional and functional lines, rather than to a single one; if that is so, how are they related? Do they obey the same rules? Obviously the answers to these questions will differ if by balance one simply understands distribution, or the massive fact that power stops power, or the delicate mechanism through which a system of several independent states is kept in existence.

The last words in our title would seem at least to provide some limits to our questions and some focus to our answers by pointing to a given period and a given problem: the nuclear age. But here again the comfort is slight, for the simplicity is deceptive. Even within the revolution in military technology, are we so certain that we live in the nuclear age rather than, say, in the missile or the space age? Obviously the differences between nation-states and the role of each vary if one considers the weapons or their delivery vehicles, and this is enough to indicate that any generalization here has to be qualified by our awareness both of alternative criteria and of conceivable technological changes. Still more important is our suspicion that the expression 'the nuclear age' implies an assumption of the decisive relevance of military technology (or, if one wishes, of the global strategic balance) which may be justified but is certainly not self-evident. The relevance of nuclear weapons to, say, guerrilla warfare, and the respective importance of these two levels and of the intermediary, conventional one, for the nature of our age and the fate of the nation-state, are open questions from the military point of view alone. They point to the wider problems of the relationship between the military and the political, between arms and influence, between the nation-state's ability to defend itself and its other roles.

We shall start with the relationship between the two relatively well-defined terms – nation-states and nuclear weapons.

74

When analysing the fate of the nation-state, especially in a context in which we are interested both in the problem of nationalism and in that of nuclear weapons, we must be careful not to confuse what belongs to the nature of the territorial, of the national and of the nationalist state. In other words, we must distinguish the material and institutional basis of the state (in terms of territorial dimensions, resources and organization), and the political, psychological or ideological ties on which the unity of the population and the authority of the rulers are based (the modern nation as opposed both to traditional dynastic or religious states, and to universalist and ideological ties); and we must also distinguish the types of attitude and behaviour towards the outside world (such as stressing one's own independence or freedom of action more than desiring to limit that of others, or stressing those objectives which necessarily presuppose conflict, such as prestige or conquest, rather than those potentially more cooperative, like peace or prosperity).[2]

If we go from the first aspect to the third, we find the same problems and dilemmas in a more and more acute or exaggerated form; the appeals, the troubles and the dangers of nationalism are those of the modern state writ large.

If we define the latter as a centralized area unit, composed of an organized group of men occupying a territory under a sovereign government endowed with the monopoly of legitimate force, we see that some elements of this definition seem hard to reconcile with the new realities of the nuclear age (this goes, above all, for the material elements, the size of the territory and the volume of resources), while others (the organizational ones like centralization and unity of command, and the moral ones like patriotism), seem to be made more necessary or at least more important by these new conditions.

If we remember that the nation-state is only one form of territorial state, we see that in most cases it amplifies both the problems of scale (the dimensions and the resources of the nuclear age being those of continents or of the world rather than those of the great majority of nations) and the advantages of unity and solidarity (which appear decisively more solid in the case of nations than of alliances, of camps and of blocs).

Finally, if we look at the objectives of foreign policy, at the ideology which inspired them, and at the action which seeks to achieve them, a new reality appears: nuclear weapons seem to encourage the defensive nationalism of separateness, distrust and self-reliance; they seem to discourage the offensive nationalism of conquest and expansion. To use Stanley Hoffmann's expression, they tend to protect the nation-

75

state both from merger and from madness. A less charitable way of expressing the same situation would be that modern conditions help nations to preserve their independence but prevent them from using it, that they make nations more jealous of their sovereignty but make this sovereignty less meaningful.

While these formulations differ only by their emphasis, the search for the ultimate meaning of the situation they describe can lead to two completely opposite views. 'Nuclear nationalism' can be seen either as defensive nationalism, a nationalism purified at long last of its adventurous and imperialistic aspects and made compatible with the international stability upon which it is based; or it can be seen as an absolute illusion which can only be either meaningless or suicidal, since, precisely, the only freedom on which it is based is that of suicide, while interdependence carries the day both in the hypothetical world of nuclear defence and in the real world of non-nuclear activities.

To decide between these two extreme and simplified views one would have to undertake a complex weighing of psychological versus quantitative data. From admittedly intangible hypotheses about degrees of credibility and of reality, the only certitude that would emerge is that nuclear weapons do not justify the sweeping generalizations of those twin 'great simplifiers', the small-power nationalist and the great-power globalist.

Their excuse is that, if one isolates it from its historical and political context, the atom is itself the great simplifier. Through the immensity of their destructive power and the improbability of their effective use, nuclear weapons are a permanent invitation to reason in 'all or nothing' terms, hence to visualize the dissolution of more complex and ambiguous wholes like alliances or like the international system itself, either by fusion or by fission: either by total integration into one community, or by total disintegration into a multiplicity of isolated nations.

The most extreme theories of peace through universalism and of peace through nationalism current today start from the nuclear fact which, by making the classical game of diplomacy and war impossible because it makes it too dangerous, must lead, according to the first, to its total suppression through disarmament or world government, or, according to the second, to its stabilization through nuclear proliferation and multilateral deterrence. If, narrowing the points of the compass, one looks at the debate on nuclear control and sharing within alliances, it is no less striking that the crisis of both the Western and the Eastern alliance should have had the atom, if not as a cause, at least as a starting point or a pretext. In both cases the deep roots are probably elsewhere, in the conflict of ambitions involving a complex and unconscious mixture of ideological preconceptions and national interests. But in both cases the existence of the nuclear factor has considerably sharpened the problems of independence and solidarity by increasing the leader's claim to centralized control and his distrust of his adventurous allies, and by the claim of the latter to sovereignty and their distrust of their too prudent protector.

Both in the universalism-versus-nationalism and in the integration-versus-multinationalism debates, one is struck by the deep intellectual resemblance between the opposite theories.

The case for the demise of the nation-state through nuclear weapons is an amplification of the case for the demise of the territorial state through air power. It has been made most forcefully by John Herz and Kenneth Boulding.[3] For Herz,

> What accounted for the peculiar unity, coherence, or compactness of the modern nation-state, setting it off from other nation-states as a separate unit and permitting us to characterise it as 'independent', 'sovereign', 'a power', was its 'impermeability' or 'impenetrability': so did the territoriality of the modern state, surrounded as it was by what may be called its 'hard shell' which protected it from foreign penetration. It is this factor which made it defensible and, at least to some extent, secure in its relations with other units. It thus made the state the ultimate unit of protection for those living within its boundaries. Today, on the other hand, the impenetrability of the political atom, the nation-state, is giving way to a permeability which tends to obliterate the very meaning of unit and unity, power and power relations, sovereignty and independence. The possibility of 'hydrogenisation' represents merely the continuation of a development which has rendered the 'hard shell', the traditional defence structure of nations, obsolete through the power to by-pass the shell protecting a two-dimensional 'territory' and thus to destroy – vertically as it were – even the most powerful ones.

Successive developments in warfare, from economic blockade through ideological penetration to air war and atomic power, have increasingly overpassed this hard-shell defence. In particular, since the advent of air warfare, which makes it possible to destroy a country before disarming its armies and occupying its territory, the roof has blown off the territorial state. This in turn means a change from distinctness and separateness to pervasion, to 'absolute permeability of each by each of the others'. Potentially at least, the power of everyone is present 'everywhere'.

Other authors have given the same idea a more formalized and economically oriented formulation, which makes it easier to test its validity. For Kenneth Boulding, the nation-state is doomed because its unconditional viability (i.e. its power to withstand any attack) has been replaced by conditional viability (i.e. its survival is dependent on the decision of others not to attack it, as distinct from their inability to do so). The reason for this is that states were protected by the existence of the LSG (or loss of strength gradient), which favoured the defensive: power tended to decrease with the distance from its home base. Today, aircraft and missiles have reduced the loss of strength gradient almost to vanishing point, thus favouring the offensive, since power can be applied from anywhere, distance involving almost no loss in time and cost. This is what Professor Modelski calls a 'perfect market' in security, transportation costs being a basic cause of imperfect competition. But while Boulding, like Herz, draws from this situation the conclusion that the world has become too small for the existence of separate nation-states, Modelski sees in it a greater chance for the survival of small nation-states: they can protect themselves and be protected by great powers against any threat regardless of geography, without the delay that was crucial in other times.[4]

This leads us to the view that constitutes the perfect mirror-image of the Boulding–Herz one. Like the latter and unlike Modelski, right-wing proliferationists such as General Pierre Gallois and left-wing ones such as Mr John Burton[5] believe that nuclear weapons act as the great equalizer, making differences in power between states meaningless; but while for the first school all states are equal because none is able to defend itself, for the second all are equal because each is able to protect itself. If everybody can destroy everybody, one may conclude either that everybody can be destroyed or that nobody will be. The unconditional viability once enjoyed by some may be over, but conditional viability, if it is universal and reciprocal, may yet provide the greatest security for the greatest number of states. The model these authors outline is one of generalized armed neutrality (as General Gallois would put it and as the French Chief of Staff, General Ailleret, would seem to imply in an authoritative article),[6] or (as in Mr John Burton's approach, which combines faith in the Afro-Asian world with faith in the bomb), of generalized non-alignment, based on what Morton Kaplan has called the unit veto system: every state being able to destroy, in retaliation, every other one, or, in a more extreme version, to destroy the whole world.[7] Obviously we encounter here the ambiguity of the 'nuclear age' idea. Neither school claims that the conditions of its favourite model are anything but foreshadowed by the situation of the nuclear powers in the present world; but both maintain that they are implicit in present trends.

For all states to be equally vulnerable thanks to the eclipse of distance, every state would have to have the weapons and the means of delivery to inflict unacceptable damage on every other one; for all states to be equally protected, each should, in addition, have an invulnerable retaliatory force. In other words, the situation described is a generalization to the whole planet of the nature of the present nuclear balance between the two superpowers. It holds between states that have achieved a condition of stable deterrence, characterized by the mutual invulnerability of their forces and the mutual vulnerability of their societies.[8] This condition is created by the extreme concentration of explosive power characteristic of nuclear weapons, but it is by no means universally given or, in all likelihood, universally and permanently accessible. At one extreme, the existence of an insufficiently powerful or protected nuclear force, at the other technological break-throughs like progress in anti-missile systems or in civil defence, can make a nation's forces vulnerable or its cities invulnerable; neither the equalization of states nor the stabilization of deterrence would then remain valid. General Gallois admits as much, since in his latest book he distinguishes three categories of state: those which, besides securing their protection through nuclear weapons, can keep conventional forces enabling them to put military means at the service of an active foreign policy directed at influence or conquest against non-nuclear states; those which can only afford a nuclear posture and enjoy the same security as the first but not the same active influence; and finally the non-nuclear states, which can hardly be called states at all since they cannot protect themselves against the nuclear ones. In the same book, Gallois recognizes that automatically stabilized deterrence on his model is likely to be a transitory one.[9] However, he would maintain as permanently valid the bias of nuclear weapons in favour of the nation-state, due to their apocalyptic destructive power. That their use means suicide can be credible only as a last-resort threat, meant to defend one's ultimate honour or one's very existence and based on ultimate solidarity and either on automaticity or on 'irrational' values; this rules out protection and alliances. On the other hand, 'proportionate deterrence' and the blurring of quantitative differences after a threshold of destruction which he puts relatively low, give this deterrent capacity to relatively small forces.

Obviously, technological presuppositions (on the ease of securing for one's retaliatory force both sufficient protection and sufficient penetration) are mingled with psychological ones, but the stress is on the latter. While the case of the 'nuclear pessimists' is based on the physical difficulties of defence, the case of the 'nuclear optimists' is based on the psychological possibilities of deterrence. Of course, if deterrence does not fail, defence will not be put to the test; but the point about deterrence is that it may fail, that in order not to fail it must be credible, which means that if not defence, at least retaliation, must be both psychologically conceivable and physically feasible. In both respects one is up against psychological assumptions which, by the nature of deterrence, cannot be verified unless deterrence fails. Whatever the wisdom of thinking about defence if deterrence fails, obviously the first consideration is to prevent it from failing. The best formulation of the two positions, then, is based on Glenn Snyder's distinction between deterrence by denial and deterrence by punishment.[10] Nuclear weapons make deterrence by denial more difficult and deterrence by punishment more easy. Deterrence by denial, as against deterrence by punishment, may always have been less prevalent in the past than the theorists of territoriality or unconditional viability assume; at any rate, deterrence by punishment seems to have been more effective in keeping the peace since 1945. On the other hand the crucial point is that 'deterrence by punishment' is more correctly named deterrence by *threat* of punishment. Contrary to deterrence by denial, it has to be believed in order to work and it leads to suicide if it isn't. Hence, while today the possibility of deterrence by punishment plays a greater role than the impossibility of deterrence by denial, we are more certain about the latter than about the former. The difficulty of deterrence by denial is possibly irrelevant but certainly solid; the feasibility of deterrence by punishment is certainly relevant but possibly shaky.

We find a similar opposition between the psychological strength and the physical weakness of the nation-state in the second dialogue, which sets nuclear nationalists not against world disarmers but against alliance centralizers. Again, both approaches look like mirror images of each other. Both conceive of deterrence in an essentially bilateral setting, with power A deterring a potential aggressor B. Both insist upon the necessity, for retaliation to be effective and hence for deterrence to be credible, of having one finger on the trigger, and a political one; they are, then, equally hostile to decision by committee and decision by delegation to military commanders.

They are unquestionably right from the point of view of the strategic optimum. What forces them to oppose each other is the fact that political reality makes this strategic optimum inapplicable, since reality is made up of a plurality of states which are close enough to be allied against a common enemy, but both too distinct to constitute a single community under a single authority, overcoming disagreements and suspicious, and too unequal in dimensions and strength for each to be able to secure its own protection by itself. The tendency of US strategists is to dismiss the first difficulty and to consider the whole zone covered by the Atlantic alliance as a single area, whose protection and defence, placed under the authority of the US president, should be conceived and whose forces should be distributed according to the strategic requirements of maximum security and efficiency.

A theorist like General Gallois answers that if the Atlantic community or Europe did actually constitute a single country, the ultimate decision on which deterrence relies could and should be entrusted to its president, but since this single country does not exist, national solidarity can only be that of existing nations, each of which must secure its own protection since all are too vulnerable to protect each other.

The Americans in their turn answer that, to secure one's own protection, national existence is not enough; the unequal distribution of dimensions and resources does not allow most countries to deter the possible aggression of a great power with any kind of credibility. General Gallois answers with his theory of proportional deterrence; a kind of pre-established harmony enables every small power, if it wants to pay the price, to inflict on every great power an amount of destruction corresponding to its own 'stake'.

At this point it becomes clear that the reasoning leads to a postulate which is just as obvious contrary to reality as the 'American' point of view postulating the negligible nature of national differences within the alliance. The coherence and simplicity of the two extreme positions are obtained only be leaving aside political reality in one case, psychological, physical, and technological reality in the other.

In real life, one cannot help having to deal with both aspects and hence with a complex reality where states unequal in power are both linked by common interests and separated by diverging ones. One must envisage various unsatisfactory compromises between protection and independence, self-reliance and interdependence, commitment and flexibility. If it does not lead to compromise, the uneven and contradictory distribution of power as physical strength, of power as freedom of action and of power as influence can lead to mutual paralysis or destruction.

One finds an enlightening reflection of the same dilemmas if one looks at the non-nuclear level, and at the debate raging in the United

81

States between globalists for whom modern communications and strategic mobility have made spheres of influence and geographical limitations obsolete, and 'neo-isolationists' for whom modern national-ism and revolutionary warfare have made great-power intervention self-defeating. The horns of the dilemma are less far apart than in the nuclear case. The loss of strength gradient and the favourable or unfavourable characteristics of the battleground for intervention from a distance, exist to a greater degree for local war; David cannot protect himself against Goliath by threatening to destroy him in retaliation. Nevertheless the same technology-versus-psychology debate does take place, and perhaps in a more relevant and realistic way than in the abstract world of nuclear deterrents.

Strategists have argued (most brilliantly and thoroughly in the case of Albert Wohlstetter[11]) that geopolitical distances tend to become irrelevant not only for nuclear but also for non-nuclear combat. Long-distance lift capacity is easier to achieve for a country like the United States than short-distance lift capacity within the military theatre. If distance is measured not in miles but in time and cost of trans-portation, the United States is closer to Vietnam than is China, since it can more easily transport troops into the country.

On the other hand, psychological, sociological, ideological, cultural and historical distances reassert themselves with a vengeance, and more so in the confused and diffuse world of conventional and subconven-tional war than in the rarefied dialogue of nuclear crisis. North Vietnam or the NLF cannot deter the United States by punishment, but they are themselves less vulnerable to 'compellence'[12] or to 'deterrence by punishment' than the Soviet Union would be, precisely because they can benefit both from their weakness and from the inability of their opponents to ascertain to what extent they under-stand his messages and to what extent they would, if willing, be able to comply. More important, they can practise denial and reaffirm, if not the impermeability of the territorial nation-state, at least the unconquerability of the nationalist territory, in a more convincing way than both modern nuclear mini-deterrence and traditional resistance to conquest. The costs of transportation have declined but the costs of intervention in human, psychological and ultimately in financial terms have increased. The appeal and the legitimacy of conquest, of an imperial mission, go against the ethos of a modern democratic society; the urge and ability to resist are encouraged in the developing nations by increasing political mobilization and organization, made possible by modernization itself; smallness, underdevelopment and new nation-hood being advantages in cohesion, solidarity, austerity and fanaticism, which increase the credibility of protracted resistance even more than some of the same features do the credibility of nuclear retaliation.[13]

The fact that the case against the nation–state has been linked to the case against geographical distance should not, however, make us identify the two issues completely. Among US globalists, the more serious ones (the strategists as opposed to the ideologists) seem to be opposed more to regionalism than nationalism. They can – as Wohlstetter does – acknowledge the resistance of revolutions to technology, yet point our that this might apply to Latin America no less than to Asia. That nationalist peoples are obstinate does not make spheres of influence any less obsolete, or regional divisions any less irrelevant – so long as they are based on geography. This is certainly true, from a military point of view, as against critics like Walter Lippmann or Hans Morgenthau who are imprudent enough to put their case against US overextension in terms of physical resources and proximity. But it is more valid for capabilities than interests, and more for the capability to move troops and to inflict destruction than for that to win friends and influence people. The point is that there is more to regionalism than geopolitics or, put another way, that political geography is made up of history, anthropology and psychology as much as of physical geography. There is nothing sacred about distance which cannot be made obsolete by changes in transportation time and cost; but the racial and cultural differences, and centuries of shared (whether hostile or friendly, usually both) experiences as neighbours, are another matter.

Militarily the United States may be closer to Vietnam than is China, just as, physically, Europe is closer to China than the United States; but psychologically and politically the United States is an Asian power in a way Germany is not, and China's presence in Southeast Asia is of a different nature again: it does not have to establish the credibility of its long-term presence, whereas the United States, in order to do so, must commit itself psychologically and materially to an extent which then drastically limits its freedom of action. Oceans may no longer constitute a physical barrier, nor is the same skin colour a guarantee of understanding, or racial difference a guarantee of hostility; but – just as for the perceived difference between land conquest and colonization by sea – they constitute points of salience, in Schelling's sense, which emerge out of history and leave their mark on psychology. They are crucially important in the case of deterrence itself, as both Schelling's observations on the relation between degrees of bloc-cohesion and territorial contiguity, and the experience of the different kind of protection extended by the Soviet Union to North Vietnam and Eastern Europe, with the latter being more respected by the United

States, have shown; how much more important, then, in the case of political relationships. The fact that, more often than not, one hates one's neighbour and enters into alliance with a more distant protector only reinforces this. This ally is valued *qua* distant and different, and the eclipse of distance may make him lose this quality without gaining an intimacy which the traditional foe has never lost. From the relations between Greek city states and the Persian empire to those of Southeast Asian states with China and the United States, or of France and Germany, the history of Asia and Europe is full of these ambiguous and ambivalent relations, where different degrees and phases of enmity and cooperation, suzerainty and conquest, of presence and absence, affect the ways in which states can understand, influence, protect and deter each other. Another relevant consideration is that of size or of position in the power balance: again, medium states will both be more jealous of other, neighbouring medium states than of a distant protector, and at the same time share a common experience as against his which a too direct confrontation (in which, precisely, the difference in size and power appears as the decisive factor) may help to revive and strengthen. Here again, the strategist and the economist will find ideas of continental solidarity or self-assertion irrelevant only if they are prepared to maintain that strategy has nothing to do with psychology nor economics with politics.

In short, the brave new (unified) world of universalists and globalists and the brave new (fragmented) world of nationalists and isolationists, both supposedly based on the lessons of technology, are abstract and one-dimensional worlds which neglect, at their peril, the complex network of solidarities, hostilities, misunderstandings, or commitments and balances, which centuries of conflict and alliance, as well as new common interests and new rivalries, have woven among nations. The political map of the world, with its mountains and its hills, its canyons and its oceans, as well as its roads and passes, is neither a series of islands nor one continuous bloc or flat surface. None of the generalizations of either side in each of our three dialogues really holds true.

It is false to claim that in earlier times no state was pregnable, or that every state could defend itself: at any time many states have had to rely on their lack of appeal, on alliances, on the workings of the international system itself for their viability. It is equally false to claim that today any state can be conquered or that no state can defend itself: the roof may have blown off, but being bombed is not being conquered, nor does domination of the air guarantee political domination.

Similarly, it is false to say that any state, even nuclear, can deter any

84

attack upon itself. And it is equally false that no state can deter any attack on another state. Nor would the opposite statements be any more true. Obviously, while the optimum situation is that of a great nuclear power, endowed with an invulnerable force and an assured destruction capability against any opponent, deterring an attack on its own territory, some residual deterrence against some threats is available both to a small nuclear power, however limited and vulnerable its retaliatory force may be, against attacks directed against itself, and also to a great nuclear power, even one lacking a 'credible first strike' capability, which wants to deter an attack on one of its allies. Weighing the degree of deterrence secured by a greater probability of retaliation, as against less acceptable damage, can be done only by the potential aggressor. Precisely because degrees of credibility are involved, the nature of the political relationship within the relevant triangle would obviously be decisive.

Finally, it would be equally ludicrous to assert that all powers are equal because none can exert influence or balance power outside its borders, and that great powers can do so everywhere and in the same way, regardless of variations not only in regional balances but in the nature of the power involved or required.

To say, then, that the international world is always changing in the hierarchy of powers, in the nature of power, in the nature of links and of balances between states, that one type of power is related to another type, but not immediately convertible into it and may sometimes be counterproductive for it, that, even militarily, no state can exert any kind of deterrence and of compellence, of defence and of conquest, against any other state, that no state is totally devoid of all four of these possibilities against every other state, and that the favourable conditions for each of these functions vary with the relationships among various states, is simply to advance a series of platitudes, amounting to the idea that no state is either all-powerful or completely powerless, and that the degrees and nature of the power of all vary from case to case. Yet sometimes it is difficult to resist the impression that beyond these platitudes one can find only either a philosophic speculation on the nature of the nation-state or an empirical analysis of the various political situations in a given area at a given time.

This impression, however excusable, would be misleading. Once one accepts the idea that it is not very fruitful to talk about *the* nation-state, and even less about *the* balance of power, there remains a broad field of inquiry about the changing and complex nature and distribution of power in the world today. Both the debate about the changing meaning and results of the use of force, and the debate about trends towards dominance by one power, bipolarity, multipolarity, or polycentrism in the international system, are genuine debates which have been abundantly illustrated by many writers, including Raymond Aron, Thomas Schelling, Robert Osgood, Klaus Knorr, Stanley Hoffmann, Kenneth Waltz, C.E. Zoppo, George Liska and Zbigniew Brzezinski. This is not the place either to summarize these debates or to add to them. One general point, however, seems worth making because it would seem to indicate the direction in which the conditions and limits of national independence, military sovereignty and diplomatic freedom of action can be meaningfully explored today for the different states.

The striking feature which recurs both within and between the various debates is a particular type of multidimensionality, or a particular combination of independence and interdependence, of separation and interaction. Dimensions that could be considered as indicators of each other because they used to be roughly inseparable in fact, or confused in analysis, must today to distinguished in a more systematic way because their discrepancy raises all kinds of paradoxes: this goes for deterrence and defence, for military force and diplomatic influence, for flexibility and security, etc. But, next to confusing them, the most dangerous error is to think that because they must be distinguished they are not related, or that because they do not automatically reinforce each other they are automatically contradictory.

A central illustration of this is the relation between the nature of power (or its different kinds), its hierarchical distribution (or the structure of the international system) and its geographical distribution (or the relation between the global system and the partial, regional subsystems). The dialogues that bear on the second and third problems can be understood only in relation to the first and vice versa.

To writers like Stanley Hoffmann and Klaus Knorr, who insist on the mutual or self-inflicted paralysis of the great powers, due in the first place to the difficulty of using nuclear weapons, and to the resulting superior freedom of action open to the middle and small powers, and in the second place to the difficulty of controlling unstable societies and the possibilities of revolutionary warfare, Kenneth Waltz offers the same reply as Albert Wohlstetter to regionalists: these changes and limits have nothing to do with a decrease in the global power of the United States or in the bipolar nature of the international system; they have to do with the limits of military power itself, which is insufficient to control the domestic development of societies, but no more so in the case of the United States or the Soviet Union today than of other powers and at other times.[14]

But surely this argument, even though literally true, is self-defeating. While accusing his opponents of confusing military power and political control, Waltz himself comes close to identifying power with military force; he can maintain that the balance and structure of power have not changed only by giving them such an impossibly narrow definition that it leaves out the very realities which he himself is interested in understanding, namely the factors making for stability and change in international relations, and the possibility of managing them. To Coral Bell, who maintained that the revolutionary guerrilla had proved the most effective means yet devised for altering the world power-balance, he replies: 'The revolutionary guerrilla wins civil wars, not international ones, and no civil war can change the balance of power in the world unless it takes place in the United States or the Soviet Union. Even in China, the most populous of states, a civil war that led to a change of allegiance in the cold war did not seriously tilt the world balance.' More than a case for bipolarity, this is a radical case for isolationism, since nothing which happens in the outside world can alter the balance of power, defined exclusively in terms of the balance between the strategic military forces of the United States and the Soviet Union.

Surely the real problem (once we have been reminded of this basic structure which, contrary to the uncritical prophets of polycentrism and multipolarity, none of the writers mentioned had even thought of denying) is to what extent and in what way this strategic balance affects the actual course of international relations: whether, where, how and to what extent, strategic arms can buy political influence. As Philip Windsor has written: 'Surely the history of the Cold War needs above all to be examined in terms of the changing requirements of effective power: to relate it merely as a shift in the centres of power, away from the European nations to the two great neutrals of 1940, is not only to project the conflict in a misleading dimension, but to make much of it incomprehensible, from the loss of Soviet authority in eastern Europe to the American stalemate in Vietnam.'[15]

In turn, these changing requirements of effective power lead to changes in the relative importance of the different centres. When Waltz writes: 'To say that militarily strong states are feeble because they cannot easily bring order to another state is like saying that a pneumatic hammer is weak because it is not suitable for drilling decayed teeth. It is to confuse the purpose of instruments and to confound the means of external power with the agencies of internal governance', he forgets what he himself points out a few lines later – namely, that the great powers do consider the internal order of weaker states as part of their global power game, that they intervene in it, directly or indirectly, with their military force, and that while they have no guarantee of success, they still have a better chance of achieving it than weaker states. If this is so, the obvious problem is whether or not the domestic order of states and civil wars, as opposed to conventional state-to-state conflicts or the danger of general nuclear war, are becoming more important, and whether the military force of the great powers is becoming less or more relevant to these types of situation.

The comparison of the pneumatic hammer needs to be carried not only one step further than Waltz takes it, but two. First, someone who has a pneumatic hammer is actually weaker than before if he finds himself in an environment where the demand for new construction works has drastically decreased, but there is a steady demand for drilling decayed teeth. But in the second place, it might still happen that he will be able to sell his pneumatic hammer at a considerable loss and buy instead, say, two dentist's drills. He might then still be stronger with the new and more relevant teeth-drilling power than someone who has always owned only one small rudimentary drill. But the difference is much smaller than either that indicated by the costs involved or that which was relevant at the time when pneumatic hammers were the instrument of progress.

In other terms, the problem is that of the indirect exploitation of superior military force and, more generally, that of the exchange rate (or loss of energy) between various forms of power.

This, rather than the intellectual pleasure derived from proclaiming that the world is monopolar because only the United States can air-lift troops everywhere,[16] or that all states are equal because Zambia can be non-aligned, should be our main concern. Obviously, such general labels are of little use in a complex world where increases in strength may coincide with losses in political control, where the economic costs of one type of military power may be prohibitive and those of another increasingly cheap, where a given state or a given type of power may be able to deter but not compel, or to destroy but not to build, where the use of force can be necessary for political influence here and detrimental there; where, to use Karl Deutsch's comparison, the power to knock a man down does not give us the power to teach him to play the piano, but where, to pursue the comparison further, it may still be useful (much less, admittedly, than in a boxing match) in order to compel a great piano teacher to do the job, or again may be counter-productive by creating in the pupil a psychological resistance to musical education; where plenty of arms may buy a little influence, where good soldiers may or may not be, as Machiavelli thought, a better means to get money than vice versa, where some do raise divisions and some do not, where small states can successfully challenge great ones most of the time and the latter may reassert their superiority in times of crisis or war, where economic giants may be political dwarfs; in short, where the strength of some can be turned into weakness and the weakness of others into strength according to the objectives, the skill and the resources of the different states, and to their position in the various (sometimes contradictory) combinations and alignments on the international map. Much work in the social sciences, from economics, systems analysis and strategy, to sociology and integration theory, can help us to clarify this economy of force and control, to distinguish potential power and actual influence, to see the limits of this distinction through the notion of 'anticipated reaction', to see that all exercise of power implies not only actual costs but opportunity costs, to compare various forms of power by confronting their respective costs, risks and achievements, to glimpse the dynamics by which success in one type of power may spill over into another or, conversely, failure in one type may lead to the resort to another one less difficult to use but even less likely to produce results.

Equally useful notions developed in international-relations theory proper indicate not only that the international system, in its various dimensions, has elements of monopolarity, of hostile and cooperative bipolarity, of multipolar concert and balance of power, of universal collective security and universal isolationism, but that it may be useful to distinguish different international systems according to the different patterns emerging from different issues, different levels or different types of power.

Again, it is precisely when one distinguishes the different patterns that one can see more clearly the causal connection between them: for example nuclear bipolarity produces political polycentrism and encourages nuclear multipolarity, which in turn encourages a reassertion of bipolarity in a more cooperative, condominium form.[17] The incongruity between various coexisting patterns has been called 'structural distance', the 'degree of distance' being 'the degree to which patterns on different phenomenal levels do not overlap'.[18] The usefulness of this notion should be particularly clear in the context of an enquiry into the fate of the nation-state.

The same multidimensionality which is to be found in the nature of power and in the structure of the international system appears today in the functions of politically organized communities. The crisis of the nation-state lies less in a uniform broadening of dimensions which would lead, naturally and harmoniously, to continental units or to a world state, than in the increasing 'structural distance' or increasing discrepancy between the dimensions required for fulfilling its various functions. Both the optimal dimensions of units and the scope of the subjective feeling of solidarity or community seem to vary if one looks at the military, economic, political, ideological or cultural aspects. While the nation-state retains its ultimate sovereignty and the loyalty of its citizens, the Common Market may be a more relevant unit for agricultural policy, Nato for military deterrence and defence, the West or, in another sense, the developed world from an ideological or cultural point of view. A common fate may encompass provinces, states, regional and ideological blocs and alliances: that of being powerless here and sovereign there, of overlapping with their rivals and being challenged by their components. Nuclear weapons can be said to strengthen the case for great political units, since their existence seems to make a world state even more difficult to achieve and their economic and geographic preconditions seem to make the nation-state even more powerless. But at the same time, through the universal danger which their use, even against a neutral power such as India, would cause to humanity, something like a collective security feeling, or the consciousness of universal common interest, seems really to be emerging for the first time, while, at the other extreme, the concentration of decision and of solidarity which nuclear weapons seem to demand, gives a new value to the national dimension. According to circumstances one dimension or the other can be decisive: one can imagine a model in which states are interdependent for actual defence and independent for the ultimate nuclear choice, or one in which they keep their freedom of action in every circumstance except precisely the ultimate one, since the choice between life and death is not really theirs.

Like the multiplicity of alignments and conflicts within the international system, this multiplicity in the size and scope of relevant territorial units makes for divided loyalties, cross-cutting cleavages, limited sovereignties. And just as with the multiplicity of roles and hierarchies for the individual in a differentiated modern society, this multidimensionality, if it is kept within tolerable limits, makes for healthy pluralism and for the relativization of inequalities and conflicts; if the degree of distance is too great, if between the various levels or roles there is not merely potential tension but flat opposition, it makes for neurosis, paralysis and disintegration.

This carries an essential lesson for the fate of the national, regional and global levels, and of their respective roles.

The nation-state does not seem on the verge of collapse; but the essence of its original conception, that of a tight and self-contained unity of authority, community, loyalty, culture, language, defence and if possible, economy, is decisively challenged and with it the basis of 'nationalist' ideology and foreign policy.

Similarly, regional federations would seem to be the ideal answer to the structural distance problem, since their function would be precisely to create units which, while having less unity than the nation-state or less space and resources than a world state or the superpowers, would have more unity than the latter and more space and resources than the former, and would be able to fulfil, more or less satisfactorily, the traditional functions of the nation-state. But it is obvious that they would mitigate the problem by reducing the degree of distance, rather than by suppressing both, since some functions would continue to be the privilege of the member states and others would be beyond the reach even of a continental one. Moreover, in the case of Western Europe, we are witnessing precisely a broadening of the horizon, at least in all European directions, and a reassertion of the national objectives of the various states. But this only strengthens the case for a modified regionalism or federalizing process as distinct from any rigid and self-contained formula. Precisely because the structural distance is widening, the discrepancies have to be mitigated even though they cannot and should not be suppressed. Precisely because of the potential gap and clash between national ambitions and universal problems, a third intermediary level is needed to maintain some communication and coordination. But this can be done only if this third level is conceived not as a substitute for the others but as a link between them.

Finally, the consequences for the world powers are best seen if one considers the interaction between the multiple dimensions of power and the multiple dimensions of political units. Some types of power suffer a huge loss of strength gradient and some none at all. Some are effective within a political community, some within an alliance or an organization, some within a given area of civilization; some are much more effective on a global scale than on a more restricted one. Ultimately the mark of a world power is that it must be able to exert some kind of influence both on every level of collective activity and in every part of the world. But the point is that on many issues and in many regions the various types of power can exercise this influence only in an indirect and hence considerably limited or modified or watered-down way: by passing through other types of power and through other powers, by adapting themselves to the specific issues and the specific areas involved.

To try to push one's influence directly by ignoring national or regional feeling, and by forgetting that the search for unmitigated control and security can only lead to unmitigated loss and danger, would be to follow Pascal's definition of tyranny: to ask in one area for what one can have only in another.

The same lesson is valid for all three levels: each has a unique and indispensable role, each can play it only if it accepts, respects and eventually learns how to influence the two others.

This is, however, easier said than done. The problem of the link between forms of power, between levels of the international system and between the states themselves is complicated by the fact that different activities and levels have not only different scopes and structures but also different functional mechanisms and requirements. The very meaning of actions like balancing, of mechanisms like stability, is different when we look at the nuclear and the conventional, the unipolar and the multipolar, the military and the diplomatic, the political and the economic, the global and the regional levels. Yesterday, under the name of the 'balance of power', one could comprehend a balance of political alignments, military power and economic resources which, without in any universal or exact fashion coinciding, could still roughly serve as each other's sanction and instrument. Today there is plenty of deliberate of *de facto* balancing in the world, but the notion of one balance of power is at best descriptive, certainly imprecise and possibly misleading.[19] Different types of balance and stability differently achieved at different levels interact and, more often than not, produce global imbalance and instability; conversely, global stability, if one must call it balance, is more often than not a balance of imbalances. This already points to what looks like the basic problem of international relations today: the relation between stability and change, or, put in more drastic terms, the frequent contradiction and necessary conciliation of security and flexibility.

Two classic dilemmas are associated with the general notion of equilibrium: should it be seen as a goal consciously and cooperatively aimed at by the various units or the automatic result of their competition, each pursuing its own interest? Should it be conceived as static and identified with a mechanism which re-establishes the status quo against disturbances, or as dynamic, as a way of promoting growth and peaceful change? The two converge into the question: should stability be the result of mutually compensating movements or of immobility, stemming either from stalemate or from satisfaction? Both are amplified in a world where the nuclear balance of terror is one, but only one, dimension of reality. They appear in this new balance itself – under the guise of the dilemmas between the search for superiority or for equality, the arms race and stabilized deterrence, the reliance on rationality and predictability of unpredictability for deterrence and crisis management. But basically the nuclear balance is biased in favour of as little movement as possible: its purpose is deterrence rather than political or military gains or adjustments. Contrary to the tactical or conventional and to the political balance of power, it is more stable if it includes a smaller number of actors, because, as stability results less from the equality of forces than from the calculus of costs and risks, allies appear more as an increase in risk than in strength, and because the maintenance of stability, that is, the absence of attack, relies more on intentions and less on capabilities, hence more on communications and on finding a common language and common ground rules which are endangered by the shifts and moves of a greater number of more heterogeneous powers.[20] At the pre-nuclear and non-nuclear level, the possibility of using war as an instrument of policy made for flexibility tempered by caution; states could shift allegiances but knew that these shifts could result in war; when war occurred, it was the great factor for change and was often followed by territorial changes and settlements. Today, the existence of nuclear weapons tends to separate war and diplomacy, and while they increase the destructive power of arms and the freedom of manoeuvre of diplomacy, to sterilize both as factors of change. Great powers have increasing strength, small and medium powers have increasing freedom of action, but the former tend to have *only* strength and the latter *only* freedom of action. Neither the number of Soviet or US missiles nor the number of French or Romanian initiatives or speeches can do very much to solve the German problem or to change the territorial status quo in Europe. The nuclear balance seems characterized by the acceptance of stalemate, the diplomatic one by the search for flexibility; but the gap between the two is narrowed by the fact that both remain abstract, the diplomatic combinations that re-emerge look like the ghosts of yesterday's realities; everybody can play with combinations reminiscent of old alignments precisely because they do not affect reality. Or rather, as with the nuclear weapons of the great powers, the power of the diplomatic activity of small and medium powers appears essentially negative, a new proof of what Stanley Hoffmann has called the prevalence of denials over gains: everybody can block everyone else's design but not promote his own. Just as the Soviet Union and the United States have, in turn, discovered the great difficulty of constraint as compared to deterrence, so the most revisionist of European statesmen discover how much more effective their veto power against the leaders of their alliance is than their positive influence.

Actual changes, then, seem to occur neither under the influence of nuclear weapons nor under that of diplomacy, but either under the impact of the direct use of force in places where conventional war is still possible, or under that of sub- and transnational forces, from ideological evolution under the impact of social and economic change to civil war and revolutionary violence. But whether slow and sub-terranean or sudden and explosive, these changes are least easy to understand in terms of balances or to regulate by diplomatic or strategic calculations. Hence the problem of contradiction and inter-action among these various trends.

To the three recognized levels of violence, nuclear, conventional and subconventional, correspond three types of politics – the nuclear dialogue between great powers, meant to maximize the security of deterrence, the classical diplomacy associated with the prevention and settlement of conventional wars, and the domestic or transnational politics concerned with the peaceful or violent transformation of the social order. Since, however, contrary to the classical relationship on the conventional level, the foreign policies of middle powers, in a situation dominated by the nuclear balance of the superpowers, seem to be almost unconnected with the possibility of war, and since, at the other extreme, politics and violence seem impossible to distinguish according to classical criteria, four basic types of situation and of stability and instability seem to appear: the nuclear balance of deterrence based on immobility; the diplomatic balance based on flexibility; the con-ventional balance based on a quantitative balance and on a mixture of flexibility and the actual use of force; and the sub- or transnational situation, based on evolution and revolution, or on power trans-formation rather than balance.

The question, then, is whether the processes which occur at each of these levels and which, whether through immobility or flexibility, deterrence or violence, may produce some stability in their own area, do not prevent the successful operation of the stabilizing mechanisms of the others? Stanley Hoffmann, in his book *Gulliver's Troubles*, calls the present system a 'stalemate system', because of the predominance of denials over gains. But at the same time he points out that at the subconventional level force continues to produce gains, while the negative use of force for deterrence, or its 'repellent' use to recover losses, are less successful. 'What is lost by war is gained by revolution.' The 'internalization of politics' is partly a consequence of the stalemate system, by creating the dilemma of thwarting domestic evolution and revolution in the name of stability, or of endangering the existing balance in the name of revolution. Similarly, C.E. Zoppo points out that 'the very flexibility of alignment which brought stability to the

balance-of-power system could become a serious threat to the maintenance of deterrence'.[21] A world patterned upon the requirements of
nuclear deterrence could be a world in which political situations,
however intolerable, would be frozen. A world which would satisfy
the aspirations of nations to independent action and of social groups to
revolution would be a world in which, at some point, unpredictability
and conflict would seriously endanger the stability of nuclear deterrence and the security of states.

To see in which direction the winds are blowing, one need only
take into account the fragmentation of the international system and the
relation of the global strategic balance to the regional, political and
military ones. Nothing is more striking than the contrast between the
situation of Europe and that of other continents. In Europe there have
been spectacular changes in alignment and, occasionally, the direct use
of force by the Soviet Union. But basically, the use of force to modify
the status quo looks increasingly impossible, with the result that the
security of Europe is incomparably greater than that of other continents, and that its unsolved political problems, like the division of
Germany, have been frozen in a status quo which may yet produce
dangerous repercussions in terms of popular reactions. At the other
extreme, in Africa, *coups d'état*, civil wars, and genocide occur without
being stopped or even being considered as a real danger to world
security. In the Middle East the use of force over territorial issues has
repeatedly, in the most traditional fashion, modified the balance and
the map, through conflicts that the great powers have managed to
contain but have not been able to prevent, In Asia, one has a mixture
of every possible situation, with domestic revolutions, external
aggression, attempts at an interstate balance, direct intervention by one
superpower against an ally of the other and indirect intervention of the
latter.

Obviously the crucial difference in these various regional situations
is their respective relation to the strategic nuclear balance. The characteristic of Europe has been of a particular regional balance identified
with the global one by the direct confrontation of the United States
and the Soviet Union, due to the tightness of their commitments and
the physical presence of their troops. Hence the sterilizing effect of
nuclear weapons and of the danger of general war has been enormous
in limiting the freedom of action of unsatisfied states and in guaranteeing their security. The freedom of action of West and East
Germany is much smaller than that of Israel and Egypt, but their
security is much greater. In the Middle East, too, the great powers are
interested, concerned and to a certain extent present and committed;

but nobody could know before the 1967 war just how strong either their commitment to their friends or their control over them would prove to be. Obviously, in the past and in the future, the regional balance (conventional today, perhaps nuclear tomorrow) appears to be the decisive one. Much faith is needed in the stability of this regional balance to believe that the prospects for peace are as good as in Europe.

Yet it would seem that the two really secure situations are either identification with the central balance or the creation of an equally stable regional one. The worst situation is the one where the great powers are committed, but without either exercising the corresponding degree of control over their protégés, or making clear the nature and extent of their commitment. Yet this is, apparently, the trend of the times. In Asia, the United States and the Soviet Union cannot abandon active interest in the stability of the area; but nor can they establish the kind of presence they have in Europe; meanwhile, revolutionary upheavals and nationalist self-assertion are growing. Nobody can assess with any assurance the risks of escalation of these conflicts to the global and nuclear level.

Any state, including neutrals, has a chance of benefiting from great-power protection. No state, not even an ally, can be certain to benefit from the same degree and kind or protection as the European ones.

In Europe itself, however, the trend is towards eliminating the peculiarities of the situation. Fortunately, domestic instability and reciprocal hatreds are not those of other regions; but the desire for independent action, for flexibility, for the loosening or the suppression of alliances, for the withdrawal of foreign troops, are there. Yet the loss in control by the superpowers must inevitably result in a loss in their protection. If alliances become looser and policies become flexible, so do the commitments. It is not true that alliances, protection, commitments and guarantees are made impossible by nuclear weapons. But it *is* true that they are made more costly and more dangerous; hence they are not really credible if, on the one hand, the protector does not keep some control over the situation which may lead to his having to act on his pledge; and if, on the other hand, there is not at least a real possibility that he may have to do so even if, faced with the event, he would like to change his mind. As Schelling has shown, the only way of proving that one's commitment is really binding is to let oneself to a certain extent be actually tied by it. Long before Schelling's work, the main basis of world security has actually been the existence of hostages. In the case of an alliance, the physical presence of troops has so far seemed its clearest and most effective form. While substitutes for troops as hostages may be found, there does not seem to be any alternative to hostages as tokens of commitment. The discussions around a non-proliferation treaty and those around a European security system must necessarily find the problem of guarantees in a nuclear age one of their most decisive ones. Yet it also seems one of the least soluble. In the nuclear age, the equivalent of the Hobbesian 'covenants without swords are but words' might be, as I have tried to show elsewhere in some detail,[22] 'guarantees without hostages are but mirages' – and not of the kind that served the Israelis well.

Nuclear weapons, if they are not to destroy alliances and hence to jeopardize the security of that huge majority of states which can no longer rely exclusively upon themselves for their security, must lead to a greater interdependence, coordination and, to a certain extent, identification of interests, policies and strategies as a substitute for territorial identity or contiguity, than ever before. There is then a contradiction between the requirements of nuclear deterrence and the tendencies of political evolution. Nuclear weapons do not necessarily produce 'fission or fusion', but they do tend, as Leonard Beaton has pointed out, to require and produce an amplification of integrative or disruptive trends. If nuclear alliances or guarantees are to be more than a secondary supplement to a deterrence exercised by each power for itself, they require not a legal document or a traditional coalition, but a real entanglement to make commitments stick. On the other hand, international politics are evolving precisely towards disentanglement and flexibility, towards the refusal to let alliances or integrated organizations restrict freedom of exploration and of combination. States cannot be asked to sacrifice flexibility for the sake of security, to subordinate every national objective to the optimum conditions of nuclear deterrence. But while, from the superpowers to the smallest nations, every state enjoys some degree of freedom of action, the very multiplicity of alignments and conflicts which gives it this freedom of choice also limits its range if disastrous clashes and agonizing reappraisals are to be avoided. The days of monolithic blocs are over, just as much as those of self-sufficient nation-states. But they have been replaced neither by absolute isolation nor by absolute freedom; independence and freedom are to be found in the diversification of ties and of conflicts, in the calculation of priorities among one's interests and of their conflict or convergence with the interests of other states.

Some interests and some conflicts are, for each state, more important than others; some, like avoidance of nuclear disaster, are common to all. Every state, then, has to weigh the requirements of a 'free hand' as against those of international order, those of flexibility against those of security.

The international world, to use the expression of Osgood and Tucker, must be seen neither in 'systemic' terms, aiming at the suppression of interstate competition, nor in 'laissez-faire' terms, letting this competition find its own equilibrium, but in 'regulatory' terms. Similarly, great powers cannot use all their strength, nor small or medium powers all their freedom of action, if they are not to endanger the very bases of the system on which their position is built. This goes especially for medium, potentially nuclear powers, and these have the greatest stake in the international system – their security depends on it even more than that of superpowers who can defend themselves, and that of small powers who may be protected by their lack of resources; their influence and their superior freedom of action are also based on the system, since these too depend on the balance between superpowers. But at the same time, by trying to act as substitutes for the superpowers, they create the illusion of an independent system of security, an illusion which might well end up by destroying the real one.

Their role should rather be to help, through alliances and regional organizations, to provide a link between the technological world of the superpowers and the emotional world of unstable nationalisms. The great danger of international politics lies in the twin and mutually reinforcing temptations of great-power paternalism based on superior strength, knowledge and pretension to wisdom, and the irrational self-assertion of unstable nationalism based on negative rebellion and on the thirst for empty prestige. Just as between the state and the individual one needs voluntary groups and communities, or between the technocrat and the beatnik one needs the politician and the citizen, the most urgent need in the international world is for an organized dialogue (both on a vertical basis, involving the leaders and the led, and on a horizontal one, involving the states of comparable background, orientation and dimensions) which can humanize the inevitable inequalities and induce everyone to accept the limits of his power. Nuclear weapons are the most powerful factor contributing to the possibility of the twin nightmares of a tyrannical and an anarchic world; by the same token, they are the most powerful incentive towards attempting to build a more tolerant and responsible one, in which nation-states would learn that cooperation is the precondition of independence and self-limitation the precondition of power.

5

Ethical Issues in Nuclear Deterrence:
Four National Debates in Perspective
(France, Great Britain, the United States
and West Germany)

Who is debating, where, when, how,
about what, and with whom?

THE MAIN problem of this paper is to identify its object. Debates about nuclear weapons certainly take place in all Western countries, with the partial exception of France. But are they debates, in the sense of forensic confrontations, deliberations, attempts at mutual persuasion? Should one distinguish between religious, philosophic, technical and political debates? Are they really about ethics, or is the ethical dimension a convenient disguise, a vehicle for polemical insinuations or for national or bureaucratic special pleading? When 'statesmen, bishops and other strategists' talk about escalation control while strategists, bureaucrats and other theologians talk about just–war doctrine, does this mean a mutually enlightening dialogue where ends, means and consequences are thought through as they should be, in their mutual relationships, or does this indicate a cacophony out of which the citizen may acquire the theological wisdom of the Pentagon and the strategic expertise of the Vatican?

Sometimes the philosophical-religious debate on ethics and the political-strategic one on deterrence seem to be worlds apart; sometimes they seem hopelessly intertwined. Very seldom is the double task of distinguishing and reuniting, breaking down and reassembling, done systematically.

Nor is the question of who should do it clear, as among the rival claims of technical competence, spiritual authority and political legitimacy in a time of crisis, or at least of transition, where no cosmological, religious or ethical tradition provides a sufficiently clear and accepted common ground. The inherent uncertainty of political choice in situations of conflict is compounded both by the uncertainty of technological evolution and by the lack of agreement about first principles. The difficulties of identifying common interests and, even more, a common code for bargaining with adversaries are compounded by the difficulty of finding common assumptions and principles for debating within the same society, across the barriers which divide specialized elites and mutually distrustful social groups.

More specifically, is the title of this paper justified? Are there, indeed, four national debates? And, if so, to what extent do they interact with each other? Are ethical issues in nuclear deterrence essentially debated within each nation, within a framework or terms of reference provided by its specific situation or culture? Or is the debate essentially international, each country holding a specific position within one general alliance-wide debate, or in answer to common questions? Or are the terms set essentially by a series of transnational debates both among and within the Catholic church, the strategic or scientific community, and the peace movement? Or are these various dimensions, the national, the international and the transnational combined in such a way that concepts and fashions, doctrines and policies which are born in one country and in one context, are transmitted, reinterpreted or rediscovered at another time and in another place? Of course the last case is both the most important and the most difficult to analyse, as is shown, for instance, by the different understandings of a notion like escalation or, even more, by the way in which doctrines like arms control or notions like security partnership or *kooperative Rüstungsteurung* (cooperative arms-steering), which originated in the United States and in Britain in the 1960s, have taken on a new life and, perhaps, a new meaning, in Germany in the 1980s.

The question is what to make of these migrations of concepts and moods. The most ambitious and satisfying interpretation would be a Hegelian one: a phenomenology of attitudes towards the nuclear problem should lead, through dialectical progress, to a logically complete system of knowledge. At the other extreme, a sociology of knowledge in Mannheim's sense would show the determination of various doctrines by socioeconomic attitudes and sociocultural traditions; it would lead either to pure relativism or, at most, to a relationism which, by showing all these social connections, would put them into some sort of perspective for the *freischwebende Intelligenz* of the conference circuit. Finally, a more rationalist position, along the lines of Max Scheler's version of the sociology of knowledge, would see the concepts and the universal alternative options, if not as permanent and universal, at least as resulting from problems which are common to the nuclear age and to the Western alliance. But their emergence and decline, the fact that at one time or another they dominate the field in this or that country, would be heavily influenced by special circumstances which must be explained sociologically and have their own historical logic.

The third type of interpretation seems more satisfactory to the extent that, intellectually, it protects the autonomy of ideas and the possibility of debate, but that, historically, it takes into account their cyclical fortunes (evidenced for instance in the periodical re-emergence of the debate on counterforce and assured destruction). However, the door should not be closed on the possibility that new circumstances, particularly in the technological field, may make old concepts entirely irrelevant or even produce new ones. Nor is it entirely unthinkable that the interplay of national, international and transnational debates and experiences should produce a deepening and a broadening of consciousness which would at least at the theoretical level, overcome (in the Hegelian sense of *aufheben*) some of today's apparently structural or intractable antinomies between ethics and strategy and within each of them.

Under what conditions is a debate on ethics and nuclear deterrence possible?

The notion of debate has to do with that of deliberation (to make a decision) and with that of argumentation (to convince an inter-locutor). In both cases, as Aristotle points out, the outcome sought can be neither absolutely necessary (in that case it would be a matter of science, hence of demonstration, not of debate, hence of argumen-tation) nor absolutely arbitrary. 'We deliberate only on questions which seem to be able to receive two opposite solutions; as for things which in the past, the present or the future, could not be otherwise, nobody deliberates about them if he judges them to be so; for it would not serve any purpose for him'.[1]

This implies that a debate on the ethical issues of nuclear strategy can take place only within a certain spectrum which excludes certain conceptions of ethics and of strategy. A religious or absolutist ethics, whether based on Kant's categorical imperative or on Weber's *Gesinnung*, proclaims the unconditional priority of certain ends, or the uncondi-tional unacceptability of certains means or certain consequences. Hence it refuses to subject them to debate, even if it accepts the legitimacy of debating the practical or hypothetical consequences to be drawn from them. Conversely, if strategy were a science, if it could be demonstrated that deterrence rests on a certain formula of proportionality, or that involuntary escalation from a limited-theatre or counterforce nuclear war to a major anti-cities war, and ultimately to 'nuclear winter' or the destruction of the planet, is certain or is impossible, most of the strategic debate would disappear and the ethical implications of nuclear deterrence would be fundamentally transformed.

Much of the apocalpytic and self-righteous tone which makes part of the peace movement (particularly in Germany) inaccessible to debate is based on the combination of an absolute ethical and (the survival of the planet) and a double deterministic prediction: the inevitable failure of deterrence and the impossibility of controlling escalation. Conversely, much of the French complacency is based on the idea (which can be seen as rationalistic or as superstitious) that since the doctrine of deterrence is systematically coherent, deterrence is stable, for its failure would be irrational and hence cannot happen. Both the ethical and the strategic debates are based on the existence of an ignorance or uncertainty gap setting in between ends and means, between means and consequences, between messages and responses and, on the other hand, on the possibility of reducing this gap by carefully weighing stakes, costs and risks. Of course debates about priorities and about subjective probabilities entail a large area of potential consensus based on factual evidence, but also one of intractable divergence based upon arbitrary acts of faith. These are made inevitable both by the impossibility of knowing the future and by the impossibility of reducing various ends to a common denominator which would permit ranking them in a permanent order.

Let's take two statements by a British strategist critical of deterrence, M. McGwire, and an American theorist who believes in its stability, R. Jervis. McGwire defends what he calls 'the sensitive assessment of probabilities, costs and benefits' of the antinuclear movement contained in the formula: 'better red than dead'. 'Many would argue that it is better to risk the remote possibility of Soviet occupation by adopting a different defence posture and style of foreign policy than to face the virtual certainty of nuclear incineration if we carry along this road'.[2] On the other hand, Jervis states: 'Just as in the past some objectives were worth a war because the damage from the conflict was less than the expected gains, so now some objectives are worth a risk − albeit a low one − of total destruction'.[3]

Now, obviously much of the two opposite arguments rests on an estimate of probabilities: if in McGwire's statement one were to interchange them and assign a 'remote possibility' to 'nuclear incineration' and a 'virtual certainty' to Soviet occupation, if in Jervis's statement one would substitute 'high' for 'low' risk of total destruction, their conclusions would presumably be very likely to be reversed. Obviously too, for those who see either total destruction or Soviet occupation as *the* absolute evil, probabilities would make no difference. But the more interesting and relevant case arises for those who, like most of us, want to be neither red not dead, for whom both Soviet occupation and nuclear war are evils to be avoided, not least because each of them contains the possibility (although not the certainty) of leading to its extreme form (the spiritual or the physical suicide of mankind).

If only for this reason, it is extremely difficult to rank them in the abstract. If the probabilities were equal, which of the two would one accept, or at least risk, as a lesser evil? Even more interestingly, if one of the two is considered as a worse evil, but it appears that a given policy holds a higher chance of avoiding both but a greater risk, if it fails, of producing the worse of the two, should it be preferred to one which holds a smaller chance of avoiding both but a greater one, if it fails, of avoiding the worst? It is this classical choice which may be closest to the real world;[4] obviously the answers will vary according to the evaluation of both risks and costs, i.e. the probabilities one gives to the two outcomes, and to the degree of difference one assigns to the two evils.

This is where ethics and strategy meet, in the twin dilemmas of deterrence and defence for the latter, of threat and use for the former. If, like Albert Wohlstetter, one believes that discrimination and control are the answer to both, that the policy which is the most credible for deterrence is also the most moral for use if deterrence fails, the only problem is how much priority one should give to the means (both technological and political) of this policy. If, however, one believes that, as L. Martin puts it, 'in all nuclear deterrence there is a complicated relationship between the horrifying nature of a threat and the plausibility of its execution' and, in particular, that the policy which is likely to be best for deterrence is also the one which may lead to the greater evil if deterrence fails, then one encounters not only the strategic and the ethical dilemmas but also the dilemma between ethics and strategy.[5] If one thinks that the ultimate dilemmas, in an extreme situation, are inherently unsolvable rationally, the real question is whether one should take one's bearings by this extreme contingency, or by the normal one. In one case, that of the apocalyptic attitude,[6] one may either in Weberian fashion choose one of the extremes through an ultimately arbitrary act of faith, or be paralysed into abstention or despair by the impossibility of making this choice. In the other, that of prudential incrementalism, one may try to mitigate the dilemmas by hedging on both cases, and devoting one's main efforts to avoiding their occurrence. One would then live by the normal case, but there are two ways of doing so: to dismiss the extreme unsolvable case as irrelevant precisely because it is unsolvable,[7] or to live with it as with a Pascalian *pensée de derrière la tête* which should not keep us from our daily work of maintaining peace but should make us see it, as well as our other daily pursuits, in a different, both more urgent and more humble, light.

It is this tension between the extreme and the normal case, between the permanent possibility of escalation to the extreme and the permanent need for control, between the need to strive for the normal and the need to be ready for the exceptional, well discussed by such different philosophers as Karl Jaspers and Leo Strauss, which may be seen at the centre of the various debates.[8]

The other basic tension which, in a way, is common not only to the ethics of strategy and to the ethics of debate, but to the very possibility of international politics and of human society is that of *reciprocity* and *asymmetry*.

Just as one of the two most universal requirements of ethics (self-control or restraint) implies a never ending struggle against its polar opposite, the endless drive of passions threatening to get out of hand, so does the other expressed in the golden rule of justice based on reciprocity imply a tension with the fact that not only are needs, aptitudes and merits unequal, but meanings and individualities are heterogeneous. Not only divergences of interest but structural gaps of communication make all human relations, let alone politics and, especially, within politics, international politics and, most of all, deterrent relationships, relations of limited distrust. The familiar Schellingian combination of conflict and cooperation, of 'imperfect partnership and incomplete antagonism', is only one aspect of this more general necessity of finding common rules for dialogue between fundamentally different interlocutors, of drafting agreements between structurally different regimes, of addressing threats and inducements to adversaries whose value systems are alien.

Nuclear deterrence sharpens both aspects, particularly when it is combined with the conflict between open and closed societies, or between freedom and totalitarianism. Just as Carl Schmitt has successively extolled the element of asymmetry and of unqualified conflict (with the notions of total war and total enemy) and that of reciprocity (with the notion of *justus hostis,* and the distinction between enemy and adversary in the *jus publicum europaeum*),[9] so do lesser authors in the same breath justify nuclear weapons by the existence of the absolute evil, i.e. totalitarianism, which calls for the use of absolute means, and define deterrence as introducing reciprocity between those who don't understand each other.[10] Disarmers look forward to the elimination of distrust and hostility between nations and regimes, but proclaim their inability to have a dialogue with those who accept nuclear deterrence. Arms controllers and advocates of mutual assured destruction tend to fall into the trap of postulating a symmetry of objectives, interests or doctrine with the Soviets. But their critics who, often with good reason, pour scorn on their attempts to preach their own gospel at the Soviets, and stress the profoundly Russian and totalitarian character of the latter's attitudes and strategies, then show themselves willing to submit to Soviet ideas by adopting the Soviet concept of deterrence through the ability to conduct a prolonged or victorious war. Nor is this all: in a further twist the same school that stressed how different the Soviets were proceeds to educate them in order to convert them to the virtues of assured mutual survival! Believers in reciprocal vulnerability tend to exaggerate the Soviet security problem and the symmetry of objectives, identifying with Soviet fears, real or assumed, of a US first strike, but they then tend to advocate an asymmetry of practice, namely, US acceptance of vulnerability and minimal deterrence, even in the face of Soviet efforts to develop a counterforce capability and achieve strategic superiority. Their critics, in their turn, tend to exaggerate the asymmetry of objectives (invariably attributing aggressive intentions to the Soviets, but scorning the idea that US behaviour could actually appear aggressive or destabilizing to others) but at the same time they postulate a symmetry of practice, believing that in the event of nuclear war the logic of bargaining and intrawar deterrence would lead the Soviets, whatever their declared policies, to respond to any US efforts at discrimination and control of escalation by doing the same.[11]

Whatever particular combination is adopted, paradox and tension persist, for they are inherent in many of the ethical and political constraints attaching to the nuclear situation. As Jaspers says, we must 'talk to the totalitarians' (i.e. to those who do not believe in dialogue). We must practise mutual deterrence with those who do not believe in it. We must accept our adversary's identity while keeping our own and while trying to communicate with him and knowing that communication changes both sides. We may, on the basis of our resistance to totalitarianism, be tempted to resurrect a doctrine of just war in the sense of the traditional *jus at bellum*, which is inherently asymmetrical, and, on the basis of nuclear deterrence, a doctrine of just war in the sense of the *jus publicum europaeum* with its inherently reciprocal emphasis on *jus in bello* (or perhaps, today, on *jus in dissuasione*), just as Carl Schmitt's *Nomos der Erde* may be replaced by a new *Nomos des Alls*.

Dimensions of the strategic debate

Of course, actual strategic debates are not posed in these general terms, which cover the structural problems of human existence and social coexistence. In more concrete and conventional terms, it may be useful to list some of the polarities which have been seen as antinomies, complementarities or competing priorities.

The most obvious one is between *politics* and *strategy*. Political goals can be seen as divided between internal consensus or reassurance and external influence, strategic ones between war-avoidance (or deterrence) and war-fighting, which itself comprises damage-limitation or war-termination and the avoidance of defeat (if not the pursuit of victory). Of course the debate concerns the question whether reassurance, deterrence and war-termination have not superseded the other series of goals. One outcome of the debate may be to point out that they cannot be considered in the abstract and divorced from political objectives, but that nuclear weapons compel us to consider the latter in a novel light. Politics is relevant as influencing the quality and the modalities of deterrence and war-termination, rather than deterrence and war-termination being made conditional on the fulfilment of political objectives. The repoliticization of the peace debate or of strategy, which Aloïs Mertes or Trutz Rendtorff have so rightly called for, cannot mean their reconventionalization. It is in this light too that the familiar polarities of deterrence and war-fighting, threat and use, denial and retaliation, defence and offence, destruction and discrimination, predictability and unpredictability (hence automaticity and control, freedom of action and commitment), as well as the even more concrete ones of countercity and counterforce, decapitation and communication, have to be seen.

Another polarity, which brings us back to politics and to the conditions of debate in general, but raises very specific questions for the strategic debate, is that of *authority and legitimacy*. If one follows the young French philosopher Bernard Manin (cited in note 1), who, in order to escape from the Rousseauist difficulties of general will and

majority rule, tries to base democracy on a theory of political deliberation, one is forced to raise stimulating questions about the nature and
conditions of strategic deliberation. As usual, nuclear weapons tend to
sharpen existing dilemmas. While the usual problem of democracy is
between the role of elites or oligarchies and that of the majority, the
nuclear decision has to be taken by *one* man and to involve consequences of life and death for *all* (which means, at a minimum, the
whole community but may mean the whole planet, including future
generations). To the extent that debate or deliberation (which is always
deliberation among several, not all, interlocutors) has a crucial role, at
what stage can it apply? To the choice of strategic postures and of the
budgetary decisions which go with them? Or to the actual decision to
use or not to use nuclear weapons? But obviously what the French call
la manoeuvre dissuasive includes not only peacetime decisions but the
process of consultation and deliberation, hence the debate itself.

The French debate on 'cohabitation' between a president and a
prime minister belonging to two opposite political camps has raised this
issue very sharply: everybody accepts that nuclear deterrence belongs to
the president ('la dissuasion c'est moi') but that the government has to
be involved in any operational decisions.

Within an alliance, particularly in conditions of extended deterrence, the same applies to the relations between the leader and its
allies, between the guarantor and the protected. And here again the
internal debate (intra-alliance or interstate) is part and parcel of the
debate with the other side.

The very existence of these various intranational debates both
relativizes and legitimizes the existence of an international, intra-
alliance debate. To some, in particular Americans, there is no real
debate because differences between allies are based on ignorance and
error, usually on the failure of Europeans to understand the truth,
embodied in the current US doctrine. At the other extreme, many, in
particular French Gaullists and German pacifists, believe that transatlantic differences are basically differences of interest (e.g. Americans
want to wage limited war in Europe or to protect their own territory,
for Europeans the former objective is unacceptable and the latter
inaccessible) or of values (the Americans want supremacy or are
possessed by technological *hubris*, the French want independence, and
the Germans want love). The notion of 'German interests' in the
nuclear field, of a specific German responsibility for peace, cuts both
ways.

Personally, I think that a real transatlantic debate is possible because
there is no ultimate scientific truth revealed to US or French strategy

and because there is an overwhelming commonality of interests and values: no country has an interest in war, nuclear or otherwise, nor in totalitarian domination; all have an interest in limiting damage and stopping war if it occurs, and are faced with the ultimate dilemmas we have mentioned if it escalates. However, within this common framework, there are differences of attitudes and priorities, based on differences of geopolitical situation, of political structure, of historical experience, of cultural tradition. And it is these which are, to some extent, revealed by the differences between the four national debates as well as by the positions taken in the common Atlantic debate.

The four national debates

Continuities and discontinuities in time and space: a brief historical sketch

When one looks back at the four decades since Hiroshima, one is struck both by the cyclical and the discontinuous character of the public debates, and by a certain subterranean continuity. The philosophical debate about the morality of deterrence has never stopped entirely, even during the periods of strategic consensus or of moral self-confidence among the general public. Some of the most critical books, such as *Deadly Logic* by Philip Green and *Strategy and Conscience* by A. Rapoport, have appeared, in the United States during the Kennedy period, or in Germany during the twenty years of general acceptance of nuclear weapons. The theological evolution in the Catholic church has been more or less continuous from Pius XII through John XXIII and the Vatican Two council till today, although some spectacular and relatively sudden changes did occur, such as the reversal of roles between the American and the European bishops.

What has varied considerably, however, both in time and in space is the relation between these more or less specialized debates and the public one. Two great waves have swept the Western world with the perennial exception of France. The first occurred in the late 1950s and early 1960s. It was, however, rather limited, and varied in character from country to country. In the United States the strategic and the theological debates were lively and convergent but they did not lead to the formation of true peace movements. In the Federal Republic and in Britain, on the other hand, the debate took on spectacular social and political dimensions.

In Germany, one of the most interesting aspects is the early raising of the legitimacy issue – among the scientists (with the Göttingen appeal coauthored by C.F. von Weiszäcker, which opposed any participation of nuclear scientists in the production of nuclear weapons), by the churches (the Heidelberg declaration, with a reluctant and provisional acceptance of the nuclear balance) and by a famous philosopher, Karl Jaspers, whose book *Die Atombombe und die Zukunft des Menschen* challenged the claims both of science and of religion to ultimate authority on these matters. Another philosopher, Gunther Anders, violently opposed him, advancing the same arguments as he was to use again a quarter of a century later.[12]

On the political level, opposition to nuclear weapons took the form of a powerful popular movement, Kampf gegen den Atomtod, supported by the SPD.

In Britain, a parallel situation existed with the Campaign for Nuclear Disarmament, the role of a famous scientist–philosopher, Bertrand Russell, that of the Dean of Canterbury, known as the Red Dean, and last but not least the unilateralist movement within the Labour Party. The difference was that the movement did not, at the time, prevail within the Labour Party and had probably less support than in Germany within the scientific and religious communities.

In France, however, an almost complete silence prevailed, the sole exception being a relatively weak movement led by the biologist Jean Rostand and a few Protestant pastors. This contrasted with (but perhaps is to be explained, at least in part, by) the earlier massive success, in the late 1940s and early 1950s, of the communist-inspired Stockholm appeal against the bomb, which gave the peace movement a bad name in French public opinion.

Elsewhere, the first wave of the peace movement receded. Partly this was due to its failure to make a decisive breakthrough at the political level in the countries concerned (Adenauer's electoral victory in 1957 and the subsequent rallying of the SPD to the Nato consensus, the defeat of the unilateralists in the struggle for the control of the Labour Party in Britain), partly to new focuses of attention and militancy such as the Vietnam war. But the most important factor was the first outbreak of detente, after the Cuban missile crisis, and its confirmation in the late 1960s and early 1970s.

For fifteen years, while the questioning of deterrence never disappeared from the preoccupations of a limited number of individuals and small groups, the moral fervour and intellectual energies of peace activists turned from East–West to North–South issues, from the avoidance of war to the fight for the mobilization of the exploited, for revolution and against 'structural violence'.[13]

If one were to give a date for the rebirth of the public debate on deterrence and nuclear war, and of the peace movement, it would have to be 1977–8, with the debate on the neutron bomb. This followed the end of the Vietnam war, and coincided with the worsening of East–West relations. The double consensus on deterrence and detente was breaking down and, combined with the world economic crisis, was opening the way to a phase of disarray and disagreement, of anxiety and recrimination about the future of mankind and about the respective reality and priority of the catastrophic dangers, such as nuclear war or mass unemployment or hunger, which the progress of technology and rationality was supposed to have eliminated. Hence, not only did the peace movement revive in Germany and Britain but it spread much more widely (everywhere, including the United States, except France) and with greater depth and strength than twenty years before: it had richer cultural and existential overtones, involving a reaction not only against the arms race but against technology in general, and a more direct and diversified political content.

While the immediate issue was, indeed, the deployment of nuclear weapons and the danger of war, it appeared fairly clearly that this anxiety, genuine as it was in most cases, also served, directly or indirectly, consciously or unconsciously, as a vehicle or a symbol for raising the political issue of relations between the two Germanys, between the two Europes, East and West, and between them and the superpowers, particularly the United States. But the prominent role of the groups that had been central to the first wave and to the central issue, the scientists and the churches, remained very much in evidence.

Perhaps, however, the most important and lasting aspects of the debate lie less in the peace movement itself than in the reactions of the establishment, both in political terms (i.e. in its attitudes towards detente and arms control) and in strategic ones (i.e. in its attitudes towards conventional weapons and anti-ballistic-missile defence). The most general phenomenon is the downgrading of nuclear deterrence in every country but France, based on the belief of public opinion in democratic countries that living with the bomb is not acceptable in the long run.

While the establishment, in the West, had defended the morality of deterrence against the peace movement in the debate over the development of Euromissiles, it was caught on the wrong foot by President Reagan's speech on 23 March 1983, declaring nuclear deterrence immoral and obsolete, as it was also, three years later, by Gorbachev's embracing of the zero option for nuclear missiles in Europe. Between Reagan and Gorbachev, between CSU and SPD, the argument seems to be less whether nuclear weapons are bad than whether the best way to get rid of them is through new technologies, conventional or spatial, or through general disarmament. This trend has been dramatically accelerated by the Reykjavik summit, where both sides agreed on the goal of getting rid of nuclear weapons within ten years (subsequent qualifications by the United States proposing to get rid only of ballistic missiles were not very convincing, or very durable, or very reassuring), and by the cascade of 'zero options' and the Washington summit. To be sure, the adoption by both superpowers of the anti-nuclear theme has produced some counterreactions: West European governments have reaffirmed the legitimacy and necessity of nuclear deterrence and some European opposition parties, particularly the SPD, have confirmed an existing trend, in opposition to SDI, towards the acceptance of nuclear deterrence. This acceptance does not extend, however, to theatre nuclear weapons, or to the first use of nuclear weapons or to counterforce flexible options. In other words, while the abolition of nuclear weapons is not very credible, movement in this direction, via a minimum deterrence lacking both plausible targets and credibility, seems almost universaly desired.

To put it another way, nobody except Ronald Reagan and a small part of his administration, believes in the feasibility of getting rid of nuclear weapons through defence, but nobody except the French denies the desirability of the goal of moving away, at least partially, from nuclear retaliation.

The French exception is not purely negative, however. The question persistently raised by France, explicitly or implicitly, ever since de Gaulle, is that of the desirable *political* structure of the international order. This is a powerful challenge to everyone else's abstract or planetary discourse, which tends to jump from ethical imperatives or technological projections to visions of collective security systems or a defence-dominated regime jointly managed by the superpowers, without really considering their political preconditions and consequences.

While the general mood seems to be shifting from the fear of nuclear weapons to the hope of universal reconciliation through 'new thinking', one feature seems to remain constant: the rejection of old-fashioned considerations of politics and power.

The American debate

This general criticism would seem to apply particularly strongly to the American debate. As is often the case in the United States, it is strongly influenced by history and politics, but in a half-conscious and rather unsophisticated way. The retrospective shock of Hiroshima, the feeling of cosmic or Promethean responsibility, the traditional moralism which leads Americans to oscillate between punitive righteousness and self-flagellating guilt, strongly influence the debate. But its content, rather than emphasizing politics or history, is both technical and theological; it has to do with the destructive power of nuclear weapons and with the moral intentions of those who have to decide on their possession, their abolition, their threat or their use.

The first question, then, is that of the absolute novelty of nuclear weapons. Do they call for a revolution in our way of thinking not only in strategic terms (as in the ever-quoted sentence by Bernard Brodie about their only utility being to prevent wars, not to fight them) but also in political terms (do they make the nation-states obsolete?) and in ethical terms (does the number of victims affect the nature of the ethical problem? does the survival of the planet or of the species pose a different ethical problem from that of one political community?) and even in theological terms (have the traditional criteria of *jus in bello* and *jus ad bellum* lost their validity?). Or should one attempt to domesticate nuclear weapons by submitting them to traditional wisdom, such as the Clausewitzian primacy of political objectives or the 'just war' principles of proportionality and discrimination?

The alternative answers to this question lead to alternative perspectives and attitudes on the second, action-oriented question: to possess or not to possess? to threaten or not to threaten? to use or not to use? Underlying a variety of possible answers there is a basic duality in outlook, which Freeman Dyson has described as reflecting two worlds − that of the strategic establishment or the military decision-makers, and those who work for them and accept their perspective (the *warriors*), and that of the peace movement, or the general public whose feelings and fate it claims to represent (the *victims*).[14] It is interesting that in his defence of the Strategic Defence Initiative, G.H. Keyworth accepts this duality and associates himself with the camp of the victims.[15]

It is even more important to note that the whole attempt of nuclear theory and practice since Hiroshima has been to avoid the dilemma of the warriors and the victims. Just as everybody wants to be 'neither red nor dead', the whole point is to be, as Albert Camus put it, 'ni victimes ni bourreaux', neither victims nor murderers. The concept of deterrence is meant to do precisely that. Hence the normal predominance of what Robert Osgood has called the 'mitigationist' school, as opposed to the 'maximalists' and the 'minimalists'. The question is whether, by holding the middle ground of the deterrent threat which prevents actual use, the dilemma of the warriors and the victims is solved, or only postponed in favour of the dilemma of the deterrers and the self-deterred. Can one deter without accepting the risk of becoming a warrior? Can one refuse to become a warrior without being self-deterred, hence risking becoming a victim? Or can one be a warrior without murdering innocents? Or can one be self-deterred and yet avoid becoming a victim? A negative answer to the last two questions would expose the advocates of discrimination and those of 'existential deterrence' as, respectively, warriors and capitulationists in disguise.

This alone is enough to show the dependence of both the strategic and the ethical or religious debate upon *technological* assumptions. But, as Robert W. Tucker has pointed out with great force,[16] they are at least as dependent upon the *political* climate. Reassurance through pure deterrence is only as good as the belief that deterrence cannot fail. And this belief is linked both to a certain state of technology which makes retaliatory forces invulnerable and populations vulnerable, and to a certain state of political relations, namely detente or at least a continuous dialogue between the nuclear superpowers, which makes war by aggression or by misunderstanding sufficiently unlikely to be psychologically unreal. As Paul Bracken indicates, the fact that there never was a full-scale nuclear alert is as remarkable as the fact that there has never been a nuclear exchange, and contributes powerfully to the belief that there will never be one.[17]

What has happened in the late 1970s and early 1980s is a double lapse of faith, in deterrence and in detente. The new features of the arms race taken, rightly or wrongly, to be destabilizing because favouring a first strike, and the new features of the superpower relationship taken, rightly or wrongly, to be destabilizing because favouring aggression or at least unpredictability and misunderstanding, have produced the double fear that technology and hostility may get out of hand. Disbelievers in deterrence and disbelievers in detente are sometimes the same but they can also go in opposite directions. Those who combine the assumption that detente and deterrence will fail with, on the one hand, a distrust of US leaders, of their peaceful intentions or moderation, and on the other hand, a distrust of discrimination and control as such and a belief in inevitable escalation if deterrence fails, can only be in favour of the abolition of nuclear weapons, or at least their stationing abroad, and of extended deterrence. Those who believe that deterrence may fail, but who trust US objectives and leadership and think the new technologies increase the possibility of discrimination and control, are for conventionalization in the same sense as the former (i.e. replacing nuclear weapons by conventional ones whenever possible) but also in the sense of applying to them the same criteria as to conventional ones. Both groups sometimes converge towards the Strategic Defence Initiative, which has the ability to produce strange bedfellows, such as the couple, Dyson and Keyworth, already mentioned, or Robert Jastrow and Jonathan Schell. But most of those who question either the morality or the credibility of deterrence fear even more the destabilizing trends unleashed by a new arms race in search of strategic defence, the offensive potential of the new technologies (even if those who promote them use the language of defence), the danger of making war more likely if one wrongly believes one can control it or limit the damage. They tend, then, to side with those who put their faith in minimum deterrence or mutual vulnerability, with whom they share a belief in the danger of searching for superiority and a disbelief in the possibility of avoiding escalation if deterrence fails.

However, since Reykjavik and, even more, since the Washington summit and the INF agreement, Reagan's attempt to outflank the peace movement on the left is beginning to meet with greater success than at the time of his March 1983 speech. The perception that the two leaders are engaged in a sincere search for peace leading if not to the abolition of nuclear weapons at least to the de-escalation of the arms race, and that the remaining villains are the smaller European nuclear powers, is gaining ground in the peace movement.

If one combines the criteria of optimism or pessimism about deterrence on the one hand, about discrimination and control on the other, with the practical consequences to be drawn from them, it is possible, if one takes one's bearings by the discussion between Albert Wohlstetter and François Gorand in *Commentaire*,[18] to distinguish four basic attitudes. The first is that of *optimistic determinism*. According to this position, control and discrimination are impossible, but this impossibility preserves the stability of deterrence and peace. This would be the basic position of Jervis, of Mandelbaum, to some extent of Schelling and of the various shades of believers in pure deterrence. This is also the classic French position.

The second position is that of *pessimistic determinism*. This position combines pessimism about escalation with pessimism about deterrence and the arms race. If nuclear weapons exist, they will be used, and if they are used they will go all the way. The only logical conclusion, this side of complete despair, is complete abolition of nuclear weapons, but various partial or intermediary solutions (no first use, no extended deterrence, no modernization) are envisaged as ways of at least postponing the moment of truth.

Optimistic voluntarism. This is the position of A. Wohlstetter as described by François Gorand, or of Fred Iklé. Deterrence may fail (and, according to the latter, is even likely to) but new technological possibilities in the direction of precision and information make it possible to strengthen the credibility of deterrence and, even more, to avoid both defeat and genocide if deterrence fails. Wohlstetter stresses more the possibility of a happy ending to the conflict (through discrimination and control if it breaks out), Iklé the possibility of a happy ending to nuclear deterrence itself (through a defence-dominated environment).[19]

Finally there is a fourth position, which I would call *pessimistic voluntarism.* In this interpretation, deterrence may well fail, control and discrimination are unlikely to work at present, due both to the limitations of technology and to the rigidities of bureaucracy, and will never have much chance of succeeding because of human passions and impetuosity. But there is still a moral and political duty to try to play the game both of deterrence and of damage limitation, as long as the uncertainty of their effectiveness is recognized. This would be the position favoured by this writer, as well as by Robert Osgood and Laurence Martin.[20]

There is very little practical difference between what one might call a maximalist version of the fourth position and a minimalist version of the third one. Both tend to go in the same technological and strategic direction, if with differing degrees of enthusiasm and assurance. But optimism and pessimism do make a difference not only in declaratory policy but also in the respective priorities given to the two goals they both deem desirable – of controlling escalation in the case of nuclear war and of avoiding the latter's occurrence in the first place.

The fourth position has, in turn, many versions which range from what Wohlstetter, attributing it to one phase of McNamara's thinking, calls 'madcap' (the policy of mutual assured destruction), or from Secretaries of Defence J. Schlesinger's or Harold Brown's attempt to gain some measure of flexibility and control while remaining sceptical as to the ultimate result, to an emphasis on war-termination as advocated by L. Wieseltier,[21] or to the combination of minimum deterrence and of city-avoidance which seems to emerge with ever-greater force from the combination of the new detente, the new economic constraints and the moral objections against MAD: it is advocated by members of the Princeton Project on Finite Deterrence (Harold A. Feiveson, Richard H. Ullman and Frank von Hippel)[22] and, more explicitly, by David Lewis, also from Princeton, under the labels of 'Finite counterforce' and 'Buy like a madman, use like a nut',[23] by Harold A. Feiveson in his article on 'No first use and no cities'[24] and by Henry Shue.[25] This last trend, which would seem to be very much in tune with the recommendations of the American bishops as translated by McGeorge Bundy (with his combination of 'existential deterrence', and the search for a limited non-escalatory response), is particularly vulnerable to the charge that it goes so far in avoiding a military use of nuclear weapons that its only logical consequence is of no use at all. This is recognized almost explicitly by H. Feiveson, who relates his proposal to the very low degree of plausibility of the Soviet threat.[26] Whatever its particular merits or faults, however, it shares one feature with the other versions; while they all may appear incoherent or incomplete in the eyes of the true believers in pure deterrence or in a war-fighting capability, their apparent inability to bridge the gap between conflicting requirements or between prediction and prescription may in fact constitute their main virtue.

While being heavily influenced by moral considerations, they remain, however, within the confines of strategic discussion proper. The relationship between the latter and the religious or philosophical debates on ethics and deterrence deserves to be spelt out.

The religious debate has its own dynamics: for instance, the increased legitimacy of pacifism as against the just war tradition, in the view of the American bishops, a trend which emerged well before the recent peace movement, is linked to the Vietnam war. On the nuclear issue itself, the distinctions between threat and use and between combatants and innocents have dominated religious discussions at times when the first was accepted and the second rejected far more categorically by the strategic consensus. Of course the focus of the religious debate is on the relevance of just-war thinking and, above all, on the moral rectitude of intentions. But these cannot be judged without reference to the plausibility of results, and there religious discussions have to bow to the dominant conclusions of strategic reasoning and to the current state of technology. In this consists the fragility of the much discussed pastoral letter of the American catholic bishops in 1983.

The specific contribution of religious authors to the debate would seem to lie in two opposite casuistic reasonings. One is 'double effect' theory, illustrated in particular by Paul Ramsey, which justifies civilian casualties if they were not intended as such but occur as collateral damage produced by counterforce attacks. The other is 'existential deterrence' (an expression coined by McGeorge Bundy to summarize, approvingly, the position of the Catholic bishops), justifying the possession and, perhaps, the implicit threat of the use of nuclear weapons but forbidding the explicit threat and the use itself. Both insist more on intentions than on consequences, and postulate that the minimum requirements for target discrimination in the first case and credibility in the second, without which the good intentions would be self-defeating, will somehow be met. In reality, however, their status is not fundamentally different from that of the ethical arguments used against each other by the advocates of pure deterrence and of defence, i.e. of accepting mass murder or making it more likely by promoting the illusion of limitation: whatever their legitimacy in terms of intentions (and it is likely that the intention of both sides is the eminently moral one of keeping the peace), they stand or fall, in terms of their consequences, by who has the better of the technological and strategic arguments. More specifically ethical or religious arguments are concerned with the ethics of partly forgoing one's freedom of action and whether humility and reciprocity can be reconciled with regarding one's cause as good and the opponent's as evil.

On balance, probably the most important contribution to the debate on ethics and deterrence to come from the religious side lies in bringing home a dimension which diplomats, strategists and ideologists may risk forgetting because of their occupational (and to some extent necessary) bias; when country A threatens country B with nuclear retaliation, or when one discusses the struggle between freedom and totalitarianism, ultimately the subject is the same, that of human beings threatening to kill other human beings. This has one specific consequence for nuclear strategy, the unconditional opposition of Vatican Two to targeting of civilian populations; and one, more general, less clear-cut but no less important dimension: the appeal not to let individual responsibility and duty towards fellow men be masked by theoretical, national or ideological abstractions.

The other side of the coin, i.e. the possible tension between private and public morality, or as Niebuhr put it, between 'moral man and immoral society', is given less attention, at least in the United States and at the present time.[27]

Interestingly, the philosophical discussion on ethics and nuclear deterrence runs in close parallel to the religious debate, even when it is conducted by pragmatists and positivists. In their introduction to the special issue of *Ethics* on ethics and nuclear deterrence, Russell Hardin and John Mearsheimer write: 'Perhaps this is the most important lesson moral philosophers offer for the debate over nuclear policy: the popular view of the Soviet-American conflict as us against them and of nuclear retaliation as an act of vengeance cannot be squared with the threat of immolating tens of millions of children.'[28] More generally, as the same authors point out, in the symposium that formed the basis for this special issue, philosophers were on the side of intentions just as much as strategists were on the side of consequences. Of course, American philosophers are no more united among themselves than American strategists. But the main division, between deontologists, who concentrate on means and principles, and utilitarians, who concentrate on ends and consequences, is still articulated in terms of individual duties and calculations. The central question is 'whether we may do – or threaten – evil that good may come',[29] or, as I think would be more correct in the case of deterrence: 'that evil – a greater or the same one – may not come'. This brings us back to the double problem of the distinction between threat and use and between absolute and relative evil, which lies at the heart of the religious discussions.

Even the most comprehensive attempt at putting the various positions in perspective in terms of an ethic of ends, means and consequences, and at reaching prudent and practical conclusions (Joseph Nye's book on *Nuclear Ethics*) conforms to the style of abstract and somewhat mechanical calculations that is common to the tradition of utilitarian philosophers or economists and to that of theological casuists. The discussion remains at the level of what the Hegelian tradition would call subjective or universalistic morality, without really entering the second, political, and the third, historical, dimension, which are underlined by Dieter Henrich's contribution to *Nukleare Abschreckung*.

Of course, many philosophers and social scientists, from Michael Walzer to Karl Deutsch or Richard Rummel through Stanley Hoffmann or Michael Doyle, have tried to bridge the triple gap between the *ought* and the *is*, the abstract and the concrete, the individual and the political, or the historical. In particular, the typically American discussion about the compatibility of nuclear weapons with individual rights, and the suggestions for institutional checks and balances meant to offset the inherently monarchic bias of nuclear decision-making, combines philosophical, legal and political considerations, even though it lacks in strategic realism.[30] But the current vogue of ethics and the discussions it has inspired, while illustrating the unique American sense of moral responsibility, still bring to (a non-Anglo-American) mind the remark made by Octavio Paz about Rawls's *Theory of Justice*: 'This is a book of moral philosophy which leaves politics aside and does not examine the relationship between morality and history.'[31]

The German debate

Like the American one, the German debate has been characterized by the major role played by the churches and, to a lesser extent, the scientists; but it has been focused much less on strategic doctrine and on problems of choice if deterrence fails, and linked much more to politics.

Perhaps the most interesting period is the first. In the discussions by Catholic theologians about pronouncements made by Pius XXII, particularly in 1957 and 1958, when the prime movers were Gundlach and Hirschmann, all the elements of the present discussions on limiting and controlling nuclear war and on the relation of the nuclear threat to the totalitarian one were already in place. As already mentioned, the triangular discussion between the churches, the antinuclear scientists and the philosopher Karl Jaspers has remained paradigmatic. *Die Atombomb und die Zukunft des Menschen* is still the most comprehensive and most rigorous philosophical analysis of man's predicament, faced with these two inventions of our age, nuclear weapons and totalitarianism. The work of C.F. von Weiszäcker, over the whole postwar period, has, in its own way, covered the various dimensions of the nuclear debate, including the scientific and the religious ones, in an equally magisterial if less specifically philosophical way. Both exemplify an integrated approach which, with the partial exception of Raymond Aron whose emphasis was more strategic and political, is not to be found outside Germany.

The debate on force and the theoretical criticism of deterrence (exemplified by Dieter Senghaas's important book, *Abschrechkung and Frieden*) were discreetly pursued within the churches and within 'peace research' throughout the 1960s and 1970s. But public confrontation, as we have seen, ceased, first with the acceptance of German rearmament and Nato by the SPD, then with detente. The opposition to the neutron bomb marked the beginning of the new phase. It is interesting to note that it was launched with a remark made by Egon Bahr, about the diabolical and capitalist character of a weapon which destroyed people but spared possessions. It is also interesting that the same late 1970s were the years of a certain rekindling of interest in the national question on the German Left, partly through the influence of intellectuals expelled from the GDR and partly because of the birth of the Green movement and the struggle against civilian nuclear power.

As these examples show, the ethical dimension is indeed present in the new peace movement but it is different from that of the late 1950s and, even more, from American discussions of just war or nuclear freeze. Three wings may be distinguished. The first, closer both to the churches and to the fringes of the strategic establishment but also represented by independent philosophers like Ernst Tügendhat,[32] tries to demonstrate that rationality is on the side of the peace movement.

It argues in empirical terms (nuclear deterrence, and in particular the INF deployments, make nuclear war more and more likely) and in absolute moral ones (nuclear war is the ultimate moral evil, hence it should be unconditionally avoided, even if nuclear disarmament would make conventional war more likely).

Following on from that, there are two possible versions. If, like Professor Tügendhat one begins (as he rightly does against A. Glucksman) by pointing out that the ethical alternative is not between red and dead but between red and murderer, and continues, as he does, by arguing that no goal can ethically be pursued by murder, one is on the way from nuclear pacifism to absolute pacifism and arguing, as Karl Barth did in an earlier generation, that 'modern weapons have completed the self-revelation of war in its true nature', which is 'purely and simply murder'.[33] If, on the other hand, it is not murder but nuclear war which is an absolute evil, one enters, as Tügendhat does, the realm of strategy and technology and the search for an alternative, nuclear-free, defence: but this is also the realm of relative or prudential judgments and of comparative risks, and the discussion will turn, as in the American case, first on whether nuclear war is indeed necessarily of a different nature, in its consequences, from any other war and, second, on whether the abandonment of extended deterrence and of first-use options, and even the abandonment of nuclear deterrence altogether, do not make nuclear war, through escalation from conventional war or through undeterred attack, more likely rather than less.

This way of posing the problem may not be, however, what gives the German peace movement its originality or its deeper ethical inspiration. Our hypothesis is that this is to be found more on the two other wings.

One can discern a more romantic, or existential current, which corresponds more or less to the Greens (or at least to their 'funda-mentalist' wing) and whose ethics is more one of aspiration and self-fulfilment, of authenticity and community, of purity and love, than of duty and responsibility: the models here are the Sermon on the Mount and St Francis. Best known is Franz Alt, who in terms of book sales is the German equivalent of Jonathan Schell.[34] The other current is more political, and stresses above all the need for dialogue with the other Germany and the Soviet Union, and the avoidance of 'demonizing' the opponent, This attitude is prevalent on the left wing of the SPD. The first focuses on the extreme, or apocalyptic case; the second on the duty of reciprocity. As the nuclear danger has seemed to be receding with the new superpower dialogue, the second position has become more and more prevalent. It has led both to the document, signed by the SPD and the SED on 27 August 1987, on 'Ideological competition and common security' and to innumerable religious writings preaching reconciliation with the East. The idea of getting rid of stereotypes of the enemy has become an omnipresent theme in German political discourse. Both currents adopt the point of view of the 'victim' as opposed to the 'warrior': a way, perhaps, of distinguishing themselves both from past German warriors and from potential American ones. More than anywhere else, the Protestant churches, partly thanks to the complexity of their structure, fulfil a mediating function by encouraging a dialogue between politicians and youth at Kirchentage and between the two Germanys via the relations and the common declarations of the two churches.

Characteristically, these have taken a more and more political and radical character. In their fourth 'common word' since 1979, in March 1986, they, on the one hand, condemn war of any sort, and on the other, enter into the specifics of the strategic and political East–West discussion by expressing their reservations about strategic defence in space, their support for a nuclear test ban and their encouragement for the special relations and joint mission of the two German states, as well as for the strengthening of human rights and fundamental freedoms within them.[35]

This active involvement of the churches in the general dialogue may contribute to the fact that the revival of religious-ethical thinking on war and peace has taken the direction less of just-war doctrine than of a 'peace ethic' (*Friedensethik*), an attempt to 'think in the perspective of peace' (T. Rendtorff). At the April 1985 meeting of the project to which this essay is a contribution, the most apparent division was neither between strategists and philosophers, nor between hawks and doves, but between Americans and Europeans, particularly Germans, such as Professor J. Delbrück, concerning the relevance or obsolescence of traditional ethical, legal or theological thinking about war.

Another difference concerns the role of philosophers and the existence and nature of a debate among them about the ethics of deterrence. Philosophical concern with the issue is to be found less in specialized journals or conferences than as one dimension of the religious and political debate. Most of the directly ethical discussion seems to adopt as a frame of reference the Weberian distinction between the 'ethics of conviction' and the 'ethics of responsibility', as in the discussion between F. Alt and W. Hättich.[36] But this can hardly be said to constitute a philosophical discussion. The latter, in its limited way, takes place on a more general level, using the Hegelian opposition between *Moralität* and *Sittlichkeit*, between an ethics based on universal principles and on the individual conscience, and one based on the accepted traditions and institutions of a given society. In their simplest form, these views would be represented by Professor Tügendhat and Luebbe. A third view, represented by Professor Henrich, insists that the 'messengers of the apocalypse' should be taken seriously in their claim that the possibility of mankind's self-destruction signals the collapse of conventional wisdom and morality, but that this must constitute a point of departure for a call to reconstitute the foundation of ethics based on a new view of history and of the world.

The British debate

The British debate has much in common with both the American and the German debates, while retaining an originality of its own and a certain insular quality. Both within the strategic community and within the peace movement, there is a lively interaction between British and Americans, to the point of making them sometimes indistinguishable: many concepts of strategic theory are of British origin; the best-known manifesto of the British peace movement, *Protest and Survive*, edited by E.P. Thompson, has a US edition with many American contributors; British scientists (such as P.M.S. Blackett, C.P. Snow, Sir Solly Zuckerman), critical of the nuclear arms race, are (thanks to the Pugwash movement or to their own writings) household names within the American debate. Even in the philosophical discussion, which is more self-contained, there is more commonality and communication between Britain and America than between either of them and either of the other two countries. There is somewhat less communication among the churches. Some Anglican groups have gone further than their American counterparts in condemning the bomb, but the Church of England as such has been very reserved, and while the role of the 'Red Dean' of Canterbury in the first wave of the peace movement is played by a Catholic prelate, Monsignor Bruce Kent, in the second, the Catholic bishops have more in common with their European than with their American colleagues.

And yet, Britain is, in a way, the country where the peace debate has struck the deepest political roots: it had the most active peace movement in the early 1960s and it has, today, the only major Western party converted to it, since the Labour Party declared its intention to denuclearize Britain.

The specific British emphasis within the peace movement is indeed on nuclear disarmament, particularly on unilateralism. This is often combined on the one hand with Atlanticism (including sometimes the idea that the United States should keep its nuclear weapons) and on the other hand with the idea that Britain should give a moral example to the world by starting the process of disarmament or at least halting the process of proliferation. Can we not recognize here a peculiarly British mixture of idealism and pragmatism? More recently, however, there has been a decline of Atlanticism in favour both of national assertion and a certain neutralist pan-Europeanism. Polls (for instance the one carried out by the *Daily Telegraph* on 22 February 1986) show that the British nuclear deterrent enjoys a much wider acceptance than US nuclear bases (although this acceptance is by no means as quasi-unanimous as in France, particularly among defence experts). The Falklands war showed both the strength of the patriotic impulse and the narrowness (both in terms of popular roots and of issues) of the peace movement.

Intellectually and politically, its evolution has nevertheless caused it to assume a position of leadership on the European scene. This evolution has taken it from the old Campaign for Nuclear Disarmament (numerically still the more important organization) to the Campaign for European Nuclear Disarmament (END), from Bertrand Russell to E.P. Thompson. One contribution made by the latter was his theory of 'exterminism', equating the two superpowers morally and accusing them of being dominated by their respective military-industrial complexes and of inexorably leading the world to destruction. Another, less predictable, contribution by Thompson and his disciples has been an increased interest in Europe and, in particular Eastern Europe. The call for 'a denuclearized Europe from Poland to Portugal' is perfectly compatible with Soviet diplomacy, but its intention is as much to encourage East European independence as to avoid nuclear war. This has led END into a lively if sometimes stormy dialogue with East European (particularly Czech and Hungarian) dissidents and into stressing an opposition between traditional diplomatic and arms control negotiations ('detente from above') and popular revolt against the superpowers ('detente from below').

Whatever doubts can be legitimately entertained about the realism of this new approach, it has contributed to redirecting the attention of the peace movement away from insular or abstract unilateralism and from an obsession with nuclear weapons, towards political structures as factors in peace or war, and towards a broader solidarity with the victims of oppression.

One of the most encouraging aspects of the British debate is, indeed, that it is much less compartmentalized than in other countries. Between

philosophers and practitioners, between civilian and military strategists
and religious thinkers and leaders, interaction and overlaps are constant.
Defence officials such as Sir Michael Quinlan, Sir Arthur Hockaday or
David Fisher are at the same time practising Christians, ethical thinkers
and strategic theorists, and it is in this quadruple capacity that they
participate in the debate. Two compilations of writings on this topic by
British philosophers, masterminded by Nigel Blake and Kay Pole,
Dangers of Deterrence and *Objections to Nuclear Defense*,[37] are similar in
tone to the special issue of the American periodical *Ethics*; some of the
contributors are the same. The main theme concerns intentions, the
distinction between threat and use, and the relevance of just-war
thinking. But there is a greater awareness of the limits of such abstract
discussions and a refreshing willingness to examine the concrete
technological situation as well as to study alternative forms of defence
and compare them with postures based on nuclear deterrence in terms
both of morality and effectiveness.

Perhaps the classic example of this openness to dialogue is the
seminar taught jointly at Oxford, in 1983, by the master of Balliol, a
Catholic priest turned philosopher, and a defence official on sabbatical
leave, together with the two complementary but opposed books that
resulted from it. The first, *The Logic of Deterrence* by Anthony Kenny,[38]
goes further than Ernst Tügendhat's pamphlet on *Rationality and
Irrationality of the Peace Movement* in combining absolute moral criteria
and an empirical strategic enquiry in a reasonably well-informed and
logically impeccable way. In my opinion, it nevertheless falls into the
trap of using against nuclear war arguments which apply to murder in
general, and failing to demonstrate the assumption that nuclear war is
necessarily a total evil and Soviet domination a milder or more tolerable
one. The companion volume, *Morality and the Bomb* by David Fisher,[39]
makes these criticisms within the framework of a rigorous review of
just-war and deterrence theories, in what may well be the most
balanced and comprehensive statement on the debate, encompassing
the religious, philosophical, political and strategic points of view, in
prose that remains clear and lucid while treating complex issues in a
balanced and discriminating way. The same can be said of Father J.
Mahoney's article, 'Moral risks and value-balancing'.[40]

The French non-debate

None of this would be conceivable in France. The existence of a
French defence consensus and the absence of a French peace movement

are no secret. Certain qualifications may be in order: there are once again the beginnings of a debate on defence, prompted by worries first about the evolution of Germany and then about the Strategic Defence Initiative and the withdrawal of the US Euromissile. On the other hand, the public acceptance of the French nuclear force − relatively recent as far as the Left is concerned − does not necessarily mean a willingness to see it used, even as a threat, in time of crisis. The difference between the French position and that of the British unilateral disarmers may, as Herman Kahn suggested in the early 1960s, be just that between pre-emptive and preventive surrender. One thing, however, is firmly established and likely to endure: the absence of a debate on ethics and nuclear weapons.

Take, for example, the debate on the neutron bomb. In France, none of those moral arguments were raised against it that existed in Germany, in Holland and in President Carter's mind: the critics attacked it exclusively from a Gaullist point of view, as leading to an 'acceptance of battle' and to greater integration within Nato. In earlier debates (at the time of the great polemics between Raymond Aron and General Gallois in the early 1960s or of Giscard d'Estaing's and General Mery's abortive attempts at revision in 1976), as well as in later ones (with the criticisms of the official doctrine by heretics such as General Coppel or Pierre Lellouche), it is essentially the degree of independence or of cooperation and solidarity with Germany and Nato and, to some extent, the degree of operational effectiveness of French defence, which is at stake, not its morality.

What prevents the latter question from being raised, except by the most marginal Christian–pacifist groups (who, incidentally, use mainly the argument of aid for the Third World against defence expenditures) is on the one hand the acceptance of an abstract doctrine of deterrence and on the other the double political consensus on national independence and anti-sovietism. Until recently, there was a striking contrast between the systematic rigidity of the French doctrine of deterrence and the political flexibility of French diplomacy.[41]

In the first case, the French fixation on pure deterrence has led to a refusal to consider what would happen if deterrence failed. Since the strategy is one of deterrence, hence of non-war, considerations of war-fighting or of damage limitation, or even of credibility or of morality would be the sign of an acceptance of war and of a lack of faith in deterrence. The French doctrine has all the features of an ideology: it is a closed system, it claims to be scientific, it demands religious loyalty, it pronounces the exclusion of heretics. It has been, so far, very rarely challenged politically, in part because its very abstractness facilitates a consensus based upon ambiguity. But another reason relates to political allegiance: many, on the non-communist Left, who would be tempted by pacifism for idealistic reasons, are afraid of being manipulated by the Soviets or encouraging German neutralism. Conversely, many of those who, like Jean-Pierre Chevènement or Régis Debray, are closer to neutralism or anti-Americanism than to the anti-Soviet consensus see in nuclear weapons the instrument of French independence. They are ready to praise the wave of nuclear pacifism through France's neighbours, because it helps to separate Europe from the United States, but they would like France to remain the only nuclear power on the continent.

And yet there is movement, both in the political and the strategic sphere: preoccupation with the dangers of German isolation or a German tête-à-tête with Moscow is leading in France to a genuine movement away from strategic rigidity and political ambiguousness, and an identification of French security with that of the Federal Republic. This is causing the Right to emphasize extended deterrence at the expense of traditional doctrine and the Left to move in the direction of detente and arms control. But the most shocking aspect of the French position remains unchanged, namely the complete lack of concern for sparing innocent human lives. The notion of avoiding collateral damage is entirely alien to French considerations. True, if one accepts the logic of the French doctrine, the search for discrimination and proportionality, the classic just-war criteria, would mean the acceptance of limited war, and hence of the failure of deterrence. In the French debate, deterrence has been traditionally synonymous with deterrence by anti-city retaliation, at least until very recently, when some references to theatre nuclear deterrence and counterforce have started to appear. But they are inspired by the search for Franco-German cooperation or for some operational flexibility, and no claim is made of any moral intention, such as limiting civilian casualties, even as a distant goal.

When challenged on these grounds the usual French response has been to dismiss the moral problem altogether in the name of deterrence (nuclear weapons are moral since they are meant to prevent war, not to wage it) and of retaliation (since France will never be the attacker, it bears no moral responsibility for what it might have to do in response to aggression or blackmail).

André Glucksmann's contribution has been to supplement the argument based on deterrence with the argument based on totalitarianism: communist (as well as Nazi) totalitarianism is a total evil, a total evil calls for a total response, any effort to mitigate this total character of the deterrent threat of retaliation (be it through conventional response, through the avoidance of collateral damage or through strategic defence) is tantamount to pacifist capitulationism: 'La dissuasion sera sale ou ne sera pas.'

The logical conclusion is that the best way to resist totalitarianism is to murder its victims. This is apocalyptical thinking gone mad: yet it is cynically applauded by the French establishment as long as it is put to the service of the most unreconstructed French doctrine.

An interesting footnote concerns the role of the Catholic church, which also supports the French consensus (except for a minority of five bishops). On the one hand, it takes a more balanced view than the American bishops of the double threat of nuclear war and communist domination, and it is more careful not to enter strategic debates proper or make technological assumptions for which it possesses no expertise and no legitimate authority. On the other hand, it disposes of the moral problem rather complacently by making the distinction between threat and use, and via the idea that nuclear deterrence is a transitional solution for a situation of dire emergency (*détresse*). But it makes no real attempt, conceptually or otherwise, to go beyond that. Its pastoral letter makes only passing mention of the fact that anti-city targeting is explicitly and unconditionally forbidden by Vatican Two, yet proudly proclaimed to be the focus of official French doctrine.

Usually the French are accused of being cynical; the French Catholics are open to the suspicion of being, in addition, hypocritical.

Why the differences?

After this review of the four national debates, we should ideally be able to return to the questions asked in the first part of this paper and draw some comparisons and reach some conclusions about the structure and direction of the transatlantic debate. Here we shall merely try to bring out a few trends, which, more often than not, are already implicit in our four descriptions. These are: the respective geostrategic situations of the four countries, their political structures and objectives and their sociocultural attitudes and traditions.

Geostrategic situations

Among the four, the United States stands out as the only superpower, and Germany as the only non-nuclear country and at the same time the only one whose interests, because it is divided, are Central European before being global. Britain and the United States have an insular tradition, Germany and France a continental one. All this produces differences in terms of both comparative responsibility and comparative vulnerability.

Within the framework of shared Western interests, the United States is saddled with the primary responsibility in the case of crisis and war. Inevitably, therefore, the American debate looks to escalation control, and the choices that would be available if deterrence failed. It quite naturally focuses its attention on the role of the 'warrior', with all its strategic challenges and moral dilemmas. At the other extreme, Germany has the most passive role. Like all non-nuclear states, according to Egon Bahr, but to an even greater degree, it can manifest its sovereignty essentially by saying no to the deployment and use on its own territory of the nuclear weapons of others. France and Britain are in an intermediate situation. Their freedom of action is greater than that of Germany, but it is still more reduced in times of crisis than in times of detente, in war than in peace. Hence their emphasis will be more on deterrence than on defence, more on keeping peace stable than on making war just.

This difference of emphasis is, of course, linked at least as much to differences in vulnerability as in responsibility.

The new feature of the situation is that the United States is and, above all, feels vulnerable. It still is less so than its allies, however, and has more hopes (unrealistic as they may be) of becoming invulnerable again through SDI. Germany is the most vulnerable of the four, both because of its geographical position and because it is bristling with troops and nuclear weapons. Hence it quite naturally sees itself in the role of 'victim'. For geographical reasons, France is more directly vulnerable than Britain.

It is above all this inequality of vulnerability which explains why the differences between conventional and nuclear, or between limited and all-out war, are more salient for Americans than for Europeans, for Britain than for her continental allies, for France than for Germany.

Political structures and objectives

These various degrees of responsibility and vulnerability are reflected in a certain differentiation of foreign policy objectives, even at the level of the four states and their national interests as they themselves perceive them.

Obviously all four share the twofold objective of peace and the containment of Soviet expansionism. But for the United States these general objectives take the form of leadership of the alliance and global stability. At given periods, they may, in the eyes of the Europeans, lead the United States to the brink of collision (in its efforts to push back communism or its involvement in Third World conflicts) or collusion (through arms control as seen at the Reykjavik and Washington summits, or through efforts at joint control of regional conflicts) with the Soviet Union. These moves in their turn trigger European responses, of which an anti-US peace movement is one possible version, efforts for West European military autonomy another.

For Germany, the common objective of peace takes on an even more urgent and quasi-unconditional importance, due to that country's particular vulnerability; but it interacts in many subtle ways with the nation's perennial search for identity and the state's search for legitimacy. These different considerations all converge, today, on the importance of maintaining communications with the GDR and of seeking reconciliation with Germany's eastern neighbours.

The distinctive feature of French policy is the search for independence. The existence of nuclear weapons is regarded as providential, since the weapon which maintains peace through deterrence also acts as an equalizer, enabling a middle-ranking power to maintain an independent defence. Also providential is the fact that France is not in the immediate front line in relation to the main continental threat, from the Soviet Union. Behind the double screen of nuclear weapons, and of the German (or Nato) glacis, it has been able to pursue its tradition of diplomatic flexibility and the long-range project of a more autonomous, more united Europe, without either superpower of German domination. Today, however, the contradictions between the search for flexibility for its own sake and the grand design for Europe, which were already apparent in de Gaulle's time, are coming to a head: the dangers to Europe coming from Soviet power, German political vulnerability and US unpredictability are seen by many as necessitating a greater European commitment, just as the new technologies of conventional and space defence necessitate more of a joint European effort. The classical French triad of a strategic policy based on uncertainty, a diplomatic policy based on freedom of action and a domestic consensus based on ambiguity is increasingly called into question.

As for Britain, it to an even greater extent is in a period of reassessment and transition. It still occupies an ambivalent position vis-à-vis the three traditional circles of British foreign policy (insular, European and Atlantic) and still wishes to keep open all three options.

But the British trend seems to be towards Europe, and the question for the future, as for the whole of Western Europe, is whether this Europeanization should lead to an autonomous West European defence or, as the peace movement hopes, to a new security system based on a denuclearized and perhaps neutral Europe.

As important as the objectives of states are, they cannot be separated from the political structures which permit or impede their implementation and their permeability to the inspiration or demands of other domestic or transnational forces.

In this respect, France and the Federal Republic are at opposite ends of the spectrum: France is the most centralized and Germany the least. The primacy of the state in France, its remoteness from the local and regional communities in Germany, are part of the explanation for the failure of grassroots movements like the battle against civilian nuclear power in the one, and their success in the other. The political system proper has been at its most monarchic in France (where else could the head of state have announced on television: 'La dissuasion c'est moi'?) and the personalities of de Gaulle and Mitterrand have played a decisive role in preventing the peace debate from developing; in Germany by contrast, the existence of coalition governments and the role of political parties have provided channels through which the pressures of militant movements are influencing governmental positions.

Particularly since the parliamentary elections of March 1986, the French system is losing many of its distinctive differences as the country becomes less centralized, the authority of the President on foreign policy is less undisputed, and the role of the political parties looks likely to increase.

The United States and Britain are in an intermediate position: they are less centralized than France, grassroots movements and local communities have a much greater influence, including on questions of war and peace (this was particularly notable in the United States with the 'ground zero' movement), although, on the other hand, the authority of the President and of the Prime Minister is far greater than in the Federal Republic. But, particularly in Britain, the peace movement still has a chance of gaining access to the corridors of power via developments in the opposition parties.

Sociocultural attitudes and traditions

This discussion has, so far, dealt with the external, political conditions of the debate on ethics and deterrence. To speak of the sociocultural attitudes and traditions which are reflected in the debate itself, or in its absence, is both more to the point and more dangerous. Nothing is subject more to misleading clichés than the attempt to read intellectual positions in the light of national styles. These are apt to vary in surprising ways. For instance, while it would be difficult to deny that Germany has a more romantic and metaphysical tradition and that France is the country of classicism and rationalism, since the Second World War Nietzsche and Heidegger have had a more open and public influence in France and logical positivism has been more important in Germany. But the influence of great philosophical traditions is sometimes to be found less in the technical work of philosophers than in the general *Zeitgeist*.

Again the most striking and important example is that of Heidegger. Followers of the Greens and of the peace movement are indignant when the Heideggerian origins of concepts like *Mut zur Angst*, or the interpretation of Nazism and concentration camps as merely one manifestation of the general Western trend towards the rule of technology, are pointed out. The kinship, however, is clearly apparent in the collection *Friedensinitiative Philosophie: um Kopf und Kriege*,[42] and explicitly brought out in the philosophical bestseller by Peter Sloterdijk, *Kritik der Zynischen Vernunft*.[43]

In the United States, there is a two-pronged approach on both sides of the debate, which is strongly influenced both by a technological and a religious attitude. Among the 'warriors', one finds the traditional 'can-do' attitude, which regards the problems of victory, defence and control simply as other challenges to be met, as well as the no less traditional righteousness which, in the past, has led the United States to adopt a punitive role, waging total war in the service of a just cause. In the other camp, one finds an antitechnological reaction and a sense of guilt for Hiroshima or for Vietnam, which leads to a distrust both of the intentions of the political leadership and of its ability to control events, and ultimately of the legitimacy of the US cause as a justification for intervention and, even more so, the threat of nuclear retaliation.

Octavio Paz has commented on the tendency of American liberals and conservatives to switch sides on the issue of intervention and isolationism. He links it to 'the tendency of North-American intellectuals to replace historical vision by moral judgment or, even worse, by pragmatic and circumstantial considerations. Moralism and empiricism are two twin forms of the incomprehension of history'.[44]

Germany, on the contrary, is haunted by history, but in the sense in which, as Joyce put it in his own case, history is a nightmare from which it is trying to escape. With all due allowance for the existence of a pragmatic and prosaic tradition, which has dominated the first decades of the Bundesrepublik, it does seem that the debate on nuclear weapons has been marked by a propensity to self-pity, by the proclamation of vulnerability and *Angst* as positive values, by the combination of a political 'arrogance of weakness' and a romantic preference for apocalyptic thinking. The search for identity and recognition takes various forms, one of which is to seek out a special role for peace that is different from its role in the past but still allows Germany some sort of unique fate, some central role in the salvation of the world.

The French search for singularity is dressed more in the mantle of universalism. Applied to nuclear matters, it can be described in terms of the three French R's: rationalism, rhetoric and *Realpolitik*. It combines a predilection, on the one hand, for abstract, logical but unrealistic discourse (what Raymond Aron used to call 'logical delirium') and, on the other, for realistic, unsentimental power politics. At the first theoretical level, to coin a concept (like *non-guerre*, or *armes pré-stratégiques*) is to dispose of a problem. At the other level, of reason of state, it is striking that France is the only really secular country of the four: scientists and churches are less important than abstract strategists and one-sided ideologists used as the tools of Machiavellian policy.

In Britain, attitudes in the debate on nuclear weapons seem freer of hubris, whether technological, mystical or systematic. They evidence the same basic combination as in the United States, but the British form – the alliance of puritanism and pragmatism – contains a greater element of moderation and prudence than the American or German version.

A few provisional conclusions

My general conclusions will be even more sketchy than these comparative notes.

First, a factual balance sheet. Nowhere have the debates on nuclear weapons been entirely without effect. On the contrary, the positions of the peace movement have been, in one way or the other, integrated into the national consensus of each of the four countries discussed, or, to put it differently, each of the four establishments has tried to revamp at least the presentation of elements of its own doctrine in response to the peace movement. In the United States, this has contributed not so much to the invention as to the promotion of President Reagan's Strategic Defence Initiative and his strictures against nuclear deterrence. More generally, the shift away from the reliance on nuclear weapons which pervades the whole spectrum of American thinking, has helped to bridge the gap between the military-industrial complex and the peace movement.

In France, officials and advocates of the official line have claimed that, if France had no peace movement to speak of, it was because French policy was itself a policy of 'non-war' and because it was second to none in refusing to seek nuclear superiority, or in rejecting the myth of limited and controlled nuclear war. A critic of the doctrine, Pierre Lellouche, has pointed out that what made the French posture acceptable was precisely its lack of operational credibility, which reassured potential pacifists that French nuclear weapons were not meant to be used.

In Germany and Britain, the reaction (other than on the rhetorical level, where the defence of INF deployments solely in terms of response to Soviet SS20s was a bow to antinuclear sentiment — leaving the governments defenceless against the 'zero option') was felt more on the political front of East–West relations. The German government, while essentially following the US lead on strategic matters proper, proclaims its agreement with its critics on the imperative need to promote detente and reconciliation with the East and to use every opportunity for arms control and disarmament. Mrs Thatcher's Britain, while sensitive to the same need for gestures towards detente and arms control, does not assign them the same priority. But it shares with the peace movement an increasing desire to affirm its independence from the United States.

In 1986 and 1987, however, a new factor has emerged on the scene and exerted a decisive influence upon both intranational and trans-atlantic dialogues: Gorbachev and his 'new thinking'. This influence has gone some way towards re-establishing consensus where bitter division reigned in 1981–3. In particular, the German consensus seems to have focused on detente, arms control and dialogue with the Soviet Union: from Egon Bahr to Franz-Josef Strauss and Hans-Dietrich Genscher, the hope for a new age and the need for a positive response have superseded the old fears and recriminations. In a less striking form, the same trend seems to have affected relations between Ronald Reagan and Margaret Thatcher and their left-wing critics, as well as, more broadly, between the United States and Europe.

In France, the opposite seems to be true. The famous French consensus, which was so striking when all the other Western democracies were torn apart by the issue of missile deployments, is now beginning to be questioned, just at the time when the rest are becoming more united. While the French public remains by far the most distrustful towards Gorbachev, clinging to 'old thinking' in terms of balance of power and nuclear deterrence, the trend is in the other direction: the image of the Soviet Union is improving for the first time in ten years, while trust in the civilian and military uses of nuclear energy, is diminishing. The majority on the Right are reacting to the danger by an ever more stringent denunciation of Gorbachev and of the perils (usually evoked by the names Yalta and Munich) the new detente conceals. But on the Left, including President Mitterrand, one discerns a shift towards the common position of the European Left. This does not mean the socialists renounce nuclear deterrence but it does lead them to denounce both the arms race and flexible deterrence and to move towards what appears to be the new de facto consensus (i.e. the combination of detente and minimum deterrence), and away from the stationing of nuclear weapons on foreign territory and from operational considerations, both of which had seemed crucial to extended deterrence.

Beyond the French case, then, the problem raised by the new consensus is whether it will produce more political unity or more fragmentation. We spoke earlier of a simultaneous crisis of deterrence and detente. Will the rebirth of the latter lead to a rebirth of the former? Certainly it has led the peace movement to tone down its ideas, and created a certain disarray in its ranks. On the other hand, as the new detente, much more than the earlier one, is committed to the reduction and ultimate abolition of nuclear weapons, it is not exactly designed to restore belief in nuclear deterrence, or at least in a credible extended deterrence.

That, as we indicated earlier, is the crux of the matter: while nuclear abolition is not likely to be pursued seriously by the Eastern and Western establishments, its more plausible functional equivalent, that of minimum deterrence at a much lower level, imposed both by popular opinion and by economic constraints, may well be the trend of the times. This outcome may be the least bad way of combining the stabilizing effects of nuclear deterrence with the requirements of a democratic and non-militaristic domestic community and of peaceful and cooperative East–West relations. There are two crucial provisos, however: first that the persisting political asymmetries between East and West should not lead to a political manipulation of the new trends, which would leave the West military, and psychologically, more constrained and more paralysed than the East; and second, that the non-nuclear Western states, deprived of the credible and visible protection of extended deterrence, should not drift into a dependence on Soviet goodwill which would cut them off from their nuclear allies. The fear, then, is not entirely unjustified that the new consensus may lead to a political fragmentation of the West which would be less spectacular and dramatic but more structural and more irreversible than in earlier times of crisis.

I should not like, however, to end this essay on such a pessimistic note.

It seems to me that the current process of synthesis, while running the risk of intellectual confusion and political or strategic paralysis, is nevertheless a move in the right direction. Any realistic policy on nuclear weapons has to embrace the various dimensions of the problem. The US emphasis on defence (in the sense of credibility, operational effectiveness, damage limitation or a satisfactory political outcome if deterrence fails), the French emphasis on deterrence and on peacetime reassurance and influence, the German emphasis on negotiation and arms control, are rooted in the respective situations of the three countries, but must be seen as complementary and as dangerous if pursued in isolation from the other dimensions and the other allies. And this is precisely what the British sense of compromise, which has never gone to the extremes of French rigidity and US oscillations, may have been best equipped to understand.

In today's world, nuclear weapons, interstate distrust, East–West conflict are inescapable realities, which dreams of invulnerability through space shields and of community through a 'security partnership' can do no more than conceal. Clarity and prudence make it imperative to accept the political primacy of *containment* and the strategic primacy of *deterrence*. But vitally necessary as they are, they are not sufficient. They cannot be the last word of Western strategic and diplomatic policies. We need to look *beyond containment*, to East–West reconciliation, and beyond *nuclear deterrence* (especially beyond the version which relies on mutually assured vulnerability) towards a balance in which defence and conventional weapons play a greater role. The nuclear element will remain, and with it the danger of escalation and ultimately of apocalypse. Mankind cannot avoid the risk of self-destruction, but it can avoid making it the basis for its own security.

Before any structural reform of international security can take place, deterrence and containment themselves need to be supplemented in order to be credible and effective. If deterrence is to be credible we need to prepare *now* for the eventuality of its failure. If containment is to be sustained, we must *now* look beyond it, by dealing with communist governments (through arms-control negotiations) and with their societies (in order to encourage their openness towards the West and their evolution towards greater national and individual autonomy).

As for the ethical dimension of the problem, the need is to avoid the danger of escaping either towards a simple just-war doctrine through a rediscovery of proportionality and discrimination, or towards a simple peace ethics dealing with political dialogue but avoiding the hard strategic choices. Deterrence should not be made into an abstract fetish, as in French official thinking, although it should still be at the centre of our ethical reflections. Peace cannot be based on deterrence alone, and neither military preparations nor ethical soul-searching can avoid the dilemmas of defence if deterrence fails. But neither peacetime diplomacy nor wartime operations can continue as before. They dare not for one moment forget the threat of escalation or ignore its restraining hand. While one half of Churchill's famous aphorism, although perhaps true so far, may be dangerously misleading for the future, the other will always remain the case. Peace may not be for ever 'the sturdy child of terror', but 'survival' will always be 'the twin brother of annihilation'. Or, to put the paradox more plainly, we need both an ethics of peace and an ethics of war, but as part of a comprehensive ethics of deterrence, combining a moral, political and strategic perspective. Each in their own way should reflect and elaborate the principal lesson of a half-century of successful deterrence: that conflict may be reconciled with reciprocity, and resolution with restraint.

PART THREE

TOTALITARIANISM

6

Communist Totalitarianism: The Transatlantic Vagaries of a Concept

Where I feel that people like us understand the situation better than so-called experts is not in any power to foretell specific events, but in the power to grasp what *kind* of world we are living in.

(George Orwell, Wartime Diary, 8 June 1940)

TO WRITE about totalitarianism is to write about oneself. For this writer the question of how to think about totalitarianism lies at the crossroads of two personal itineraries: the first one is geographic – between Eastern Europe and the West and, within the latter, between the cultural atmospheres of France and the United States; the second one is conceptual – between the study of political philosophy, ideologies and contemporary international relations.

It is perhaps because of personal circumstances that these historical questions – Is it true that there is something fundamental in common between the Nazi and the communist regimes that sets them apart from constitutional or pluralist systems? Is this bond central and permanent, or partial and transient? Why do some people ignore it and others become so obsessed by it that they are unable to see anything else? – merge, for me, with the theoretical ones: Can one understand what is completely alien? Must the non-ideologue become an ideologue, just as, for Plato, the judge must be able to turn himself into a criminal? Faced with the reality of totalitarianism, is there no choice but to trivialize it by denying its originality and hiding it behind the diversity of its origins, its incarnations, its phases or its consequences, or to absolutize it by imitating its methods and substituting, once more, the logic of an abstract idea for the complexity of reality? Is Manichaeism forced upon us by the very nature of totalitarianism? And if the only way to understand totalitarianism is to be antitotalitarian, can one be antitotalitarian without recreating an anti-ideological ideology, an antitotalitarian totalitarianism?

These problems were faced by Arthur Koestler and George Orwell, by Albert Camus and Ignazio Silone, by Raymond Aron and Richard Löwenthal, and have inspired their moral and intellectual stance since the 1930s. But the dominant impression left by 35 years of ardent curiosity is one of constant surprise and irritation at the way in which the problem of totalitarianism has been disappearing and reappearing according to the vagaries of ideological and political, individual and collective fashions and whims.

In France, or even in Europe, the postwar debate over concentration camps and the Stalinist trials (which were central to the Kravchenko and Rousset affairs, and to the polemics among Sartre, Camus and Merleau-Ponty) did not lead to a deeper theoretical analysis, except through the great novels of Koestler and, above all, Orwell. It was in the United States, often through the works of German émigrés who had known Nazism and had started to formulate the concept of totalitarianism as far back as the 1920s, that the latter, after being temporarily shelved because of the alliance with the Soviet Union, re-emerged triumphantly in the early 1950s – a triumph soon extended to the Federal Republic of Germany and, to a lesser extent, to Great Britain. In France, those who had forestalled the wave of US books became the only ones to take it into account. A solitary review of Hannah Arendt's *Origins of Totalitarianism* (New York, 1951) by Raymond Aron, in 1954, did not succeed in breaking the wall of silence, and the book was not translated until the 1970s. Hence the surprise of opposite but quasi-unanimous attitudes in the United States and in France.

After 1956 the atmosphere changed on both sides of the Atlantic. In France, through a process witnessed again today in their attitude towards China, intellectuals began to turn away from totalitarianism as soon as it became a little less bloody and attempted a certain reconciliation with society and reality. Meanwhile, in the United States, the death of Stalin, the decline of terror and the events in Poland and Hungary led to a questioning (anticipated by Aron in his 1954 article) of the classical and maximalist model of authoritarianism (Arendt's and that of Carl-Joachim Friedrich and Zbigniew Brzezinski[1]). This questioning was shared, with various nuances and delays, by these authors themselves. But the decline in the fascination with totalitarianism led most US Sovietologists to reinterpret the Soviet Union by denying its uniqueness. In the United States as well as the FRG, the decade from 1956 to 1966 is full of polemics around the notion of totalitarianism – now charged with underestimating the complexity of the regimes to which it is applied and their capacity for change, as well as the differences between them and their features in common with other dictatorships. By the end of the 1960s, the debate seemed to be over: the opponents of totalitarianism, found guilty of Cold War bias, won by a knockout in the United States, and on points in the FRG and in Great Britain. In the 1970s, while the debate lingered in these two countries, it was replaced in the United States by a quasi-unanimity in favour of broader notions, which were either classical (authoritarianism), novel ('movement' or 'mobilization' regimes) or Westernized ('institutional pluralism', or bureaucratic and corporate models). Hence a new malaise: for what the social sciences seemed to have done was, in effect, to provide totalitarian power with a set of new clothes about as useful as those of the naked emperor.

Fortunately or unfortunately, however, the cunning of reason, that old friend of totalitarianism, did not stay idle. From Mao's little red book to the normalization of Czechoslovakia, from the new forms of psychiatric repression in the Soviet Union to the grim Stalinism of liberated Vietnam and the demonstration by Cambodia's Pol Pot that the most monstrous monster can give birth to even more monstrous caricatures, it made nonsense of the reassuring chatter of scientific Sovietology by showing that if totalitarianism was dead, it had left behind some rather strange offspring. Above all it gave totalitarianism a spectacular comeback through the acclaim of a most unexpected public – the Parisian intellectual scene.

At long last came *The Gulag*, a divine surprise for the sad and ageing cohort of Eastern émigrés and their few scattered friends. The door to criticism that had been set ajar by the brutalities of Khrushchev and Mao was now blown wide open by the revelations of Solzhenitsyn, whose impact in France was greater than in any other country. The period of indifference and embarrassment which had replaced, between 1956 and the early 1970s, the positive fascination with the Soviet Union, was now succeeded by a negative fascination with the Gulag. There was a convergence of three trends: specialists like Alain Besançon who furthered Arendt's ideas of the totalitarian 'supersense',[2] or Eric Voegelin's on its gnostic origins;[3] former Maoists or members of the New Left who substituted totalitarianism for imperialism as an incarnation of evil, the dissidents for the colonized people as a suffering incarnation of good, and looked to moral resistance against power and the state rather than to social and political revolution for a substitute to politics; and, finally, a political group, the antitotalitarian Left or the 'second' Left, who found in solidarity with the antitotalitarian revolution of Eastern Europe the occasion for challenging, from within the Left, some of the latter's traditional dogma. Antitotalitarianism meant the rediscovery of pluralism, of the rule of law, of an analysis in terms of state and society rather than of class and party, of an interest in Europe rather than in the Third World.

One could welcome this evolution and yet express certain doubts. First, the antitotalitarian mood retains the characteristics of French intellectual fashion – the combination of abstraction and romanticism, the reluctance to recognize ambiguity, contradiction and change. Second, even specialists such as Besançon, Claude Lefort and Cornelius Castoriadis describe the two worlds of party and society, ideology and reality, or the military and civilian sector, in terms of an opposition between abstract and coherent models, never in terms of transformation and interpenetration.

The reader is then in danger of falling into a state of acute schizophrenia. When he reads that one of the brightest young stars of US Sovietology, George Breslauer, seems, among *Five Images of the Soviet Future*,[4] to favour 'welfare-state authoritarianism', he reacts by thinking of the constant primacy, in the Soviet Union, of power and the warfare state, of the decay of civilian infrastructure and of the progress of totalitarian psychiatry; in short, he reaches for his Besançon or his Castoriadis. But when he sees that, according to Besançon, the concept of economy cannot be applied to the Soviet Union because the Soviet system does not know economic constraints and can apply the criterion of power without ever having to care about the consumer, he is reminded of the sums poured into agriculture and of the Kremlin's concerns about consumer dissatisfaction, and he returns to the specialists of the Soviet economy.

Of course, Breslauer can argue that neototalitarian phenomena fall under the concept of authoritarianism and that the term welfare should not be understood according to the Western model. After all, Zinoviev and Besançon themselves describe a certain type of socialist welfare, based on laziness and corruption. On the other hand, Besançon can argue that the Soviet rulers, even when they abandon their ideological jargon to speak the everyday language of the consumer's preoccupations, are disguising their real priorities, which are built into their budgetary choices.[5] Conversely, when these choices are modified in the direction of consumption, Besançon will argue that this is in order to achieve the goals of the regime, which by definition can only be the pursuit of power in the service of the Bolshevik revolution.

One is thus faced, in the first case, with the methodological problem of using concepts so broad that they become meaningless and, in the second, with the philosophical problem of whether one should judge a regime (as do both the defenders of the Soviet Union in the name of socialism and its radical critics in the name of totalitarianism) according to the goals set by its ideology or according to the daily experiences of its citizens. In both cases, one is confronted with the epistemological problem of theories which, like the ideologies themselves, do not explain anything because they can always explain everything.

If, however, one tries to get outside the conceptual framework of the two approaches so as to find a way of choosing between them, one has to acknowledge that Besançon's discourse – in spite or because of its internal logic – cannot be used to study the mechanisms and evolution of the Soviet economy, but that he is quite right when he states that those who live within, or in direct contact with, Soviet reality do not recognize their own experience when they read the learned studies of Western specialists. One may even generalize this observation. On the one hand, the evolution of Sovietology away from the notion of totalitarianism reflects, often naively and excessively, a very real evolution of its subject matter which French anti-totalitarian intellectuals are wrong to dismiss with such contempt. On the other hand, it is not by chance that Solzhenitsyn and Zinoviev have had such influence in France; their respective visions (which incidentally are profoundly contradictory to each other) fit better with Besançon and Lefort than with Breslauer or even Severyn Bialer.[6] Many East European dissidents, whose very existence refutes the triumph of totalitarianism, reproduce its classical descriptions or recognize their own experiences when they read *1984*. Somewhere there exists a hard core, a permanent kernel of truth which is the classic view of totalitarianism. The question then is whether it can be reconciled with the empirical studies produced by social scientists, particularly in the United States.

From politics to political science

The guiding theme in this essay is the double contrast between American and French students of the Soviet Union, and between the 1950s and the 1970s. In the United States, Alex Inkeles and Raymond Bauer[7] – authors of the 1950s studies which gave the totalitarian model its empirical support – had announced from the outset, as Raymond

Aron did in France, that the concept of totalitarianism would have to be linked to that of the industrial society. In 1953, Karl Deutsch[8] had already announced that the limits of centralization, mobilization and control in any organization were bound to produce cracks in the totalitarian monolith. Conversely, at every wave of attack against the totalitarian model, some brave and isolated soldiers heroically took risks to cover its retreat (Peter Wiles in 1961, Paul Hollander in 1967 and William Odom in 1976)[9] and prepare for a counteroffensive which may well be in the making. But dominant trends do exist, and they are best explained by the interaction of the evolution of the Soviet Union and Eastern Europe, East–West relations and the social sciences.

The concept of totalitarianism has never been, as many have claimed, a mere instrument of the Cold War, but neither has it been depoliticized and turned into an operational, let alone a value-free, concept of political science. It was indeed born from a political struggle, but at the same time all the basic features which dominated the postwar discussion had been present since the 1920s (with Don Sturzo calling fascism a right-wing Bolshevism and Bolshevism a left-wing fascism[10]) and the 1930s, from Elie Halévy's 'organization of enthusiasm'[11] to Waldemar Gurian's and Voegelin's political and secularized religions,[12] from Emil Lederer's 'state of the masses' to Sigmund Neumann's 'permanent revolution'. In a sense, what Hannah Arendt did was only to tie these elements together in a creative synthesis (of which Friedrich's and Brzezinski's 'totalitarian syndrome' represented the academic counterpart) by uncovering their common logic. It is clear, however, that the triumph of the notion of totalitarianism in the 1950s, particularly in the United States and in Germany, is due to the East–West struggle; antitotalitarianism had become, so to speak, the Cold War cry of the West. But conversely, if nearly fifteen years separate the American Philosophical Society symposium of 1939 on 'The totalitarian state from the points of view of history, political science, economics and sociology' from the American Academy of Arts ad Sciences symposium on 'Totalitarianism' in 1953, it was because political reasons – the same ones that had made the Left so reluctant to hear out Koestler and Orwell, namely the alliance with the Soviet Union – had made it undesirable in the meantime to stress the basic kinship between Stalinism and Hitlerism – all the more so since the former was raising hopes of improvement analogous to those connected with de-Stalinization a few years later. At any rate, the rude postwar awakening, brought in particular by the fate of the people's democracies and the trials of the late 1940s and the early 1950s, led the theorists of totalitarianism (particularly Arendt,

Friedrich and Brzezinski) to stress, in their definitions, its most extreme forms – namely, those which were rapidly to be seen in the Soviet Union and later in China as linked to the person of the tyrant: the mass terror driven by ideology but increasingly taking on a life of its own, the permanent purges, etc. The theories of the 1950s oscillated between structure and process, between the idea of a new type of regime complete with a set of criteria and operating rules, and that of a mad and constantly paroxysmal system, initially aiming at transforming reality in the name of ideology but ending up with no other aim than itself. These two ideas could be reconciled in the name of the absorption of society by the state and of the state by the party movement, but at the price of difficulties which were pointed out, at the time, by Aron and others.

These difficulties were brought to the fore by Stalin's death. The theorists of totalitarianism were unprepared for the emergence of collective leadership, the relative decline of terror, the replacement of the permanent purge by the oligarchy's concern for security, the reduction in the role of the secret police and the increase of the party's role. Hannah Arendt, whose conception was centred on the 1932–52 period of the concentration camps, the purges and the trials, did not have to change her interpretation in order to declare that it did not apply to Stalin's successors any more than to his predecessor or to Mao. In 1966 she disavowed the ideological use of the term against all the Communist Party states. Brzezinski, on the contrary, started as early as 1956 the process of revision or of what Michael Curtis was to call 'the retreat from totalitarianism'.[13] In Brzezinski's article, 'Totalitarianism and rationality',[14] manipulation aimed at total social revolution appeared as a more modern, rational and efficient substitute for terror. For a whole period, until the early 1960s, a series of formulas stressing the process – such as Lowenthal's 'permanent revolution from above' – or the system – like Allen Kassof's 'administered society' or 'totalitarianism without terror' – developed this idea of a totalitarianism modified by the 'rationalization of party control'. This period, of course, corresponded to Khrushchev's reign, with its renewal of ideological and utopian dynamism and its attempt to take the needs of society into account while reducing the role of terror and the secret police.

This phase in the odyssey of the concept of totalitarianism was called into question by the combination of a new phase in the evolution of communist countries and the desire of the Sovietologists to break out of their ghetto in order to jump on the bandwagon of modernization and comparative studies.

In the first dimension, it soon became clear that the Khrushchevian dynamic was stalled. As Löwenthal put it at the time of Nikita Sergeyevich's fall, it was no longer only terror but the revolution itself that was withering away;[15] the Party, however, was clinging to power as tenaciously as ever but limited its ambition to keeping the social aspirations to differentiation in check rather than attempting to eradicate them. The function of ideology was the legitimation of power rather than the inspiration of a dynamic attempt at transforming society. Brzezinski had foreseen the hypothesis of a totalitarian power which would keep its institutional position while having lost its revolutionary dynamism. But then, should one still speak of totalitarianism, or rather of a transformation into a one-party authoritarian regime? Löwenthal pointed out that the label was less important than the need to recognize the exhaustion of the permanent revolution from above but, like Peter Ludz, Juan Linz and most American authors, he preferred to call the postrevolutionary or postmobilization phase post-totalitarian authoritarianism.

Others in the same period were drawing even more radical conclusions from the same evolution. Looking back at the earlier phase in the light of the new one, they were challenging the concept of totalitarianism even for the period of revolutionary mobilization, or at least they were subordinating it to more general concepts which were just coming to the fore in the social sciences. For Löwenthal and Ludz themselves, the dynamics of totalitarianism conflicted with the rival dynamics of economic development and with the growing complexity of industrial society. At the very least, one had to combine the totalitarian model with the development and industrial-society models. But then, it became very tempting to give priority to the last two, which, compared to the totalitarian, had the advantage of opening the door to the world of the social sciences.

This door was pushed by three trends that can be traced to three authors: Robert C. Tucker and mobilization, Alfred Meyer and organization, and Gordon Skilling and interest groups. For Tucker the notion of totalitarianism is either too broad or too narrow. On the one hand, he stresses the personal role of the dictator[16] in the acute phase – that upon which Hannah Arendt had insisted, and which Tucker calls today the phase of 'nightmare regimes'.[17] On the other hand, he would like to include totalitarian party movements in a broader comparative framework that would include the nationalist party movements of the Third World. He thus makes a decisive contribution to the launching of the notion of mobilization regimes, which led to the Chalmers Johnson symposium and was criticized, convincingly, by Peter Wiles and Jeremy Azrael.[18]

Alfred Meyer,[19] who tended to underplay the specific role of ideology and politics, was profoundly influenced by theories of convergence and by the analogies between the Soviet Union and a huge corporation; he insisted upon the old Burnhamian idea of the managerial revolution, without drawing clear distinctions between its bureaucratic and its technocratic versions. Here, too, the criticisms of Hollander and Azrael seem close to the mark.

Last, Skilling[20] criticizes the totalitarian model mostly for hiding the complexity of communist societies and the emerging opposition of interests within them. He does not neglect the precautions that distinguish him from Jerry Hough[21] and acknowledges that Soviet-type regimes cannot be called pluralistic. The fact remains that the theoretical tendency of his work (curiously at odds with his exhaustive and empathetic knowledge of Czechoslovakian society) goes in the direction of de-exceptionalizing communist regimes and makes him vulnerable to the criticisms of Francis Castles[22] and William Odom,[23] who try to rehabilitate the totalitarian model by distinguishing between the articulation of interests and formation of groups without, however, going as far as the Franco-Czechoslovakian scholar Thomas Lowit, for whom all apparent social diversity is reduced to the hidden unity of a polymorphic party.

Matters are less complicated with the other advocates of the pluralistic model. There the double desire both to de-exceptionalize the Soviet Union in order to be admitted by the social sciences and to save detente is expressed with an almost naive candour. Thus, Susan G. Solomon declares:

> The building of real conceptual bridges between comparative politics and Soviet studies would have accomplished two objectives. First, it would have demonstrated more forcefully than any argument that the Soviet Union was not an outsider in the family of nations, a pariah. And, in destigmatizing the Soviet system, it would have moved specialists on Soviet politics more squarely into the mainstream of the discipline of political science.[24]

The result, however, is only partly satisfactory:

> Works on pluralism and on interest groups by specialists of comparative politics now routinely contain references to research conducted by Sovietologists. On the other hand, the goal of eliminating or even reducing the credibility of totalitarianism (either in pure or in modified form) has not been notably furthered.

And Jerry Hough, the most radical advocate of the pluralist model, defends it against the new fashion – corporatism – in the name of its greater effectiveness with the public in the still to be won battle against the common enemy, the totalitarian model:

> Whatever evolution in the views of the Soviet Union has occurred within political science, the old dogmatic views continue to have a deep hold in large and influential portions of the American population. Fifteen years of work on the input side of Soviet politics have made far too little impact on old images of an all-powerful state, directing society and pursuing foreign policy on the basis of a long-established master plan. It seems to me that we should keep in mind the general audience as well as the specialists as we decide what is important to study and to understand.[25]

From political science to political philosophy

What had happened, then, to justify this plaintive tone, this confession of failure, coupled with a pressing appeal to a greater political consciousness? Again, the three dimensions that we have distinguished come into play.

First, the social sciences – whose triumphant takeoff had so impressed the Sovietologists – have lost much of their prestige. In particular, theories of modernization and political development have been increasingly questioned.[26] Over the years, the notion of political development has become more and more discredited and its application to the evolution of Eastern Europe has looked more and more like black humour. In 1982 Gordon Skilling and Archie Brown, two strong supporters of the comparative model and of limited pluralism, pronounced its death in *Studies in Comparative Communism*.

The notion of pluralism, applied to communist states, is in only slightly better shape. Already in 1979, in the same *Studies in Comparative Communism*, its critics had renewed their attacks. Moreover, as Susan Solomon points out, the Sovietologists had seized upon that notion at the very time when students of Western societies were beginning to abandon it. Without going so far as to apply the concept of totalitarianism to Western 'repressive tolerance', like the Marcusian New Left in the United States in the late 1960s and in Germany today, the Sovietologists point to the sway of large organizations, to their collusion, and to their solidarity towards the outside world. They thus rediscover one of the dimensions of fascism – corporatism. Hence the fashion of neocorporatism – which the Sovietologists are tempted to embrace, but with a certain prudence. As Hough warns, they do not want to risk falling back into the totalitarian model, all the more so because they feel it risks being revived by the New Cold War.

Clearly, this second factor – the state of East–West relations – is the most conspicuous, even more so than in earlier periods. If the notion of totalitarianism is revived by some and rejected by others, the reason lies less in the evolution of the social sciences or the Soviet Union than in the fact that the latter is again appearing as an enemy and that the term totalitarianism is the most convenient way to brand it as such. This does not detract from the genuine progress in the debate about the validity of the concept. Similarly, one need not share Jeane Kirk-patrick's conclusions[27] when she uses a revived distinction between authoritarian and totalitarian regimes to argue that right–wing dictator-ships should be supported against communist ones, to recognize that she raises a genuine problem, illustrated recently in the cases of Argentina and Poland: the respective reversibility or irreversibility of the two types of regime. But Kirkpatrick's distinction remains a political argument in favour of a political attitude – the priority of opposition to communism.

As during detente what has changed is less the communist regimes themselves than Western attitudes towards them. Or rather, what has changed is less the nature of the Soviet Union than its external role and power. The Soviet accession to strategic parity, coupled with the more interventionist quality of its military policy between 1975 and 1980, and the late and partly retrospective discovery of the Gulag by the French intelligentsia – these are what motivates the new fear and hostility towards Moscow.

This reaction relies partly on a *non sequitur*. It is not inherently obvious that the military danger of a regime or the urgency or necessity of negotiating with it are tied to its internal nature. A country can be totalitarian yet turn its dynamism towards internal oppression rather than external expansion: this was the case for Stalin during the Great Purge, for Mao during the Cultural Revolution. It is by necessity the case for some small countries, often the most totalitarian ones such as Albania and, to some extent, Pol Pot's Cambodia. Conversely, a classical power can be expansionist or imperialist. One can find reasons to negotiate as well as common – albeit provisional – interests with the most totalitarian state. The fact remains, however, that long-range agreements, such as those the West hoped to achieve during detente, are made impossible by the very nature of a totalitarian regime, by its fundamentally conflictual view of the world and by the character of its own citizens. It is also true that, even in the short run, Western democracies seem to have a subjective or exaggerated view of their allies or adversaries. What had happened during the alliance against Hitler was repeated in part during detente. Similarly, in an attenuated form, the failure of East–West cooperation has produced a renewed consciousness of the alien or evil character of the Soviet Union. Since it has not become friendly or democratic, this must mean that it has not ceased being totalitarian. Conversely, the defenders of detente feel obliged to prove that they were not mistaken in claiming that Moscow had changed.

The main reason for wondering whether, by abandoning the notion of totalitarianism, the specialists have not thrown the baby out with the bath water, is what might be called the non-withering away of dictatorship in communist states. It is de-Stalinization that has discredited the theory of totalitarianism. Conversely, the theories that replaced it relied on a vision and on concepts directed towards liberalization and democratization, or at least rationalization and compromise between the party and society. The crisis of communist countries, the domestic immobility of the Soviet Union, at least under Brezhnev, the failure of the Prague Spring, the rise of Solidarity and its repression, lead one to wonder whether one should not speak of a totalitarian residue which would block potential evolutions that are comparable to those of right-wing authoritarian regimes.

It is clear, on the one hand, that the Arendt–Friedrich–Brzezinski model is untenable for the present phase, and that its advocates have had to sacrifice its attributes one after the other – first terror, then revolution. But on the other hand, it is clear that this theoretical striptease is never completed and that the advocates of modernization, technocracy and pluralism are forced to operate an analogous retreat in the opposite direction.

Can one say, with Michael Walzer,[28] that every existing totalitarianism is a failed one, but in addition that all post-totalitarian liberalizations and democratizations have equally failed? Should one conclude from that double failure a cyclical, ever undecided struggle between system and society? Perhaps, but to defend such a statement with any confidence one would need both an empirical inquiry about the various forms of this struggle and a philosophical and moral gamble on its ultimate significance. Moreover, perhaps both this inquiry and this gamble should deal less with the system than with the societies.

Where the study of totalitarianism went wrong is not in what it said about the system but in its insufficient attention to the opposite pole, to the civil society and national cultures which it destroys but which re-emerge, which it transforms but which keep resisting. Or are this renaissance, and resistance, only an illusion? Could it be that they are only the mirror image of a transformed totalitarian power whose ultimate triumph would consist precisely in society producing its own 'totalitarianism from below'? That is the question. Everyone seems to agree with A. Smolar[29] that the dynamics of the 'revolution from above' has withered away but that the institutions of the totalitarian system persist. Should one then conclude that the latter, faced with a nascent or renascent civil society, is on the defensive, as seems to be the case in China today according to Jean-Luc Domenach, or, on the contrary, that it no longer needs to be dynamic and to impose revolution from above precisely because it has succeeded in destroying or digesting civil society? We would be dealing (everywhere, according to Besançon, except in Poland) with another society, one where communism is a reality, or even with a new type of man, Zinoviev's *Homo sovieticus* or *Homocus*.[30] For Jacques Rupnik, the answers coming from Central Europe are profoundly different (whether in the name of civil society as in Poland, or of the market economy as in Hungary, or of European culture as in Czechoslovakia) from those provided by Zinoviev. It seems fair to agree with Rupnik's conclusion that while the system is always the same, how one lives it, adapts to it or resists it differs according to cultures and historical experiences.

Can one go beyond and try to indicate some features which would be common to the present phase of communist regimes?

It seems reasonable to accept the notion of posttotalitarian authoritarianism, provided one gives it a meaning that is not too different from that of postrevolutionary totalitarianism. In other words it is true that totalitarian power, as it loses part of its dynamism and ability to control an increasingly complex and resistant society, tends to restrain its ambitions to make them more compatible with its means, and thereby to come closer to an authoritarian power; this certainly seems to be a more plausible view of Eastern Europe's evolution, and probably of the Soviet Union's, than Zinoviev's vision. But it is no less true that it does not become an authoritarian power like any other. Posttotalitarian authoritarian regimes are, in a way, a decadent phase of totalitarianism itself; at any rate they are profoundly shaped by their origins.

It seems difficult to deny that we are witnessing, in Milovan Djilas's words, a 'disintegration of Leninist totalitarianism'.[31] But, as Djilas himself pointed out, this disintegration pertains less to the organizational and ideological framework of totalitarianism than to its content. Totalitarianism seems always present in the background, functioning as a negative point of comparison which makes the current situation look more acceptable, as a threat that may be more and more unreal but projects its shadow upon real life.

Mass terror has declined considerably but enough is left to make its return not entirely unthinkable. What has replaced the threat of labour camps is the threat of being excluded from the social and economic system. What Inkeles called 'the institutionalization of anxiety' remains present even though it conflicts with the gerontocracy's aspiration to security.

A certain diffusion of power does take place, but not in the guise of a balance of interest groups. Rather, there can be on the one hand, a renewal of elites and an interpenetration within the ruling class (KGB-ization, militarization, technicalization), through co-optation within the party apparatus; and there can be, on the other hand, an increased tolerance towards the second economy and even towards a certain anomia that would be its social equivalent, even though, beyond certain limits, the party tries to reassert its control. The conflict, as William Odom points out,[32] is less between institutions and groups than between centre and periphery, between the various levels of a hierarchical system. The structure remains the same but there is a decline in central control and a withering away of revitalization mechanisms like terror and purges.

Similar tensions and contradictions are found at the ideological level. There is an increasing search for substitutes to Marxism–Leninism as legitimizing ideologies. These can be traditional (national-ism, including, today, in the GDR, where it once seemed impossible) or modernistic (the scientific-technological revolution). Soviet literature today seems to aim more at privatization than at mobil-ization and to encourage nationalism and the cults of work, nature and the past more than devotion to socialism[33] – although tendencies to a reassertion of the old priorities are also visible. There are more and more open windows on reality. And yet the wooden language of ideology survives, both as a symbol and a code of power and of its legitimacy which cannot totally dispense with the two permanent myths of dark conspiracies and a brilliant future.

Finally, foreign policy. One can accept that world revolution has ceased being an operational goal of Soviet policy, if it ever was one; that the latter is driven more by *Realpolitik* than by an irresistible ideological dynamism; and yet one must maintain that its lack of traditional or democratic legitimacy keeps the regime in a state of permanent insecurity; that, to preserve their power, the rulers must keep their empire and their society under control; that, towards that aim, they must protect them against external influences; and for that, in turn, they need an ideology that entertains hostility towards the outside world, and a power that enables them to control, at least potentially, any threat coming from their environment; and finally, that all these defensive and conservative reasons can push Moscow towards expansion and conflict as unmistakably as a triumphant messianism.

These few vague and banal indications are meant only to point out that while change and complexity are characteristic of the present phase, they are not free of the Stalinist heritage. Now more than ever we lack the instruments which would enable us to identify the role of this heritage within the different existing varieties of imperfect and decadent totalitarianism.

At any rate, it does not seem likely that these instruments will be found in the social sciences. It is the great literary works (Orwell, Solzhenitsyn, Zinoviev, Grossman) and philosophical interrogations which, periodically, force us to recognize that something escapes the conceptual frameworks and the empirical research of the social sciences applied to Sovietology, and that this 'something' has something to do with totalitarianism. Should it not be sought in the direction of Arendt's 'supersense', Besançon's 'surreality', Orwell's 'doublethink' and 'newspeak', Jaspers' 'institutionalized lie', Kostas Papaïoannou's 'cold ideology'[34] or Leszek Kolakowski's 'great lie'[35] – in other words, in this articulation between language and power analysed by the East European authors quoted by Rupnik?

If so, the mistake of the theory of totalitarianism would have to be located in the transition from Arendt to Friedrich and Brzezinski, in the attempt to translate what can be caught only by a global view, intimately linked to a political philosophy into a set of empirical criteria.

As Lefort pointed out,[36] it is perhaps only through the experience of democracy and human rights, through the relations between language and society, or between philosophy and politics, that the political scientist can understand the different forms of authoritarianism and grasp the meaning of totalitarianism.

In the end, if one wants to speak of totalitarianism, one can avoid neither a political-philosophical commitment nor a historical gamble.

Of course, abstract antitotalitarian rhetoric is no substitute for the empirical study of totalitarian regimes, and a prevalently political or ideological approach like the French one has much to learn in this respect, from American social scientists. But in the last analysis, the concept of totalitarianism does not belong to political science.

This does not mean, however, that the concept of totalitarianism is not important for political science. On the contrary, political science as a discipline is in the same situation as the theory of totalitarianism: the only way either can progress is by acknowledging its limitations. As Pascal would have said, nothing is more in agreement with political science than this disavowal of political science.

7

An Elusive but Essential Notion

PROFESSIONALLY speaking, I am not an expert on totalitarianism. My field is East–West relations, and it is from that perspective that I have developed a particular interest in the way experts in the West or from Western societies view the Soviet Union and communist countries, the images they form of them. In addition, speaking now from a personal point of view, I was born in Romania and experienced, as a Jew, first the German and then the Soviet occupation of my country – first the Iron Guard and then the communists; consequently, although it may not be a topic for an academic presentation, whether these two phenomena had anything in common is a matter that has absorbed me all my life.

In 1984, I wrote an article on totalitarianism that echoed this twofold emphasis, incorporating the autobiographical theme and also reflecting the subject of my research which, unlike today's symposium, focused more on communist than fascist or Nazi regimes.[1] I shall do no more here than touch briefly on a few points, offering my personal reactions to what previous contributors [to a symposium on 'Communist totalitarianism and Nazi genocide'] have said and giving my thoughts on the usefulness or otherwise of the concept of totalitarianism, and whether the use of the term serves to deny or trivialize the uniqueness of the holocaust, of Nazi genocide.

Second, I should like to explore a little how my knowledge of present events squares with my previous analysis. Does the direction the communist regimes have taken, and in particular the Gorbachev phenomenon, challenge the validity of a totalitarian analysis, or does it simply mark the opening of a new chapter? I was very interested in what my colleague Roland Lew had to say about the crisis in modern society. I will attempt in my turn to speculate out loud on the openings modern societies offer today for totalitarianism, whether it is a phenomenon tied to the era of Hitler and Stalin or whether it may still, in whatever manner, be regarded as a potential threat.

On the first point, I conclude that we are more or less all in agreement that totalitarianism is not a scientific concept: when we talk of a totalitarian regime, we are not talking about something that would occupy a fixed position in an academic classification of political regimes.

On the second point, I do think, reservations notwithstanding, that the description of totalitarianism applies equally to Stalin's Soviet Union and Hitler's Germany – even if there are many more differences than points of resemblance in space and time between communism and fascism, and even if, in both cases, we are looking more at a conjunction of forces than a system with an internal logic of its own. George Orwell and Hannah Arendt have both put their finger on it, with their definitions, not of a military regime, but of totalitarian ideology and, beyond that, the totalitarian *impulse*, the totalitarian *dynamic*. There is something here that one cannot take on board in the mid-twentieth century except with a sort of moral recoil. In this perversion of rationality – Hitler using his lorries to kill Jews rather than wage war, Stalin stripping the Soviet army of its officers on the eve of Hitler's attack, the 'infernal machine' of the great purge of the 1930s, the Moscow show trials, the forced confessions, etc. – there is a blend of magic and madness, of bureaucratic and technical rationality and an ultimate irrationality, that constitutes something unique, something we can never reflect on enough.

I personally believe that the link Hannah Arendt established between ideology and terror goes back further, beyond ideology and terror as such, to that implacable dynamism that proceeds inexorably, crushing everything in its path. Whatever the inadequacies of the concept of totalitarianism for the comparative theory of political regimes or for the study of history, that is something we must not let ourselves forget.

But is it a new phenomenon or as old as the world itself? Like Messrs Backes and Klepsch, I believe it to be a modern phenomenon. Of course, the toll of human victims was always as high, given that most societies were founded on the collective rather than the individual principle. But that is what is so shameful: this is a post-Christian crime, it postdates the Enlightenment and modern rationalism. It is a perversion of both religion and science, more of religion in the case of Nazism, more of science in the case of Marxism. As writers such as Louis Dumont and Claude Lefort have pointed out, coming after the emergence of the idea of equality, the concept of modern man, the separation of society and state, it represents an attempt to make everything uniform again. Its essential feature is its manic ferocity, the permanent war in which it engages against human nature and against man's social instincts, forcing him to seek out an enemy. What characterizes it above all is the notion of total mobilization, total war, as in the telling phrase Carl Schmitt adopts as the title of his contribution: 'Totaler Stadt, totaler Feind, totaler Krieg' (total state, total enemy, total war). In that equation it is not the total state that is important so much as the total enemy, the fact that everything, the battle for productivity and for the harvest, external war or the elimination of the enemy within, should be conceived of as a fight to the death, or total war. That this phenomenon arises in societies that have experienced Christianity and science constitutes both the distinctive nature and the shame of totalitarianism.

But do we not lose the uniqueness, indeed the distinctive nature, of the Nazi regime, if we set it in that broader context? Here an important methodological point needs to be made. Comparison is often confused with identification. Comparisons are held to be odious because they submerge the originality of a phenomenon, whereas in fact they can do precisely the opposite and actually highlight its uniqueness. It seems to me that the phenomenon I have described in general terms has not ever manifested itself anywhere else with such an intensity of hatred, resulting as it has done here in the destruction of entire classes of people, Jews, Gypsies, homosexuals, excluded mentally and physically from the human race; a paroxysm of hatred that accounts at the opposite extreme for the crazed quest for absolute unity and purity, *ein Volk, ein Reich, ein Führer*. That seems to me distinctively Nazi, perhaps picking up on certain distinctive features of German history, a formal bureaucracy that we may link to blind obedience to a universal law, and a romantic perversion linked to antiscience, antirationality, anticivilization, the worship of nature, the earth and the gods, to which earlier speakers have referred.

Stalin's totalitarianism, on the other hand, I see as far less intense, but more extensive. For the millions of his victims, it is true, the point is academic. But the two ideologies and the spirit behind them are clearly very different. Of the two, fascism and totalitarianism, I believe the theory of fascism offers a much better account of the origins of the regime, of its social dimensions and ideological content. But totalitarianism, as we said before, explains the moment of murderous collective madness, a madness that needs to find for itself both a pseudo-religious and a pseudo-scientific justification. Certainly we may say that communism has broader and more all-encompassing ambitions – there is the idea of taking over civil society completely, of transforming the nature of man – whereas we know that for the average German, as long as he was neither Nazi nor SS, or on the other hand Jew, homosexual or Gypsy, he could remain exactly as he was. It therefore seems to me that we can isolate from these general categories a quite specific and distinctive Nazi horror, never to be forgotten.

Even more reason why we should not forget it, is that it may spring up again in other places directed at other races, and, most importantly, under other guises. Like all of us, I am against the idea of the term genocide being used too easily. But Pol Pot's campaign in Cambodia, that was genocide, its 'communist' and 'Nazi' features indissolubly linked. Inspired by Maoism and perpetrated mostly by fanatical leaders and a youth brainwashed to regard its own people as the enemy, it also contained the elements of a return to the land and to nature, in the face of corrupt modern civilization, and, pre-eminently, racial hatred: among the Cambodians, the prime candidates for extermination were those from the provinces nearest to Vietnam, accused of a lack of Khmer purity, and singled out for execution by the wearing of a distinctive emblem.

With respect to European communism, and here I am on firmer ground, we increasingly discover (not only restrospectively but currently) that even here the desire to turn all members of society into cogs in a machine (Heller's *La Machine et les rouages* in my view describes very well the intention but not the reality), the attempt in other words to use the system to create the new man, here too that has failed; here too, society continues to exist in all its diversity, a multiplicity of national cultures survives or is reborn and routine is restored after the white heat of the terror.

The theoreticians of totalitarianism mounted a rearguard action in the face of de-Stalinization, attempting to describe this new phase in terms such as 'the administered society', 'totalitarianism without terror', 'totalitarianism without revolution', all of which revolve around the idea of making totalitarianism into something normal and ordinary – and I think there is a lot of truth in this. In their most recent phase, these societies were not the same as they were at the time of the great purge or the great terror, yet nor were they liberal societies or in the classic sense authoritarian regimes. This was something new. It was, if you like, the phase described in Zinoviev's *The Yawning Heights*, which corresponds very accurately to Brezhnevism, the point at which you might say Soviet society touched bottom and started anew. Ideology ceased to be the spur for a crazed mobilization of forces and became the source of a routine legitimacy: no one believed in it but it was needed defensively to maintain the legitimacy of power in Eastern Europe and the Soviet Union.

The East European writers who re-examined the notion of totalitarianism (an excellent account is given in the chapter by Rupnik in the publication *Totalitarismes*[2]) describe a schizophrenic state of affairs, in which everyone says the same thing but without believing it, continuing to live the lie and lead a sort of double life. In the Soviet Union, authors like Zinoviev or Heller tended rather to describe the creation of the new man, *Homo sovieticus*, the subsuming of society into the system, a totalitarianism from below. Today, it seems to me, that phase too is over. Even in the Soviet Union, Western influences are undoubtedly at work (and here I think we must congratulate ourselves that the triumphant or doom-laden scenarios associated with the creation of the new man have not come to pass). In the closed world created in the totalitarian mould, denying both the past and the outside world, this represents something entirely new. First, there is the influence exercised by the outside world, so that even the ideology in the end becomes submerged under the weight of innumerable imports from the West, with people adopting the language of the Greens, ecology, capitalism, coexistence, the market, etc. But the past too is being rediscovered: in some vast collective phenomenon, everyone is reliving his or her Russian, or Georgian or Baltic past, questioning Stalinism and even the revolution itself. But how are we supposed to react to all this? In a way, there is good reason to celebrate the victory. In the sphere of ideas, the second greatest enemy of freedom has been defeated. Democracy, the rule of law, even the market, these ideas all seem to have acquired new life. In a sense we are returning to a paradigm of the nineteenth century that was reduced to absurdity by the twentieth century. The two main challengers, fascism and communism, no longer dare advertise themselves. The Hungarian and Polish leaders recognize the superiority of the multiparty state. The ideal promulgated on all sides – and perhaps rather more than those of us on the Left would like – is capitalism, the market, Mrs Thatcher and liberal democracy.

But that is far from being the end of it. There are two phenomena connected with Gorbachev that I should like to discuss. On the one hand there is the attempt to remobilize following the stagnation of the Brezhnev years, which were characterized by a social contract guaranteeing each individual a more or less acceptable material life in return for paying lip service to an ideology in which he did not believe. But on the other hand, there is Gorbachev's desire to take the reins of power entirely into his own hands, a dangerous move denounced by Sakharov – although, rightly in my view, he still backed Gorbachev. This it seems to me has not a little in common with the Cultural Revolution. In order to stand up to the party bureaucracy and his enemies, Gorbachev is trying to summon up the forces of spontaneity, to create a sort of populism, an alliance between leader and people. All he really wants is to get society moving, but he ends up provoking nationalist movements and arousing an intellectual ferment that risks bringing him down. For that reason, it seems to me that violent and uncontrollable events lie ahead, rather than any gentle progression towards democracy and liberalism. We have had Stalinist terror, an attempted dynamism under Khrushchev, which did not succeed but of which certain traces remain, stagnation without terror under Brezhnev, and today a further attempt at dynamism and remobilization that, with the worrying exception of Armenia and Georgia, is also without terror.

But can one manipulate a society like the Soviet one without, at a given moment, using terror and repression? It remains an open question. I do not think there can be a return to Stalinism or a totalitarian regime (if such a thing exists) because there is a new openness to the West, because of the element of pluralism, because the Soviet Union needs the rest of the world. I do not think so, but my relatively optimistic view now, in June 1989, is less securely founded than before the events in Beijing, where the repression that took place demonstrated that certain classic elements of totalitarian terror and totalitarian wooden language can resurface, aggravated by the presence of television, even after the ideology itself is dead. If Hungary and Poland pose the question, whether there is life after communism, China poses the question, whether there will be a return to Stalinism.

Meanwhile, what is happening at the moment in the Soviet Union corresponds to neither situation, but represents something entirely new. A writer of Czech origin, M. Hybler,[3] has spoken of the three stages of totalitarianism: action and terror under Stalin; language and lectures – wooden language – under Brezhnev; and under Gorbachev, image, action for action's sake, image for the sake of the image, the image of dynamism. I think there is some truth in this, although I wonder if we can still use the word totalitarianism when it has become no more than the desire for an impression of action or dynamism? There is no equivalent of this in Eastern Europe, but there is rising tension accompanying economic dissatisfaction, with one whole sector of society more or less condemned to what has been called Third-

Worldization. And also, the renaissance of nationalist phenomena, the attempt, as we see in Yugoslavia with the Serb leader Milosevic, to create a distraction through the combination of national hatred and a strong charismatic leader. The problem of the minorities has come greatly to the fore again in the Soviet Union and in Romania and Bulgaria. In one sense, I do believe that democracy and freedom have won the ideological battle, but when you see the effects of Western influence on communist and Third World societies, you are aware of all sorts of tensions and reactions against, for example, our wealth, our modernity, whether this takes the form of Khomeini-style Muslim fanaticism or of a reaction against liberalism such as can be seen today in the Soviet Union, Poland and Czechoslovakia, and even among the Chinese students who, in demanding greater democracy, also protested against the new inequalities that resulted from economic reform. Perhaps the most dramatic problem is that of immigrants and refugees. That most democratic of countries, Sweden, has for the first time repatriated Soviet refugees on the grounds that the Soviet Union is now liberalized and they must therefore be economic migrants and not political refugees. In Asia, particularly Hong Kong, the forced repatriation of the boat people is the order of the day.

In one sense, the West has won, but it is frightened of the effects of its own victory on the masses, not only in the Third World but in Eastern Europe and elsewhere, who want their share of the cake. As people fight to defend their square metre of land, there is the possibility of a resurgence of fascism directed against immigrants, as we see in France with Le Pen and also in the FRG with the electoral exploits of the republicans and the NPD. There are also the specifically modern phenomena to which Mr Lew has referred, the fact that the individual is cheated of his power of decision by the sheer complexity of modern society.

We also possess, and here I will finish, the power to manipulate images. If you look at the last US election campaign, you are in a sense struck less by the topics raised, for fascism and communism play no part and everyone is in favour of liberal democracy, than by another far more disturbing phenomenon: the power of the image. To show Mr Dukakis at the same time as a black criminal guilty of rape while on parole from prison (something that is in no way peculiar to Dukakis's home state of Massachusetts) creates a highly potent association, a negative image calculated to generate hatred. Worse still was the terrible about-turn that occurred in China, as the whole world watched over a period of a few days how television moved from being an instrument of liberation and universal soldidarity to becoming an instrument of intimidation, denunciation and Orwellian rewriting of history.

Modern society offers a hold not only on the dangers of techniques of manipulation that exist because of technological progress, but also on those represented by a resurgence of ancient fears and hatreds, whether racial, territorial or something else entirely. One could never swear that the combination of ancient and modern that is totalitarianism is dead and buried and gone for ever.

PART FOUR

NATIONALISM

8

Nationalism and International Relations

The nationalist surprise

A SPECTRE is haunting the world – the spectre of nationalism. It may seem surprising to open this modest, interrogative essay with such a ringing and grandiloquent phrase but its parody of the opening of the *Communist Manifesto* points up a certain analogy and ironic comparison, and at the same time focuses on a problematic phenomenon which I believe lies at the heart of our subject.

Let us pursue the parallel by recalling the second paragraph of the 1848 text: 'Where is the party in opposition that has not been decried as Communistic by its opponents in power? Where the Opposition that has not hurled back the branding reproach of Communism, against the more advanced opposition parties, as well as against its reactionary adversaries?' We have only to listen to the exchanges that take place today between communists, between Westerners, between old states and new, and what do we hear: a hail of mutual accusations, of chauvinism at every level, of designs of economic or military hegemony, of desire for glory or anachronistic isolation, of white racism or black racism. All have one thing in common, particularly within blocs or alliances (and whether the opposing parties be ethnic groups, races, nations or states, implicit or explicit nationalisms, in the strict or broad sense of the term), and that is that they are indicative of anxiety, confusion, indignation or outrage about the values, ideologies and even the historical consciousness of these same blocs and alliances, or about the international world overall. Just as ideology is the name we give to another man's beliefs, so nationalism may very often be the name we give to another man's politics. There are of course some who come straight out with it and openly declare themselves nationalists, but even they are aware that naked nationalism is regarded as problematic in the world of today, and attempt to dissociate themselves from unfortunate precedents, shield themselves against criticism and exculpate themselves of future crimes. At the very least – and sometimes they pride themselves on it – they are conscious of acting as iconoclasts, rising up against received ideas and present realities. They are conscious they present an alternative to previous notions of the proper direction of the *industrial civilization* (as described by Marx in the section of the *Manifesto* reciting the achievement of the bourgeoisie and its promised fulfilment by the proletariat; as analysed these days by everyone from Rostow to Perroux; as lived by societies who experience the dominant ethos of business and the markets and, above all, the diversity of technologies and life styles). They also represent an alternative view of the postwar *international system* (dominated by the bipolarity of two militarily centralized alliances, led by two multinational states of qualitatively different dimensions from the rest, and inspired by two dominant ideologies). It follows from the above that they must reject also the *common inspiration* of these two ideologies.

That common inspiration, it seems to me, provides us with our starting point.

If we ask what liberal democracy and communism have in common, the obvious response is that they are global ideologies in which the highest good is the individual or the class, not the nation or the race. We can also say, as an extension of the above, that in the last analysis both of them, however their supporters may behave in practice, subscribe to the modern values of peace, prosperity and individual happiness, as opposed to the traditional values of struggle, sacrifice and collective glory. We may at once conclude that both are different from nationalism. And indeed, implicitly or explicitly, their view of international relations is inspired ultimately, if sometimes unconsciously, by the philosophical notion of a universal, homogenous society. Their declared belief and specific objective are the achievement of harmony of interests, whether between democratic republics respecting one another's differences and deferring to the authority of an international organization or law, or between socialist states whose social regimes are intended to ensure the absence of selfish ambition and mutual antagonism.

If there was any form of nationalism these ideologies could view with indulgence or encourage by their policies, it was that of colonized peoples, which they saw rather as a movement of liberation to escape political or economic repression, a means of enabling the nations concerned to rejoin the ranks of one or other of the global ideologies. True nationalism, which until recently strode across the world scene in increasingly monstrous guises and with increasingly terrible consequences, seemed by 1945 to have been defeated ideo-logically as well as militarily.

For, in the shadow of technological advances in weapons, produc-tion and communications, of the hierarchical bipolar structure of the relationship of forces, the communist and liberal ideologies (the latter notably in its functionalist and integrationist manifestations) had silenced or quashed the traditional territorial or ethnic conflicts within their respective spheres, to the point indeed that the continuing existence of the nation-state was in question. In a remarkable little book published in 1945, Professor E.H. Carr gave a highly lucid account of, inter alia, the future philosophy of European integration. While emphasizing the limitations of forecasts concerning international relations, he risked one prediction which he regarded as more or less a certainty: 'We shall not again see a Europe of twenty, and a world of more than sixty "independent sovereign states".' The 'past confusion of a vast number of nations, great and small, jostling one another on a footing of formal independence and equality' would be replaced by 'the emergence of a few great multi-national units in which power will be mainly concentrated'.[1]

Twenty years later, a rude awakening; the more so as it goes to the heart of these blocs and ideologies. That the number of states should in the event have multiplied instead of decreased, that the continents formerly under colonial rule should have fallen prey to both balkan-ized and expansionist forms of nationalism, retrenched as well as aggressive – that would have been acceptable. In any philosophy of history or theory of political development, it could be accounted for as the sins of youth, and there would be no need to revise the overall prediction of a decline of nationalism. Rather the reverse, indeed, given that its rampant proliferation among the new and under-developed countries, allied to its dormancy in the mature indus-trialized countries, would if anything tend to confirm that it is social and technological development, and more particularly industrialization and a raised standard of living, that spells its death knell. This assess-ment of the current situation, taken more or less at random from a text by Ernst Haas,[2] appears to represent the universal opinion: 'The established nation-state is in full retreat in Europe, while it is advancing voraciously in Africa and Asia. Integration among discrete political units is a historical fact in Europe, but disintegration seems to be the dominant motif elsewhere.' And it is not seen as a major challenge to the ideologies of the industrialized world or to the theory of international relations.

What however is fundamentally new, what places in jeopardy the very direction of historical development, is that in France of all places a voice was raised in 1964 proclaiming the victory of Nietzsche (or at least of the interpretation of his ideas then current in Germany, in fact a misrepresentation of his views) over Hugo, Jaurès and Marx.[3] And, also in 1964, from the heart of communist Eastern Europe, from the country that was the most repressed politically and most closely bound economically to the Soviet Union, from Romania in fact, came the most trenchant affirmation of the indivisibility of a nation's sovereignty over its economic affairs, and of the 'perpetuation of nation-states and national differences until socialism has achieved victory on the world scale, and well beyond'.[4]

In neither of these cases should we leap to the conclusion that some fundamental truth or universal law has been revealed. If a European state rejects the European Defence Community (ratified by the rest) or (to the indignation of its partners) operates a unilateral veto against Great Britain entering the Common Market, that does not mean Europeans generally reject a community approach to military or political affairs. If a communist state in Eastern Europe rejects the Comecon plan or gives nationalist desatellization priority over liberalizing de-Stalinization, that merely shows the extent of its differences from the rest. That someone, or some country, was able to do it at all proves it was wrong, or premature, to think it could never be done; it can have a copycat effect, it can provide encouragement to others, or it can provoke the opposite reaction; whatever the case, it is the exception that proves the rule, it is not the proof that the rules themselves have been changed.[5]

Yet that takes nothing away from the impact on the global ideologies of disagreements between allies, whether typical or not. And what makes matters worse is that the proponent of nationalism coolly holds up a mirror to the outraged Big Brother, inviting him to contemplate his own nationalism: what you accuse me of, he says, is the 'kettle' of my desire for independence against the 'pot' of your desire for domination. Hence the fact that the debate is conducted on two levels, structural and ideological, corresponding to the very different spheres of international relations or nationalism. First, the leaders of a coalition or ideological movement tend to define the political nationalism of the other in terms of its centrifugal or separatist tendencies; they see it as a force for conflict and anarchy, a mark of placing selfish interests above those of the group overall. Those who stand accused, on the other hand, tend to define the nationalist element in politics in terms of its imperialist or hegemonic character:

they accuse Big Brother of claiming to safeguard the general interest, while in fact wanting to reserve for himself the right to define terms, so enabling his personal interests to prevail; for them, the desire for diversity is a normal and straightfoward part of life, while the desire for unity is the mark of all-conquering nationalism. In this dialogue, Little Brother would most often lay himself open to the charge of cynicism, and Big Brother to that of hypocrisy. In so far as it represents a desire to break away, Little Brother's nationalism will appear the more radical, because it opposes the ideology that once held the group together (even though he can still shelter behind that ideology, either in a purely caricatural or symbolic manner, like Romania opportunely discovering a text by Marx in which it was assigned Bessarabia, or more seriously, and more genuinely, like China posing as the representative of an ideological orthodoxy which Big Brother chauvinism has betrayed). Big Brother's nationalism (if such it is), because it aims to maintain a unity and orthodoxy under (and defined by) its own authority, will not manifest itself so overtly. Consciously or unconsciously, hypocritically or sincerely, it will present itself as the defender of unity for its own sake, acting in the name of common feelings, interests, rationality or ideology; it will not manifest itself as, or lay claim to, nationalism as such, but in terms of definitions of these interests, that rationality, this ideology. The heterogeneity of positions brings in its wake a heterogeneity of definitions of the bipolar and hierarchical characteristics of the international system.[6]

The existence is thereby revealed, second, of two modalities of what we may call the *nationalist surprise* (in the sense that Raymond Aron in *The Century of Total War* spoke of the 'technological surprise'), meaning the encounter between the global ideologies and nationalism, and the relative victory of the latter.

Instead of collision, open conflict, the violent replacement of one ideology by another, what we find – particularly with the big multinational empires, leaders of ideological movements or coalitions inspired by or opposed to these movements – is a contamination, a symbiosis or synthesis between nation and regime, between national interests or objectives and global ambition or obligation, between local patriotism and broad ideology. This in large measure renders superfluous the question whether US politics has the interests of the free world at heart or those of the United States, whether Soviet politics has its rationale in Marxism or belief in Russian dominance, or even if Mao Zedong is more Leninist than Chinese. If one were tempted to reply to the above (the interest in so doing residing in the fact that each case is slightly different), it would be to the effect that the

United States can no longer (or cannot yet) refrain from having a global or world view of its own national interest as well as a US view of the interests of the free world; that the Soviet view of its national interest cannot but be conditioned at least minimally by the ideological background of its leaders and, probably, their sincere belief in Marxist doctrine as they conceive of it, and hence that they cannot but identify the interests of world revolution with those of the Soviet Union; and finally, that Mao combines Marxist conceptual frameworks with a nationalist sensibility, as Stuart Schram has demonstrated.[7]

Returning to the instructive examples of the United States and the Soviet Union and their respective dialogues with France and Romania, it would undoubtedly be silly to push the parallel too far. In no conceivable scenario or analysis can one imagine the postwar United States not revealing itself as both less ideologically motivated and less nationalistic than the Soviet Union; where the latter annexed its neighbouring lands and imposed a bilateral relationship that precluded any other, the United States, in offering its help and support for European unity, actually created the very conditions necessary for the growth of a rival power. It is absolutely right to point out, as Stanley Hoffmann does with his habitual brilliance and trenchancy, that they are beginning to be afraid they have created a Frankenstein; like Pygmalion, they wish they could reshape the statue they have brought to life.[8] The fact remains, they took the risk in the first place, and to an extent they knew the risk they ran. Generosity and absence of narrow self-interest there certainly was, but also ignorance and lack of foresight, a naiveté that one is bound to acknowledge is the absolute antithesis of the global vigilance and mistrust characteristic in my view of a nationalist approach to foreign policy, beyond ideological distinctions. Nonetheless, there are sufficient parallels between the United States and the Soviet Union to recognize a certain truth (allowing doubtless for some exaggeration of the element of nationalism) in one English commentator's concise assessment, that 'in fact, just as the real strength of Russian ideology lies in the fact that it is Soviet rather than Communist, so being an American in the world today is in itself an ideology. It is a combination of nationalism and social aspiration which is characteristic of both countries.'[9]

This 'nationalist surprise' may be said to have dominated the history of international relations since the French revolution. There have been successive irruptions of nationalism into conflicts between the traditional global ideologies (conservative legitimism, liberalism, socialism), with the encounter taking one of two forms (replacement or synthesis, abolition or contamination). The current predicament of the dominant ideologies, faced both with nationalism that is opposed to them and nationalism that subconsciously influences them, does not take on its full significance until (pursuing our reading of the *Communist Manifesto*) we realize the extent to which both Marxism and liberalism underestimated the phenomenon of nationalism in 1848, how little Marx foresaw of the nationalism that would attach to the revolution of 1848, the extent to which (in so many respects the disciple of liberal cosmopolitanism) he agreed with Cobden that free trade and the world market would cause differences in foreign policies to disappear, leading up to if not actually prefiguring the definitive elimination of international conflict, ushered in by the revolution of the proletariat as foreseen by the famous declaration: 'In proportion as the antagonism between classes within the nation vanishes, the hostility of one nation to another will come to an end.' Already the bourgeoisie is bringing to an end national differences and divergencies in the economic and hence also the intellectual and political spheres.

> To the great chagrin of Reactionists, it has drawn from under the feet of industry the national ground on which it stood . . . In place of the old local and national seclusion and self-sufficiency, we have intercourse in every direction, universal inter-dependence of nations. And as in material, so also in intellectual production. The intellectual creations of individual nations become common property. National one-sidedness and narrow-mindedness become more and more impossible . . . National differences and antagonisms between people are daily more and more vanishing, owing to the development of the bourgeoisie, to freedom of commerce, to the world market, to uniformity in the mode of production and in the conditions of life corresponding thereto.

In 1852, speaking of England, Marx still saw the free-traders as the party of the moment and of the future, the party of modern society and of the bourgeoisie, the party for which national and religious shackles, royalty, national wars, even the state itself, were no more than the *'faux frais* of production' – unnecessary expenses. Yet a few years later, as Kostas Papaïoannou has pointed out, England was awash with jingoism and humming with the spirit of imperialist expansion.[10] On the continent, the revolution of 1848 had already twice given the lie to Marx, on the one hand by the failure of international revolution and the mutual hostility between the nationalities involved, and on the other hand because Germany, having failed to achieve national revolution, had also disappointed his hopes of an immediate social revolution. The 1848 revolution has been identified as the moment of truth, when nationalism diverged from liberalism and socialism, becoming an autonomous force and soon-to-be-victorious rival; also the moment when the futility or frailty of any 'International of nationalisms' was demonstrated for the first time.[11]

Even before 1848, but especially afterwards, we are faced with the eternal spectacle of nationalism and the 'warring brothers' of the global ideologies performing ever new versions of their old minuet, so that the historian or philosopher is hard put to know where his sympathies lie. The nationalism of the French revolution, allied to popular sovereignty, changed in the course of the events of 1792 from a defensive posture to one of rampant global expansionism. Its influence continued to spread partly by the example it offered and partly by the opposition it provoked. Napoleon awoke European nationalisms by shaking up the legitimate dynasties, but also by making peoples conscious of national solidarity as they resisted his attempts at conquest (the eternal dialectic of imperialism or expansionist nationalism, whose yoke gives rise to nationalism or at least national consciousness in the subjugated people).[12] A temporary *rapprochement* of liberalism and nationalism was cut short as modern thinkers registered their inherent contradictions, and revolution began its militant advance. The restoration of the legitimate dynasties brought about a further *rapprochement* between the two, this time united in opposition: for Metternich, liberalism, socialism, nationalism were three modern, popular movements, all equally formidable; 1848 caused them to diverge, but again there were new syntheses as conservative statesmen exploited nationalism and made it serve their own purposes. Bismarck was no nationalist, but he presided over the triumph of German nationalism. Cavour, a liberal, achieved a comparable synthesis. A few 'sick men' apart, the era of *Realpolitik* seemed to have overcome the opposition between the old states and the nationalist movements.[13]

Of the internationalist movements, only socialism seemed to offer an effective opposition, and nationalism dealt it a crushing if paradoxical blow in 1914, when the proletarian masses placed national feeling above class solidarity, the leaders of the Second International happily followed the lead of their troops, and Lenin, disgusted at the betrayal of internationalist ideals, set about organizing the revolution that would in the event lay the foundations for that nationalization of socialism and socialization of nationalism so many fine minds have seen as the distinctive contribution of the twentieth century.[14]

If reactions in 1914 may be said to represent the low point for Leninist socialism, then the consequences of 1918 represent the low point for Wilsonian liberalism. Like John Stuart Mill or Mazzini in the previous century, Woodrow Wilson believed that nationalism and self-determination went hand in hand. He believed in the natural harmony of free nations. Yet of all the liberal thinkers, the plaudits deserve to go to Lord Acton, whose sober warnings that the nationality principle would lead only to tyranny and disorder appeared to be borne out by the enthusiasm with which a Balkanized Central Europe launched itself into chauvinism and minority squabbles. Worse still was the fact that before long liberals and socialists, capitalists and communists were forced to contemplate, with horror and incomprehension, the rise of fascism and Nazism. You may, like Hannah Arendt in *The Origins of Totalitarianism*,[15] reject the description of either of these (as well as of Pan-Slavism or Pan-Germanism) as nationalist, because their goals are of unlimited expansionism; yet they make their appeal to ideas of community, territory, blood and war, rather than to global rationalism or pacifism, and by their acts they discredit, if not nationhood, then at least the nationalist ideal.

We are back where we began, in the bipolar world established in 1945. But better placed now, in the light of the above digression, to appreciate the ambivalence and complexity of the situation and of any judgments upon it, whether made in the name of the various ideologies or in the name of peace and freedom, which everyone today claims to support. In the Eastern world, the need to resist German and Japanese aggression acts as a powerful influence in nationalizing Soviet and Chinese communism. For the Soviet Union, proletarian internationalism means that each and every communist has to make the security of the revolution's homeland his or her absolute priority. Is this then the triumph of nationalism? Clearly the answer is yes, though in a sense also of internationalism since so many communists throughout the world agree to become in effect 'foreign nationalists' or 'separatists', and they do so because of their sincere commitment to the ideology. Local nationalism is encouraged, for tactical reasons, in the Western countries and especially the current or former colonies: Lenin, already, distinguished between good and bad nationalism. But the good becomes bad when the same opposition between colonized and colonizers, between underdeveloped and industrialized, finds expression within the bloc. We may note that the excellent American historian Richard Pipes has no qualms at all in predicting for the Soviet Union a future in which it consists of nation-states, as an indispensable stage along the road to modernization.[16]

In the West, the situation is not much clearer. We are celebrating the last days of nationalism, if not of the nation-state; and the manner in which national conflicts between hereditary enemies are resolved (as over the Saar problem), the question of how a world power ought to behave (the Marshall Plan), and the planning and implementation of European integration, would all appear to confirm the natural alliance between liberal democracy and internationalism vis-à-vis past or future adversaries. But there are two phenomena that seem once again to revive the ghosts of Mazzini and Wilson, as the West aligns nationalism with freedom, and vice versa. First, there are many who take the view that in decolonization or colonial conflicts independence is to be equated with personal dignity and freedom or, in the language of political polemic, they regard the nationalism of the colonized peoples as being of the Left and that of the colonizers as being of the Right. Second, in Eastern Europe, particularly since the Hungarian revolution, nationalism has once again entered into an alliance with liberation, as one of the forms of resistance to tyrannical oppression and the imposition of its ideal of uniformity.

Yet in neither case could liberal enthusiasm be said to be undimmed. Even with the new states, it is very much the same old story, a situation compared in an article in *The Economist* emphasizing the ambivalent nature of nationalism, to a dynamo that, once it has been started for the best possible reasons, cannot be stopped[17]: necessary for the cohesion of the community, salutary during the phase of liberation and nation-building, nationalism refuses to fall quietly back into line after completing the task allotted to it at birth by its fairy godmother. If the seventh floor of the State Department is contemplating Indonesian nationalism with increasing concern as each year passes, so too should the watchers on the thirty-eighth storey of the UN building. From the Soviet position, it is possible that the nationalism of the underdeveloped countries appears even more a matter of contrasts: even more useful at first, even more of a threat later on. That at least is what the examples of China and Eastern Europe would seem to indicate. Of the latter, and Yugoslavia in particular, R.V. Burks has written: 'This terrain of nationalism and national conflict is in the long run the most treacherous for the Communists, but in the short run the most fruitful.'[18]

Nationalist developments in Eastern Europe are even more complex and raise problems that go beyond the communist world and impact on the international scene. Hostility, rivalry, territorial and minority conflicts between small states, all play an important part in communist revolutions (cf. Yugoslavia, Albania, the role of national factors in the

Greek insurrection, etc.). Within nations like Yugoslavia, within the monolithic Eastern bloc (with the relationship between Romania and Hungary for example), the traditional rivalries seem to be eradicated or at least sublimated by the internationalist doctrine of communism. The split between the Soviets and Yugoslavia, the Hungarian revolution, demonstrate that in this respect at least the Soviet Union constitutes a unifying factor, although more by the opposition it provokes, as local nationalisms unite against it, than by direct influence. In this phase, it is particularly striking how ancient enmities appear to vanish: the Hungarian revolutionaries issued a declaration saying they had no territorial claims over Romania. But we must ask whether we are now entering a new phase, whether the loosening of the bonds of ideology and Soviet domination will not simply reveal all the old oppositions between states and ethnic groups to be still intact, whether the reborn nationalisms will not now turn on one another; certainly, in the case of Romania and Hungary, the traditional quarrels over the situation of the Hungarian minority and the status of Transylvania have started up again, perhaps thereby enabling the Soviet Union to practise a no less traditional policy of divide and rule.[19] Hence the question posed in the article previously quoted: if they truly recover their independence, will these renascent national identities in Eastern Europe, welcomed by President Johnson and President de Gaulle alike, contradict the experience of history, will they overcome chauvinism and become part of new groups and federations?

In the West, there are different but parallel questions which, taken in conjunction with the above, place a giant question mark over the global situation. Is the transcendence of nationalism real or imagined, is it a transitory or a permanent phenomenon? Is it the result of the combined effects of traumatic historical experience, immediate external threat and powerful external stimulus? Does that therefore mean that if these three factors cease to act in concert or their proportions are altered in any way, the poisoned chalice of nationalism will return as though it had never been absent? Or does economic and technological development impose on medium-sized industrial states 'too small to be big and too big to be small',[20] a permanent alteration not as yet experienced by the very big and the very small? Does the development of military technology spell, as some believe, the end not only of nationalism but of the territorial nation–state, incapable any longer of ensuring its defence by making its frontiers impregnable, or does it mean the end, as others believe, of everything but nationalism, since it alone could back its deterrent by asserting its right of suicide? Has the experiment of European economic integration reached the point where it is sufficiently irreversible to restrict the freedom of nationalism to manoeuvre, or does it depend on the continual renewal of a pledge by the states concerned, and hence on a renunciation of nationalism that has not happened and that therefore already restricts the potential for such integration? If one single state chooses the nationalist path, is it condemned by its isolation – or is the example it sets condemned to be followed? If nationalism, conscious of the limitations of the classic nation-state and the material and mental barriers to classic expansion, is determined on transcending itself, is it, as some still insist, in the ultimate sense of translating national ambition into European ambition: the creation of a European power disposing of all the classic means of diplomacy but on a vastly increased scale, and of course vastly more vulnerable to the no less classic risks of nationalism? Or would the nature of the game be changed with the change of scale? If national ambition were to be translated right now to the world arena, would it be to preside over an alliance of all the nationalisms against dependency of every kind, against the 'dual hegemony' of the superpowers, against entrenched coalitions as well as against the intervention of international organizations in the internal affairs of states? Or would it be to establish, on the other hand, a sort of directorate of perhaps three or five major powers acting in concert, as was proposed in 1960 over the Congo, to combat instability and internal disruption in new states still seeking to find their measure and establish an equilibrium and national identity?

In a world that is characterized by the sheer diversity of types of nations and nationalisms, there are as many views and disputes among historians and theoreticians as there are states and ideologies. Arnold Toynbee, seeing nationalism as 'the outcome of a perversion of Industrialism and Democracy through the impact of these new forces on the old institution of Parochial Sovereignty', denounces 'this disastrous corruption poisoning the political life of our modern Western society'. He regards as even more disastrous its spread to the rest of the world, where the combined cultural, historical and economic conditions for the nation-state do not yet exist. Rupert Emerson, who quotes these passages in his fine book *From Empire to Nation*,[21] responds with a chapter that is at once ironic and eminently sensible, entitled 'The virtues of nationalism'. Here, without in the least concealing his uncertainty mixed with anxiety as to the ultimate effects of the phenomenon, he tries to demonstrate the possibility of a positive role for nationalism in the newly independent countries. Another respected historian has no such doubts. In his review of a book on the Middle East, Geoffrey Barraclough recalls a prophecy by

Ali Suavi in 1870 that 'problems of nationality would cause our ruin' (not so very different from the views of Lord Acton), and attacks support for the nationalism of new states as a new incarnation of the Wilsonian myth of natural harmony between contented nationalisms. Lenin, he declares, was right, as compared with Wilson, in seeing nationalism as an evil, something it was useful for others to have but definitely to be avoided on home ground. He concludes that 'it is not necessary to share a communist ideology to realise that national autonomy and self-determination are no answer to the problems of the world today, either in Asia or in Europe or in Africa', and that, in the phrase used by the author who is the subject of his review, Professor B. Lewis, nationalism in the form we have known it so far can only 'disrupt and destroy'. He praises communism for having at least recognized that fact, one from which the West has to date retreated.[22]

Far from being exorcized, the spectre of nationalism continues to haunt the historical consciousness of professors and peoples alike. But whether it is invoked or cursed, placated or camouflaged, depends on the period, the region, and the particular point of view. Anyone who attempts to discuss the subject must veer continually from one extreme to the other. Abandoning any attempt at global logic or scientific objectivity, he must just keep on asking the same question: is it a good thing or a bad thing?

Nationalism and foreign policy

Up to this point, I have attempted to describe the problem of nationalism and its international ramifications as they seemed to me to impinge on the contemporary consciousness. Keeping to the level of description interspersed with opinion, I have attempted a few analytical judgments as and when they sprang to mind, but in general have faithfully reflected the confusion of ideas that is characteristic of the phenomenon, approached in this way. Time now to ask whether the key to a theoretical understanding, as well as the answer to the question posed at the end of the previous section, does not lie in a more rigorous definition of the criteria for and types of nationalism.

Moreover, some such attempt to arrive at definitions and draw distinctions follows naturally from what has gone before. In the previously quoted text, where André Malraux contrasts the world of nations with the world of internationalism, he dismisses the objection that nationalism is a dangerous concept in the following terms:

> The chief transformation has been that of nationalism itself. In the nineteenth century, funadamentally there was just the one all-embracing nationalism, which Germany made in her own image and called the nation *über alles*, the nation above all else. It was this sentiment that internationalism opposed, and it seemed that great nation status could not be viewed as inseparable [= could not be viewed separately?] from the desire for hegemony. When we defend the nation, we are told: you mean war. Take good note that, for the past hundred years, no major war has ever in reality been started by national feeling: all have been started by hegemonism. There has never been a threat of a Swiss war, in spite of the highly developed state of Swiss civilization, because there was never any possibility of Swiss hegemony. And whatever anyone may say, there is no desire for war of any kind in our country at the present, because there is no possiblility of French hegemony. But there is a desire for a national consciousness in a century where the historical destiny of peoples reposes in nations . . . We give France absolute priority, not because we believe it to be a land *über alles*, but because it is the shape of our destiny.[23]

Thus there is an initial distinction to be made between hegemonic nationalism, which is the dangerous sort, and the desire for a national consciousness, which implies that an 'absolute priority' be given to the nation above any other political objective ('General de Gaulle was not being superficial but extremely profound when he said: for twenty years, I have been making France through foreign policy, I have been making France through internal policy; I have made, I am making and I will make France'[24]); this has more to do with Swiss–style national feeling than German nationalism, because it does not imply a desire for hegemony, and hence a risk of war.

To this distinction must be added a second:

> There are countries that are never greater than when they are deeply entrenched in their own defence – the Battle of London is a fine thing in human history. But there are countries that are never greater than when they are being great for all the rest, that perhaps are only ever great in those circumstances. All the roads to the East are lined with the tombs of French knights. The roads to the West

out of the Pyrenees are lined with the tombs of the soldiers of the revolution. There is probably no place in Western civilization where France is not represented, not because it wanted to take, but because it wanted to give. There is the imperialism of taking and the imperialism of giving.[25]

This second distinction contrasts the desire for a national consciousness that is isolationist or directed inwards and a desire for national consciousness that is universalist. What, according to Malraux, enables French nationalism to bridge the two categories is the contrast between imperialism that takes and imperialism that gives, the idea of a universalism that is fundamentally altruistic and, *pace* the reference to knights and soldiers, also fundamentally pacific. One may make a further distinction (not in fact made by the author in this text, which does not pretend to be an exhaustive analysis): the two forms of universalism may be contrasted in respect of their objectives (taking or giving) or the means they employ (militaristic or pacific). While there is certainly a considerable overlap between the two pairs of alternatives, surely we could also conceive of, or alternatively may already have experienced, militaristic universal movements whose declared objective was to give rather than take, and pacific imperialisms more concerned to take than to give, even though not by militaristic means.

We may add a fourth distinction which is implicit in the quoted text without ever being spelt out, that between the desire for a national consciousness and the accordance of absolute priority to the nation – conceived of as shaped by destiny – over any other value or objective of internal or external policy (the President of the Swiss Confederation might say 'I have made, am making and will make Switzerland', but it will not mean the same as the comparable statement by the President of the French Republic). That concludes our list of the main categories in terms of which we have attempted to distinguish good and bad forms of nationalism, in respect of their effects on international relations. To sum up, the categories are: (1) affirmation or prioritization of national sentiment; (2) isolationist or universalist nationalism; (3) selfish and possessive or generous and missionary universalism; (4) militaristic or pacific universalism.

From whatever angle we look at it, what we come up with once again are the three classic oppositions. There is the *terminological*, distinguishing between the predominant usage in the Anglo-Saxon countries, where nationalism and national feeling are very often regarded as synonymous, and the French usage which distinguishes between the two, reserving the term 'nationalism' for the desire to build, defend as a priority or glorify the nation. There is the *ethical/ political*, which refers to relations with other nations and other nationalisms, and distinguishes between nationalisms that restrict themselves to constructing, affirming or defending their own nation and those which, because of feelings of superiority, a desire for domination or a tendency (conscious or unconscious) towards expansion, constitute a threat to other nations and the international order. And finally, there is the *historical/geographical*, which draws the distinction between nationalisms associated with a predefined nation and nationalisms that are in search of a nation, further distinguishing, in the first of these cases, between the self-affirmation of a nation that has not yet achieved recognition (which may easily be confused with the second case) and the defence or glorification of an existing nation.

The second distinction, which I have called the ethical/political although it could equally be called *relational*, is the one that interests us here. But it is instructive as well as illuminating to consider how its relationship to the other two distinctions may vary, depending on the definitions a particular author employs. Thus, the Egyptian scholar Abdel-Malek proposes to employ the term 'nationalitarian' to describe what we would normally call Egyptian nationalism, on the grounds that the condition it refers to has nothing to do with excluding others and everything to do with self-affirmation. The term 'nationalism' would imply something negative, and perhaps imperialist aspirations, while 'nationalitarian' would indicate 'a process of autonomous growth, a true and profound assumption of identity bearing no comparison with the early struggles to achieve sovereignty or sort out petty grievances'.[26] Professor Hans Morgenthau, on the other hand, contrasts the nationalism of yesterday, dedicated to building the nation but also recognizing the right of the others to do the same, with the nationalism of today, which is directed against other nations and accepts no limitations on its actions. He regards only the first as deserving of the name nationalism, while the second would more accurately be called *nationalist universalism*.[27] Within this second type, he seems to be on the brink of a further distinction which he does not make explicit, but which it might be useful to spell out here, between two particular combinations of national base and global objective: the first might be called *universalist nationalism* – where the nation in question has a special and superior global significance or mission – as in the Fichtean concept or in German nationalism; and the second *nationalist universalism*, where the nation in question is seen as constituting the contingent incarnation, initial springboard or temporary bastion of an ideology or international movement, as in the rationale of proletarian nationalism.

In contrasting the true nationalism of the past with the false nationalism of today, Morgenthau is thinking of totalitarian imperialisms of European origin. But another writer whom we have already quoted, John Kautsky, makes a comparable distinction (taking the opposite path from Mr Abdel-Malek, terminologically speaking) with reference to newly independent countries. He contrasts the true European nationalisms, which correspond to nations that exist actually and potentially, because of a common language, common culture and common participation in political life, with the nationalisms of underdeveloped countries, where the word seems to him a contradiction in terms, since these are nationalisms without a nation, they are not based on common language, for none exists, territorial framework, either unclear or bequeathed by the colonial power, or popular participation, which is non-existent given the non-participation of the peasants, but instead define themselves against the colonial or ex-colonial power and in terms of some global enterprise such as industrialization or modernization.[28]

Neither the terminological dispute, which is a matter of convention, nor the more fundamental question of the national bases of the new states are of interest to us in themselves in the present context. Let's simply note, in the context that concerns us here, the obvious absurdity of any answer based on the idea that one could put all the European nationalisms together in one group (according to Kautsky's criteria, would not certain countries in Central or Eastern Europe be as close to some Afro-Asiatic countries as to some Western countries?) and, even more inconceivable, the nationalisms of Third World countries all together in another.[29] Some of these latter have no real national base, others exist within the framework of proper, defined, contented nations, yet others, probably the most significant in terms of international relations, attach to states where undeniable national sentiment coexists with poorly defined or disputed territorial boundaries. And finally, in the Arab countries for example, there are nationalisms that combine a degree of national consciousness focused on the state with a trans-state ethnic awareness that itself makes an appeal to nationalism: here once again, the key is in the variety of local situations, certain countries being, like Egypt according to Abdel-Malek, more attached to their national tradition, and others more aware of the artificial character of their states and attuned to the idea of the Arab nation. The problem for us is that this ambiguity and fluidity may also lead, on the one hand, to tolerance, acceptance, the invention of new forms, either federal or confederal, which would help to move the international system on from the old 'billiard balls' idea, the model of warring sovereign nation-states that constitutes the implicit philosophy of nationalism, or, on the other hand, it may lead to a state of permanent dissatisfaction and tension, as happened with Pan-Germanism and Pan-Slavism.

Let's return therefore to the relational perspective. If we look to it to provide a principle for classifying nationalist attitudes in the international sphere, it is in full awareness of the diversity of possible interpretations. In fact, the distinction between the two nationalisms, constructive and negative, tolerant and conquering, may be seen as a distinction either between two *kinds*, or between two *poles* or between two *phases* of nationalism. The contrast of the two types or kinds is the most accessible, and in a sense provides the starting point for the other interpretations. But there are many writers, including Malraux and Morgenthau in the quoted texts, who are content to leave it at that contrast, which they believe reveals a fundamental duality. An English writer, John Bowle, takes the contrast of Mazzini's and Treitschke's styles of nationalism as the keypoint of his book on the international dangers of nationalism.[30] But one cannot help wondering if the polarity does not create more problems than it solves, or if, the point no sooner made, it does not at once obscure the real problem, which concerns the internal dynamic the two types of nationalism have in common.

First, it seems definitely to be the case that each of the two contains, potentially at least, elements of the other. The great British historian Sir Lewis Namier spoke of Mazzini's ideas in the following terms: 'National self-glorification and claims to moral superiority were of their core; which entails a measure of depreciation of other peoples, and is not conducive to international comity.'[31] Treischke, on the other hand, and even Hitler himself, did up to a point recognize the nationalism of others, or at least certain others.

What is more, as Benjamin Akzin remarks, 'the birth of a nationalist movement under liberal, humanistic and universalistic auspices, with self-determination as its only goal, does not guarantee that at some future date this movement will not assume an aggressive character. We have seen this occurring in the cases of the German, Italian, Hungarian and Polish national movements, and there is no basis for assuming that the new emerging nations of Africa and Asia are immune to the danger'.[32] This would represent the development of good nationalism (in the liberation and nation-building phase) into bad (the phase of expansion or deviation, making use of newly acquired independence and power, or energies and feelings of hostility hitherto channelled into the struggle for independence). The oppressed becomes the oppressor, out of hubris, revenge or as a result of being led astray. It is the development described by Carr, Morgenthau and Rosecrance, in the works quoted above, as well as by many other writers with reference to many different situations.

But it is no less common to find precisely the opposite development being regarded as inevitable: from bad to good, from the aggressive exuberance of youth to the tolerant wisdom of maturity. Nationalism would then be seen as a problem that contained the seeds of its own solution. It would at first refuse to subject independence, all the more appreciated for being still recent, to limitations that seemed like a hangover from or return to a detested dependency; then, having become more confident, having less need to prove itself in action, having to a degree exhausted the charms of absolute sovereignty and seen its limitations, it would bend its efforts more to internal tasks, and would be more inclined to agree to substitute cooperation or passive participation for conflict and violence in foreign affairs. Thus another British writer, C.M. Woodhouse, in a book also devoted to the international consequences of nationalism, particularly that of the underdeveloped countries, compares nationalism with juvenile delinquency, adding 'but juveniles are expected to grow up'.[33] He distinguishes three stages in the normal development of the attitudes nationals adopt towards international relations: nationalism; acceptance of limitations on sovereignty; internationalism. Although less positive, a similar vision informs Raymond Aron's judgment that the desire to make a stand for its own sake, or the refusal to accept any sort of bond, are normal for a young state but not for a state that is a seasoned veteran, which he reproaches for 'that infantile sickness of an old nationalism'.[34] And certainly that vision receives no less confirmation in history than the previous one, as is at once apparent if we compare Western Europe and the Third World, territorial disputes over Alsace-Lorraine, or indeed the Saar, with African or Asian examples.

But are the two historical sequences mutually exclusive? One can see how it would be possible to combine them in an optimistic, Hegelian dialectic of wide application. There would be a first stage (affirmation or thesis), in which nascent nationalism would be content to demand its independence and look to the building of the nation; a second stage (affirmation of the opposite, or antithesis) where it would become intolerant, aggressive or expansionist; and finally a third stage (new affirmation, or synthesis) in which, tamed by fatigue, experience or failure, it would retreat into itself, either becoming an element of the status quo or else submerging its identity (to start the cycle all over again, or perhaps to find an ultimate resting place) within a greater affirmation, a higher unity.

Arguably, that is very much the sequence of events that the European states have lived through. Equally one may say that it is consistent by implication with the philosophy of history that treats the destructive aspects of nationalism in certain underdeveloped countries as a purely transitional phase. But one may wonder whether, dialectic for dialectic, such an interpretation does not suffer from assuming that nationalisms undergo a sort of quasi-biological internal development, the characteristics of which are predetermined. Is it not equally likely that the encounter with other nationalisms may set up a dialectical relationship that is more powerful still, but negative? This is what Rosecrance calls the cumulative or boomerang effect.[35] Positive (or as Rosecrance calls it 'coalescent') nationalism becomes negative (or 'expansionist'). But along the way, just as Napoleon provoked into existence the European nationalisms, among them the German variety, so it provokes 'coalescent', defensive or positive nationalisms, and these in their turn, like German nationalism, will become great, and therefore also expansionist, and will provoke 'coalescent' nationalisms, and so on and so forth. In this way the good becomes the bad, out of which good is created, which in turn becomes bad, etc. Thus a vicious circle of good and bad is established, but a vicious circle whose logic is to spread the damage ever further and wider.

Even so, is it not possible that at some point a general lassitude might creep in, allowing a dialectic of the first description to seize its chance? And conversely, is not this first sort of dialectic always at risk of being halted and reversed, at its second stage, by encountering the second sort of dialectic, ergo, because of the logic of hostility? In so far as nationalism implies comparison with or hostility towards others, it is impossible to study its sources or its nature outside the context of international politics. The dream of philosophers, from the Plato of the *Republic* to the Rousseau of the *Government of Poland*, has been the creation of, in effect, chauvinistic Robinson Crusoes, patriotic citizens living in isolated cities with no external ambitions and no reason to fight, but whose civic and patriotic virtues, indispensable to them as individuals and for the internal running of the city, should logically imply a belief in its superiority and hence a hostility towards foreigners – although that hostility and those warlike qualities would not in fact be exercised. In the real world, they are exercised, and there are people against whom to exercise them. The essence of nationalism is also its tragedy, that it does not have the world to itself.

But if this dialectic of imitation, contagion and opposition exists, echoing the logical dilemma that poses the problem of security for the Hobbesian state, ought we not to ask ourselves, when one nationalism meets another, not only what they say to one another, what they feel and how they perceive one another, but also what they actually do? To put it another way, in order to reach the point that interests us here, that of relations between nationalisms and especially the relationship between those relations and the international system, it seems to us that we should start by distinguishing between, and then combining, two different approaches. The first, starting with national-ism itself as a set of ideas, values and feelings, would examine its consequences for the foreign policy of the state in question and of other states. The second, starting with international relations and the different elements of a theory of foreign policy, would examine, on the behavioural level as it were, the criteria that permit one to regard a foreign policy as nationalist, and also the reciprocal influence of this type of behaviour and the situation of encounter and rivalry, co-operation and competition between foreign policies, within the international system.

Perhaps the central question of a study on the theme of nationalism and international relations has to do with the extent to which the two approaches overlap. Supposing that the first approach defines national-ism as an ideology, an attitude, a historical movement, then to what extent has this nationalism actually given rise to (or will it inevitably give rise to) a foreign policy that may be defined as nationalist, according to the criteria of the second approach? Conversely, has a foreign policy so defined always and inevitably been inspired by nationalism? Above and beyond questions of vocabulary, the problem is of knowing on the one hand if, with respect to nationalism, we can make a distinction between behaviour and consciousness, nationalism *en soi* and nationalism *pour soi*, and on the other hand whether the modern phenomenon of the nation and the allegiance, both popular and intellectual, affective and active, that it provokes, introduces a new dimension into relations between political entities or whether it merely conforms in this respect to the existing framework, which will continue unchanged.

This brings us up against that most classic of problems, the sense of the word 'international' in the definition of the discipline or reality of 'international relations'. There is general agreement that the latter term should be taken to mean the relations between political entities, as defined by a territory, people or government, not necessarily exclud-ing entities other than the nation such as cities or empires, and by no means ignoring the individual or social relations that exist between one entity and another over and above the interstate relations that are our central point of reference. If therefore we give the name 'international relations' to the relationship of coexistence, conflict and cooperation between a number of political entities constituting autonomous decision-making bodies and independent of any higher common authority, then, size and historical background apart, we can situate their attitudes, behaviour, politics, conceptions of themselves and others, and of the relationships between them, on an axis with, at one pole, accordance of priority to the individual political entity, its independence, power and freedom of action, and at the opposite pole, accordance of priority to the bonds between entities, to the system, society or community that they constitute, or more succinctly, to the suprastate and infrastate relations by which they are subsumed and underpinned.

In one respect this abstract analysis of international relations is immediately reminiscent of one aspect of the ideology or attitudes of nationalism proper, namely the emphasis placed, not merely on national values, but on the qualities that distinguish the nation or set it apart from others, such as its unity, independence, superiority or originality, rather than qualities like security or prosperity. But this type of attitude towards foreign policy may be associated with motives or ideological justifications that have little to do with nationalism, indeed it may be associated with political entities that have little to do with the nation: one thinks of the concept of *raison d'état*, of Machiavellianism, *Realpolitik*, the Hobbesian idea of state, the essence of political interplay or rivalry between independent entities, or at least the interpretation placed upon it by princes and philosophers long before the advent of the modern nation. If it is true that Machiavellianism (in Meinecke's sense), power politics, sovereignty and national sentiment have been acting in close concert since the sixteenth century, it has also been suggested that the notion of reason of state was no more than an intermediate stage, historically and conceptually, between the interests of princes and the politics of nations, and that the latter represented in effect a continuation of a system, the original sense of which was only properly understood by the former.[36]

One does not have to espouse this view to recognize that there are many possible ways of defining the nationalist attitude vis-à-vis, for example, the problem of alliances,[37] that of national interest as against the moral choice,[38] those − which seem to me perhaps the most revealing - of the distinction between the extreme and the normal case, of the priority of foreign over internal politics, of politics as the search for a maximum freedom of action for oneself or a minimum freedom of action for others, and that all these various definitions extend in fact way beyond the historical or geographical context of the modern nation and hence of nationalism.

That being the case, the question with which we began – whether nationalism had become redundant in the present international system and in the modern world or whether on the contrary it was its characteristic and distinguishing feature – must now be posed on two different levels, separate but linked, having to do with the size of the political entity, and its relations with others, both leading to the problem of its nature and vocation.

It was widely thought that nationalism had become redundant because the nation-state was no longer of a size, economically or militarily, to cope with the problems of today. But that could also mean that it had become redundant because it was no longer of the right size for the international power game. Yet this game itself, and also nationalism as the maximalist strategy associated with it, would continue and prosper, and even discover new resources of energy in their transformed role: by this token, the decline of the nation-state would actually facilitate the rise of nationalism in the continental state. But although this interpretation is salutary as a means of guarding against the illusion that a change of scale automatically means a change of behaviour, that the further you move away from the nation the closer you are to humanity's existing in a world at peace, it is quite possible that it too will be rendered redundant by a new turn of events.

Since 1945 we have seen the triumph of regionalism – ideologically, politically, militarily and economically – as in some mysterious fashion it has succeeded in overcoming the classic opposition between nationalism and globalism. But this success has been due in part – and it is particularly marked in the case of European economic integration – to its ability to adopt, use and accelerate the process known and described as functionalism, whereby sectors, interests, alliances and conflicts are interrelated and interconnected, so that, as they cross frontiers and bypass governments, they effectively erode nationalism from all sides, without and within.[39] Is there not today at every level a movement towards diversification, complexity and disequilibrium? Are not the ideological blocs or alliances experiencing the same fate as the nation-states, of becoming in certain respects redundant yet revivified in others, sovereign here and prisoners there, allies of this opponent on one issue but opposed to that ally in another?

If, for example, we consider the role of atomic weapons, is it not true, on the one hand, that the political units they seem to call for are broad groupings (the worldwide organization that would enjoy a complete monopoly of such weapons being rendered perhaps even more unlikely by their existence, and the nation-state rendered even more impotent by their geographical and economic constraints); but on the other hand, that because of the universal danger their use would represent (against a neutral like India as much as against an ally) something resembling collective security seems for the first time a real possibility; and that, in the concentration of decision-making and degree of solidarity their deterrent use implies, the national viewpoint, at the opposite end of the spectrum, takes on a new value? If the crisis of the nation-state arose not simply out of a change of scale, a uniform increase of dimensions, but from the fact of a disparity between the various dimensions, if it were the case in our day that not only the optimal size of entities and but also feelings of solidarity or community differed in different spheres (economic, military, political, ideological, cultural, etc.) and circumstances (normal life or life-and-death situations), then the federation or broad alliance might up to a point be the means of reducing these gaps or correcting these disparities, but it would not change the general drift. There would continue to be a movement towards a plurality of contradictory but necessarily concomitant relations of alliance and conflict, towards the creation of a network of interconnecting communications, of different extent and direction depending on the particular sphere, permitting an indefinite number of manoeuvres but restricting their individual scope and reach.

That would spell the triumph of nationalism, since the smallest entities would recover a freedom of action, and power to combine, that appeared lost; at the same time, it would in a more profound sense spell the downfall of nationalism, since the political process would continue, but in changed conditions and according to different rules. This would have the effect of imposing limitations on the smallest entities' powers of action and combination, limitations all the more imperative for consisting in links established at both the infra-national and supranational levels. The governmental decision-making level would usually be no more than one among many, more like a sort of umpire, *primus inter pares* rather than sovereign.

Over and above the problem of the nation, and even above that of the relations between political entities or between states, perhaps the fundamental problem – legal, sociological and philosophical – is that of the nature of these political entities or states: more specifically, the indivisibility or 'separability' of sovereignty,[40] decision-making and solidarity, in all the different spheres and circumstances.

Having begun with a historical/ideological description and having sought to establish a number of abstract objective criteria, we should probably resign ourselves to being unable to arrive at any judgment of the place of nationalism in international relations that is not also a diagnosis of our age and the statement of a position on the essence and vocation of political communities.[41]

9

Cultural Identity and Civil Society: The New Nationalist Challenge

ONE QUESTION dominates the European scene since the fall of the Berlin Wall: does the defeat of communism mean the victory of liberalism or that of nationalism? The European revolutions of 1989 can be called cultural revolutions in the deepest sense: on the one hand, they were led by intellectuals, on the other, they express a general rejection of communist legitimacy and a general aspiration to rejoin the mainstream of European culture. But the most widespread notion to emerge from them is that of *civil society*, its rebirth and its affirmation against totalitarianism and its ruling elite, the nomenclature. Yet after victory, questions abound about the content and orientation of both cultural identity and civil society. Communist totalitarianism acted as a negative, unifying force. Its demise brings forth conflicts between levels and orientations, between social strata and between cultural traditions. Domestically, the bipolar opposition between 'us' and 'them' or between 'civil society' and 'the system' is replaced by more complex and contradictory oppositions between town and country, secular intellectuals and the church, young activists and old conservatives, new rich and new poor, etc. Internationally the bipolar opposition between East and West is replaced both by the homogenizing influence of modern technological and consumer society and by the differentiating search for identity through the rediscovery of real and mythical, ethnic, national and religious roots. The interplay among these various factors, which are present everywhere but in different proportions, may create new divisions or revive old ones within Europe – between East and West, between North and South.

Europe in the 1990s, then, will be neither the partitioned Europe of the Cold War, not the united Europe of an integrated community extended to the continent, nor a reunified Europe on the model of a reunified Germany. It will be a differentiated Europe whose formerly separated parts will be much more exposed to mutual influence but, also, to the temptation of mutual rejection and self-closure. As the military and ideological confrontations tend to vanish, economic, social and cultural differences will follow contradictory trends. They may be blurred or reduced in some respects when compared to those of the Cold War period, but they will be more salient, more sensitive, and hence more resented, particularly in comparison to the hopes awakened by the crumbling of the Berlin Wall. Indeed, new walls and new curtains, as well as new gaps may emerge as a reaction to the shock of openness and contact, whether it be the impact of consumption models from the West or immigration waves from the East. But these new divisions, while partly coinciding geographically with the old ones, will transcend the old borders. They will be (or, rather they already are) felt within the West and within the East and, indeed, within individual European countries.

The key to these divisions is the interplay among political, economic and sociocultural dimensions. Ralf Dahrendorf has illustrated both the crucial and the paradoxical character of the latter by stating that if the revolutions in Eastern Europe are to lead to open societies on the Western model, three things are needed: a constitutional state, the market and civil society, but that while a democratic constitution could be set up in six months, six years was needed for the market to operate effectively, and sixty years for the emergence of a real civil society.[1] The catch-22 in the situation is that while neither democracy nor the market can function properly in the absence of a civil society, they cannot wait the decades necessary for a civil society to emerge; and the latter, in turn, could be jeopardized by the failure of the former.

The question is whether this dialectic leads to a vicious circle – e.g. that often observed in Latin America or in interwar Eastern Europe, with Western-type political and economic institutions being introduced but failing to take root because of contrary social and cultural attitudes which, in turn, give rise to anti-Western political and economic movements – or to a benign one, in which education in democratic and capitalist ethics can build upon pre-existing elements of civil society and national culture and lead towards an original synthesis.

In a sense, society is present wherever several individuals relate to one another or, at least, wherever these relations have a private or autonomous character which escapes the control of the state. But what is the relation between, on the one hand, this broad sense of society and, on the other, civil society, in the sense of the self-assertion of the people against a totalitarian system, or in the more difficult or demanding sense of a civic culture, i.e. of a set of norms and attitudes governing the relations of people with one another and with common institutions, involving the arts of tolerance and honesty in economic and political behaviour, of voluntary association and peaceful competition, of respect for diversity and of a sense for the preservation of unity?

To say that the chances for civil society are heavily influenced by the political culture of a given country is both true and frustrating, since it leads from one complex and ambiguous notion to another. When speaking of culture, we cannot simply adopt the broad, anthropological definition which includes all the attitudes, values and customs of a society. Nor can the definition remain within the bounds of the narrow, classical sense of *Bildung*, involving the cultivation of the mind, i.e. education and the symbolic dimensions of human existence, such as art and science, religion and philosophy. What is necessary is the intermediate level, involving attitudes towards politics and, more generally, towards the art of living together, within and between communities. But, particularly today, this intermediate level is, precisely, the ever moving result of the tension between the other two.

The tension can be seen on at least three levels. The first one is that of types of culture. Never before has culture, even in the narrow sense, been so torn between conflicting forces and trends. The most obvious and widespread division is, of course, between 'high culture' and 'popular culture'. This has been given a new dimension by the spread of literacy and, above all, by the explosive progress of science and technology. Within high culture, it has led to an increasing gap between what C.P. Snow has called 'the two cultures', the scientific and the literary, or, more broadly, the technological and the humanistic.[2] But perhaps the most far-reaching consequence has been the transformation and the division of popular culture itself, under the impact of the mass media. The new communications technology tends to produce a mass culture which is naturally cosmopolitan, as it reflects the influence of the more powerful societies, particularly the United States, and of the simplest and most direct values, such as consumption or sex, whereas the traditional folk culture transmitted from one generation to another tends to be predominantly particularistic even if it follows universal patterns. Of course the former is gaining over the latter. But this produces powerful culture shocks (of which the experience of East Germany through its contact with West German society, first through television and then through direct contact, is the most vivid example). Even within the modern culture of the mass media, which, on balance, has a socially and internationally homogenizing effect, there are tensions and splits between the rock culture of the young (with its polarities of brotherhood and violence), and the consumer or social-climber culture conveyed by televised games and soap operas.

Hence the second, more indirect, division, the sociopolitical division between the intelligentsia and the masses. This is well known in countries in transition towards modernity, whether nineteenth-century Russia or the twentieth-century Third World. But it takes on an even more acute and complex character in former communist countries, in which (unlike both traditional and Western societies) intellectuals have been both the greatest favourites and the leading (sometimes the only active) opponents of the regimes. This distinction between the intelligentsia and the masses is often combined with related but not quite equivalent ones, between the young and the old, and between the towns and the countryside. The latter is particularly evident in Bulgaria (where, until recently, the opposition was holding the cities and the communist rulers the countryside), in Hungary (where the traditional opposition between 'urbanizers' and 'populists' is renewed in the predominance of the intellectual-based and universalistically oriented Alliance of Free Democrats and in the Young Students Movement, Fidesz, in Budapest, whereas the more conservative and national Democratic Forum and Small Land-owners' Party are stronger in the rest of the country) and even in Russia (where the municipalities of big cities like Moscow and Leningrad have been conquered by reform-minded, westernizing, intellectuals).

It is most acute where the absence of a civil society has so far not permitted an articulation of either political programmes or economic interests. This is most striking in Romania, where the universalistic culture of some intellectuals and many young people is separated from the nationalist culture of the majority (particularly older generations, workers and peasants, but also many city-dwellers, very often of recent peasant origin, as shown during the violence involving the miners in Bucharest in June 1990). Yet even there the situation is more complex, with some cities, like Timisoara, being more open to cosmopolitan influences while many intellectuals are rediscovering the nationalistic (sometimes bordering on the mystical or the chauvinistic) accent and themes of the Ceaucescu past, or even the days of the Iron Guard.

This leads to the third division, which is most relevant to this essay, the regional one. Is culture a factor of European unity or of national and regional divisions? Are there any stable intermediary units in the realm of modern culture between the traditional village and McLuhan's 'global village'? Is the German journalist R.W. Leonhart correct when he writes that 'from Ulster to Georgia the only *Heimat* is the region'?[3] Or is it the nation? Europe? Or are they all responding mainly to the common trends of modern society?

The question in each case is one of the respective influence of three major factors: the modern technological and consumer society, the legacy of communist rule (with its bureaucratic and authoritarian attitudes, which outlast their institutional bases) and specific, cultural traditions. With respect to the last, the additional question is whether the former partition of Europe along East–West lines coincides with a sociocultural division as well as with military and ideological divisions.

In other words, are Eastern and Western Europe defined not only by the presence of Soviet and US troops in 1945, determining the nature of their political regimes, but also by different sociocultural structures and traditions? Or are the latter distributed along different lines which are now re-emerging and re-creating the cultural geography of Europe, brutally distorted by the bipolar division?

This, for instance, is the view of Milan Kundera, who, in a famous article, defined Central Europe as 'a kidnapped part of the West'.[4] But such a definition raises as many problems as it answers. Are Europe and the West identical? Is Russia to be seen as not belonging to Europe? Has East Central Europe the same sociocultural characteristics as those of Western Europe? Conversely, has the latter a cultural reality distinct from that of the United States?

To these questions, which have been the source of innumerable polemics, there are no objective answers. One can only warn against drawing too quick and too facile inferences from the political to the cultural, and vice versa. Those (like French historian Emmanuel Todd[5]) who see a strict correlation between family structures and political regimes, run up against the obvious objection that communism was brought to Eastern Europe by the Red Army, not by native evolutions or revolutions based on demographic developments. Some tend to base schemes like de Gaulle's 'Europe from the Atlantic to the Urals' and Mitterrand's 'Confederation', including Russia but excluding the United States, on the notion that American civilization is based on technological optimism and lacks the historical depth, the attachment to tradition and the experience of suffering which characterize European (and Russian) history and literature. Others can point out, with greater plausibility, that, to use Heidegger's expression, 'Americanism is something European', that the American revolution is born of European religion and philosophy, whereas Russia has not experienced the Reformation, or the Enlightenment, or the bourgeois revolution. More convincingly still, one could point out that cultural traditions are both ambivalent and constantly being redefined in the light of current social developments and political choices.

This is particularly true of the two former superpowers. Their relation to Europe is clearly ambivalent and takes on a different character according to phases in their respective histories. The United States is completely European in its historical roots but has been set up precisely to offer a contrast with the political and moral corruption of the old continent. Moreover, it may be becoming less European by becoming more intercultural and turning its interests to Latin America and Asia. Russia, ever since Peter the Great, has had a love–hate relationship with Europe. It has been torn between imitation and hostility, between feelings of cultural inferiority and messianic superiority. Its present revolution can be seen as a desperate attempt to join Europe for good followed by disappointment and resentment. But however sincere its search for acceptance may be, it cannot wipe out, if only in the minds of East and Central Europeans, the legacy of a profoundly different past.

But isn't the same problem present within Western Europe and Eastern Europe proper? While Europe is integrating politically and economically, are not differences between an Atlantic and a Middle European, a Nordic and a meridional orientation becoming more apparent within the Community and even within some of its countries, like Italy, at the very time when mass communications and migrations are exploding traditional communities?

The question assumes even greater relevance for the future of Eastern Europe. The revival of the Central European idea both in Germany and in Czechoslovakia, in Hungary, in the northern republics of Yugoslavia and to a lesser extent in Poland or even in parts of Italy, has both a cultural and a political meaning, but the two are not identical. Culturally, the Central European theme is essentially nostalgic. It refers to the literary and artistic splendour of the decaying Habsburg Empire. But the two peoples who provided its common inspiration, the Germans and the Jews, have been eliminated in favour of more ethnically homogeneous national units. While middle-aged

intellectuals dream of Central Europe, the young are attracted either by
nationalism or nativism, or by the West as such, which, at the level of
mass culture as well as of technology, means America at least as much
as Europe.

Politically, the affirmation of Central Europe had a clear, negative
meaning. For part of the German public in search of its national unity
and identity, it meant the refusal of the division of Europe, the refusal
of amputation and Americanization. For East Europeans it meant the
refusal to be cut off from the West and identified with the Russian
invaders seen as culturally inferior and less European, or with the
politically dominant and economically inferior Serbs in the case of
Croatia and Slovenia. The question is what will remain of this notion
under conditions of all-European *rapprochement* and the disintegration
of the Soviet empire and of the Yugoslav state.

One practical answer is both political and cultural: it lies in the
rebirth of old regional solidarities which were artificially severed by
the Iron Curtain: between Scandinavians and Balts in the North,
between Central Europeans, between heirs of the Habsburgs,
between states of the Balkan peninsula. This corresponds both to the
desire of former communist states to grasp any possible anchor in the
West and to that of Western states like Germany, Italy and Austria to
use traditional ties or affinities in order to increase their political,
economic and cultural role in the new Europe. The obstacle,
however, lies in the social problems raised by these very contacts,
especially by the movements of population which they are supposed
to facilitate.

Even when regional rivalries and ethnic conflicts do not prevail over
solidarities (as in the Balkans), the flux of migrating workers and
wandering and unwanted minorities like the Gypsies tends to provoke
reactions of self-closure rather than of openness from the richer or less
poor countries. German unity has raised a new economic and social
barrier between the former GDR and Poland while suppressing those
which used to separate the two German states. More generally, visas
and border guards and protectionist measures between Germany or
Austria and Poland or Romania, but also between Poland and
Czechoslovakia, as well as between Soviet republics, are on the increase and may for a time at least hamper the re-emergence of
Europe's older regions almost as much as the Iron Curtain used to do.
The balance between the resentments created by such self-closure and
the ties created by Western influences in the East and Eastern
migrations to the West, which nobody can eliminate entirely, will vary
from case to case.

The other answer is analytical: it tends to attribute differences in the political developments of European, particularly of formerly communist countries, to their respective historical legacies and especially to their cultural and religious backgrounds. The distinction emphasized by Kundera between a Catholic or Protestant, formerly Habsburg Central Europe which, alone, would be truly European, and the orthodox, formerly Byzantine countries such as Russia, but also Romania, Bulgaria or Serbia, re-emerges in many interpretations of the political events since the opening of the Wall. The idea would be that the democratic transition is smoother and more promising in countries blessed with a legacy of historical contacts with the West, of independent centres of power (e.g. the Catholic church), of individual autonomy (promoted by Protestantism); the Balkans, on the other hand, submitted to Ottoman rather than Habsburg domination and under the influence of the Orthodox church, have no feeling for the distinction between spiritual and secular power which is the precondition of liberalism, or for the rule of law or the rights of the individual.

There is obviously something to this explanation, as shown by the differences within a multinational state like Yugoslavia in two paradigmatic evolutions, those of Slovenia and Serbia. Yet exceptions abound: within Yugoslavia itself, Serbia has at least as much a democratic tradition as Catholic Croatia which, along with Catholic Slovakia and Catholic Lithuania, experienced some of the most brutal forms of fascism during the Second World War. Greece, while not a model of Western democracy is certainly not a model of religious totalitarianism either. In the interwar period, before 1938, Romania had a Balkan form of parliamentarianism which, while weak and corrupt, was closer to democracy than to the dictatorship in Hungary and Poland.

Above all, these remarks go to show that cultural patterns are only one element among the many that tend to influence the search of European nations for a new identity. The character of recent communist rule is just as important (perhaps decisive in the case of Romania). So are the influences of a changed international environment.

All are looking for an identity and a new role by finding an original and necessarily unstable balance among the state, the international (European and global) economy, subnational aspirations (represented by the challenges of ethnicity and of regionalism) and transnational challenges, both those of the environment and those of population movements.

The last two elements cannot be overemphasized: nothing has done more to awaken Armenian and Baltic, Ukrainian and Belarus nationalism than environmental issues, particularly Chernobyl. Nothing is more explosive and more conducive to a rebirth of nationalism, in East and West, than the issues of immigration, economic rivalry and cultural shock of what *The Economist* has called the 'huddled masses, on the move'.[6]

Sociocultural malaise and political identity: nationalism in Eastern and Western Europe

Nationalism may be more a consequence than a cause of this 'new situation'. What has happened is the collapse of the division of Europe based on Soviet domination of east Central Europe and on the division of Germany. What caused it, however, was not so much nationalist reassertion in the East, Romanian-style, or an irredentist West German nationalism; the decisive factor was the economic and spiritual failure of the communist system and the success of the Western one. The collapse came as much as a surprise to the Western leaders as it did to Gorbachev. Once it happened, however, it inevitably meant the removal or at least the loosening of supranational bonds which were containing or hiding old nationalist feelings. To these were added new temptations and fears.

Nationalism has thus become the primary cause for concern about the future of Europe. But while the widespread comparisons with the pre-1914 Balkans or with the Europe of the 1930s are not entirely groundless, they run the grave risk of failing to consider historical and regional differences. A greater national consciousness or attachment to national interests does not necessarily mean a revival of nationalism; a nationalist revival does not necessarily mean a return to the warlike racist and fanatic nationalism of the Nazis or the Iron Guard. On the other hand, a revival of xenophobia linked to the increase of immigration and to the difficulties of coexistence between diverse religious and cultural communities should not necessarily be identified with nationalism, although it may pose at least as great a threat to the spirit of tolerance and universalism.

Finally, the most common feature may be a general anxiety about identity, which is to be found among individual and ethnic minorities as well as among middle-ranking and superpowers, uncertain about

their role in the face of both economic and technological interdependence and the end of the bipolar world. But while, at this level
of generality, the questions are common, the reactions and the answers
are strikingly diverse.

Eastern Europe: old-style nationalism?

The most general statement one can make about the region is that old
national, ethnic or religious conflicts which have lost much of their
relevance or at least their intensity in Western Europe, are still alive in
the East, either because its countries are at a different stage of historical
and cultural development, or because they have been isolated from the
great movement of social and economic interdependence which has
engulfed the Western capitalist world, or because the communist
regime has exacerbated nationalist tensions either by ignoring them or
by deliberately fostering and exploiting them.

Within this general context, however, it is necessary to distinguish
three obviously related cases: the crisis of the multinational states, like
the Soviet Union and Yugoslavia; the rivalries or hostilities between
independent nation-states; and the sub- or transnational tensions
affecting relations between communities, from xenophobia to racism,
from the treatment of minorities to that of immigrants.

The first case is the most serious, both in its historical significance
and in its immediate consequences for the peace and the shape of
Europe. It is here that past history seems most relevant. The Russian
empire is finally succumbing to the fate of the Ottoman, Austro-
Hungarian and Western colonial empires.

Second, it has often been remarked that the victory of the principle
of nationalities in 1918–19 was not complete: the dissolution of the
Austro-Hungarian empire has given rise to a series of Austro-
Hungarys, almost as diverse and as beset by minority problems as the
double monarchy itself. In one case at least, the successor state may be
as unviable as the original empire. This is, of course, the case of
Yugoslavia. And the striking fact, particularly from the point of view
of nationalist tensions, is its similarity with the Soviet Union.

In both cases, the content and style of the movements for independence vary considerably according to geographical and historical,
economic and religious factors. Slovenia and the Baltic states are
following the evolution of East Central Europe towards democratic
pluralism; they feel they are part of Europe and are trying to rebuild
their respective Scandinavian or Central European ties and to detach

themselves from their poorer, orthodox, less developed and (according to them at least) less democratic, but more powerful and more numerous Serb and Russian hegemonic neighbours. The Croats and the Ukrainians represent another crucial case. Their respective sizes and economic importance make them strictly indispensable to the survival of Yugoslavia and the Soviet Union. Hence they are both the most dangerous opponents and the most anxiously coveted partners of the Serbs and the Russians. Both the potential conflict and the desperate attempt at avoiding separation are strengthened by the presence of substantial Serbian minorities in Croatia and Russian ones in Ukraine. This overlapping of nationalities is one of the most important reasons that no generally satisfactory solution can be found to the problem of nationalities in either of the two federations.

More widely, in the final analysis the problem of nationalism in the Soviet Union and in Yugoslavia is less that of centrifugal forces than of centripetal ones; in other words, less that of insurgent nationalisms fighting for their independence (or at least their autonomy), for the dissolution of the Union (or at least its radical transformation), than that of the conservative or reactionary nationalism of the two largest republics, Russia and Serbia. The latter have been politically domi-nant, though economically behind, and are tempted to react violently to secessionist attempts in the name of their historical mission, of the greatness of the Union or of the protection of their brethren in the other republics.

Which way will Serbian and Russian nationalism go? This is the central question. In both countries populist nationalism, in which neotraditionalist or religious elements, conservative communist ones and parts of the armed forces would be allied, is a temptation. There are also forces in both countries which prefer progress towards democracy to the struggle to maintain the empire and which think that their nation can only be revived if it does not exhaust itself economically, militarily and psychologically by trying to maintain its supremacy over others.

At the time of writing, the first trend seems to be prevalent in Serbia, judging by the harshness of the repression exercised in Kosovo and by the persistent (although decreasing) popularity of Milosevic. In Russia, on the other hand, the election of Boris Yeltsin as head of the Supreme Soviet and, above all, the fact that under his leadership Russia decided, as did the Baltic States and Uzbekistan before it and Ukraine after it, to declare its autonomy and the primacy of its laws over those of the Soviet Union, and to open direct contacts with the other republics, was perhaps the best news of 1990 for the Soviet Union. It indicates that perhaps a way can be found which (rather than the confrontation between centre and periphery played out between Gorbachev and the Lithuanian government) may lead to a progressive and consensual separation of republics. They would all then negotiate a network of bilateral arrangements with one another rather than with the Kremlin, which would rapidly slide into irrelevancy.

Of course, inequalities of power and wealth, depending on the domestic paths taken by the various republics and on their ability to find other partners outside the Soviet Union, will necessarily reassert themselves and make some common rules and central or international arbitration both indispensable and extremely difficult. Hatreds, resentments and social revolt may also provoke new explosions at any time and jeopardize the process. Certainly, the attitude of Gorbachev and that of his new military allies, as shown by the bloody events of January 1991 in Vilnius and Riga, is not encouraging. Yet one also senses among both Russians and Balts, as well as among other European nationalities, a certain fear of being drawn into the spiral of violence and a certain capacity for control and restraint. But moderation can prevail only if the myth of Soviet unity is exploded and if the Russian nation accepts and welcomes the withering away of its imperial role.

Similarly, it is likely that the only way a mutual escalation of Serbian and Croatian nationalism (not to mention the other peoples of Yugoslavia, particularly the two extremes, Slovania and Kosovo) can be avoided is if Serbia develops an identity which does not presuppose a unitary (let alone a Serbian-led) Yugoslavia. In both cases, only on the basis of separation can a multipolar, decentralized reassociation have a chance.

This does not mean that it would necessarily succeed. Independence – or the right to declare it – may be a necessary condition for peaceful coexistence of national identities once they have achieved self-consciousness. It is not, however, a sufficient one. This is well illustrated by a second category of East European nationalism, that of states which have reached independence at least by the nineteenth century, if not much earlier, in one form or another (e.g. the three historical nations, Poland, Hungary and Bohemia).

As already mentioned, it is clear that mutual ignorance, mistrust, jealousy if not outright hostility, seem more prevalent among the nations of the region than among countries in Western Europe (with the not coincidental exception of Greece and Turkey). In spite of the common fate suffered under Soviet domination, which would lead one to predict a predominantly anti-Russian feeling, old animosities seem to have survived under the cover of socialist internationalism: old rivalries (e.g. between Romanians and Hungarians) still provoke minority problems (e.g. Hungarian minorities in Romania, Yugoslavia and Czechoslovakia, or the Turkish minority in Bulgaria) or unsolved border problems (e.g. between Romania and Bulgaria or, in a sense, the Soviet Union). But leaving aside for the moment the question of why such territorial or minority issues have stopped poisoning relations between Western states like France and Germany or the Scandinavian countries and are still alive in the East, it is striking that even between countries which are not divided by such problems (e.g. Poland and Czechoslovakia) mutual popular feelings tend to be negative in spite of the efforts of internationalist leaders like Vaclav Havel.

There are three main general explanations for this situation. The first, deepest and broadest has to do with the history and culture of East and Central European nations. The British political theorist John Plamenatz has drawn a contrast between Western and Eastern nationalism. Going from West to East, he distinguishes between states (e.g. France and England) in which the growth of national identity has been parallel to that of the state; those in which the nation has preceded the state but where national consciousness was based on a genuine community of language or culture (e.g. Germany and Italy); and those (e.g. Slavic states and Third World countries) in which nationalism is above all a reaction, made up of attraction and repulsion, or irritation and hostility to Western influence or domination.[7]

More specifically, the great Hungarian historian Istvan Bibó and his disciple Janos Szúcks have emphasized the distinctive features of the political development and culture of Central Europe which lead to a distorted or pathological national feeling. Caught between West and East, prevented by the three empires (Austro-Hungarian, Ottoman and Russian) from an evolution towards the nation-state on the Western model, these countries have suffered from a permanent insecurity about their identity and their borders. This had led, according to Bibó, to a kind of 'hysteria' (already present in the German case) expressed in the vital importance given to any territorial or minority dispute, since at any moment nationhood had to be tested against the competing claims of neighbours whose own national legitimacy also relied on mythical or at least debatable historical or linguistic claims.[8]

The second explanation has to do with more recent history, that of communist rule. Above all, of course, this has cut Eastern Europe off from the economic and cultural evolution which has led Western Europe towards more cosmopolitan postnational or at least post-territorial attitudes. More specifically, the negation of national (as well as of social) differences in the name of socialist internationalism or Soviet patriotism has served to exacerbate them: repressed, clandestine feelings re-erupt with a vengeance when given a chance.

The new situation brings new water to the nationalist mill, and this is the third explanation. There is a general desire to 'return to Europe' or to the West. But, on the one hand, since it is obvious that not all former communist states will enter the presumed paradise of the Community together, there is a race to determine who is more truly European and a search for unique Western links, which lead to jealousy or disparagement of Eastern competitors. On the other hand, the repudiation of communist ideology has naturally led to the search for long-repressed traditions as a guide or a refuge in a new and unknown world. Hence, the tendency towards polarization between an orientation towards the West and international interdependence and one towards the past and national identity.

This opposition, which is a new version of the nineteenth-century struggle between Slavophiles and westernizers in Russia, or of the interwar struggle between populists and urbanists in Hungary, is the key to the difference between the two main Hungarian parties, the Democratic Forum and the Alliance of Free Democrats or between the two factions of Solidarity (around Walesa and around Mazowiecki) which have recently split. The opposition is at its starkest in Romania: the leading National Salvation Front exploiting the distrust of the population — influenced more than was expected by decades of national communism in favour of the financial powers of the West and the former emigrés of the bourgeois parties — is following an indigenous path in open defiance (whether on the occasion of the Ceaucescu trial or of the violent intervention of the miners in Bucharest on 14–15 June) of the moral and legal traditions of the West whose help at the same time it solicits.

Recently this has led to a marked difference of emphasis — which may indicate either an emerging split or a division of labour — between Prime Minister Roman and his team of young technocrats, who are trying to reassure the West, and President Iliescu, who shares platforms with the ultranationalist group Vatra Romînească.

The Polish elections have revealed an even more complicated situation, which calls into question any excessively schematic division of the opposition between traditionalists (nationalists) and modernists (westernizers). Walesa's victory is, indeed, that of the Church and the defeat of the secular intelligentsia; but the new president has pledged to continue the same Western-oriented economic and foreign policy. More interestingly still, the amazing election results of the third candidate, Tyminski, reveal the existence of a mood which is both strongly procapitalist (since Tyminski's central promise was instant enrichment) and anti-Western (since he accused Mazowiecki of selling the Polish economy to the West and preached economic warfare).

Of course much of the development of these opposing trends and alternative paths will depend on the success or failure of the entry to Western Europe and on the latter's reaction. Following Plamenatz's definition of Eastern nationalism, nothing can encourage its pathological forms more than failing to join the group of modern democratic or capitalist nations and being rejected by them.

While, in this case, insistence upon national pride and sovereignty and the search for diversion or scapegoats in conflicts with their respective neighbours are likely, interstate wars over territorial issues, as in the past, is not the most serious. Whatever the bitterness of feelings between Hungarians and Romanians, a war between the two states, while less unthinkable than, for instance, one between France and Germany, remains very hard to imagine, certainly much more so than civil war in Yugoslavia or the Soviet Union. Other conflicts between independent East European nations are even less likely to take the form of classic wars. The widespread analogy with the Balkan conflicts and their supposed role in triggering the First World War are therefore misleading. The restraints on interstate warfare imposed by the existence of nuclear weapons, the absence (unlike the situation in the past and in the Third World) of demographic pressures, the primacy of civilian values (whether economic or democratic) and attitudes over military ones, illustrated by the European Community, are likely to constitute powerful disincentives to war.

This relative optimism about interstate hostilities does not, however, necessarily extend to the more diffuse social forms of nationalism. But is nationalism the right word for this phenomenon? The allusion, of course, is to the third level (besides the conflict over the future of multinational states and classic conflicts between nation-states), namely, the twin forces of racism and xenophobia. These do not necessarily follow the boundaries of nation-states. Even more than their neighbours, the targets of their hostility are sub- or transnational groups – only some of which, like national minorities, are actual or potential challengers for territory or sovereignty. Some, like Gypsies, who are the most despised and rejected group almost everywhere in the region, have no territorial claims at all; this is seen as another reason to deny them the legal status and guarantees of national minorities. Others, like Jews, given their drastically reduced numbers all over Eastern Europe, are no longer serious competitors for economic or even political power, but are still (along with freemasons) the object of hostile fantasies inherited from the past. Immigrants and foreign workers are perhaps the most immediate targets of hostility, particularly when the fear of competition for salaries and jobs is combined with racial or ethnic prejudices, as in the case of the Vietnamese workers (brought in by the former regimes and today widely attacked and discriminated against, before being expelled) or Poles (in East Germany). Finally, a more general feeling of distrust and jealousy, if not fear and resentment, towards the outside world, and particularly towards cosmopolitanism and the rich and lucky West is, as already mentioned, very close to the surface in large portions of the population. It does not seem dominant anywhere, with the possible exception of Romania, but it could become so everywhere (judging from the ugly scenes between the most peaceful and bland of the East Central European peoples, the Czechs and the Vietnamese workers) if things turned sour.

The reasons for mutual hostilities among nation-states are more or less the same as those already discussed: insecurity about the identity of an individual, group or nation; seclusion through Soviet rule — hence, the absence, in particular in the GDR, of education about the Nazi past and the cosmopolitan present; disappointment with what is or would be perceived as the disdain of or rejection by the West.

Two particular points, however, merit consideration in the context of the second and third explanations. Interestingly, if discouragingly, the most explosive social issue, that of attitudes towards immigration and foreign workers, cuts both ways. The hostility of East European populations to Vietnamese workers is increasingly likely to find its reflection in West European hostility towards East European immigrant workers. This is the best illustration of the way in which the fates of the two halves of the continent are linked even though the strains of their reunion may lead on both sides and particularly in the West to the desire for a new separation.

One of the main reasons for rejecting pessimistic and deterministic prediction lies in a crucial difference compared with the interwar period. Three models competed then for the souls of East and Central European peoples: Western democracy, which seemed to be tired and declining; fascism, which seemed to be energetic and on the rise; and communism, which appeared to be a dangerous threat to most and an inspiring hope to some. Today the fascist and communist models are dead or discredited, and the liberal-capitalist world appears not only to be the only model available but also to be a great success economically and politically. It is not clear what countermodel the nationalist forces in the East could look to, unless the West prompts them to find one because of its own crisis or retrenchment.

Western Europe: new-style nationalism?

Neither of these two dangers can be easily discounted. And yet it would probably be even more misleading to sound the alarm about Western Europe undoing the work of decades of integration and falling back into the conflicts and violence of the past. Any serious analysis must above all try to avoid the twin dangers of complacency and catastrophism, the two facile assumptions that history is dead or that it must repeat itself.

Something essentially new has indeed happened. One should not minimize the contrast between the disintegration of the East and the integration of the West, the creation of a 'zone of peace' or, to use Karl Deutsch's expression, of a 'security community'[9] between states whose mutual borders are not guarded; war has become unthinkable because of the constraints on their freedom of action and, even more, because the societies they represent have become civilian societies, in which the economic dimension prevails over the military one and individual satisfaction prevails over collective sacrifice.

By the same token, however, one should not be blind to the fact that this new situation creates new problems and awakens old nostalgias, that international peace and interdependence do not exclude inequalities among states but are likely to create new ones, that they do not suppress domestic violence but rather may encourage it in compensation, that the opening of borders does not suppress the need for community, solidarity and exclusion (or at least for distinction between 'us' and 'them') but may, on the contrary, exacerbate such feelings out of frustration.

As in the case of Eastern Europe, these reactions and attitudes cannot necessarily be identified with nationalism in the strict sense, but here again, they cannot be entirely dissociated from it. Again three cases may be distinguished. The first is that of the new inequalities of power, and of the temptations, jealousies and fears they may provoke among nations. Of course the central phenomenon in this respect, in 1989–90, was the unification of Germany.

The second case is the reaction against the anonymity and uncontrollability of modern society and the loss of identity it entails for traditional groups or institutions such as the nation–state. Here the progress of European integration increases these fears and is sometimes used as a scapegoat.

But, as in Eastern Europe, both the main scapegoat and the real problem are the increase in immigration and the economic, social and cultural strains it increasingly entails. This is the main source of political danger from the extreme Right.

Among these three phenomena, of course, much confusion, but also many genuine combinations, compensations or reinforcements, are to be observed. But this is no reason not to try to look first of all at their specific features.

In particular, precisely because of its central importance for the construction of Europe, its racist past and its exposure to the problem of immigration, from the south and the east, it is important to be precise about the German problem, about German power and about the nationalist reactions it may provoke among Germans and non-Germans.

First, no one should deny that in the world of interdependence inequalities of economic power exist and that they have political consequences. Within the European Community, the Federal Republic has been the most powerful partner. In spite of temporary difficulties, unity will reinforce this inequality. The role of the Federal Republic's economic strength inevitably produces (contrary to the thesis of some German academics, according to whom, as a result of European integration and domestic pluralism, Germany has reached a postnational stage at which the economy can no longer be used politically) a political and a psychological fall-out. This was obvious in the attraction which the Federal Republic's economic strength exercised both on the population of East Germany and on Gorbachev, and which was used by Chancellor Kohl with great political determination and effect. A new German self-confidence, already visible economically, has made its appearance on the political level.

On the other hand, before speaking of the danger of German nationalism, the other side of the coin should not be overlooked. There is not the slightest evidence of German militarism or of the romantic, mystical, missionary or conquering nationalism which characterized several periods of German history even outside the Nazi period. The mood of the population is predominantly pacifist and welfare-oriented. The undeniable new assertiveness is basically an arrogance of wealth and competence (the 'Deutschmark nationalism' criticized by Habermas[10]) certainly not, at least in this generation, of military power. For instance, there is still the same reluctance to play even a peace-keeping role outside Europe.

Of course, German unity may usher in a new period, going beyond the bourgeois satisfactions and the quest for acceptance of the postwar Federal Republic. There are some signs of this search for a new (or renewed) identity. One is the 'historians' quarrel' of the late 1980s, although it ended with the defeat of the revisionist school. The strength of the Right in the former GDR is another. But, again, one cannot overemphasize that the uniting of Germany was neither preceded nor followed by any great mood of national exaltation. It was essentially the effect of the opening of the Wall and of the inability of the East German economy to function without being separated from the West German one. The government, the opposition and the population of the FRG had all accepted the division. Certainly, Chancellor Kohl seized the opportunity of exploiting the inevitable and becoming the Chancellor of German unity. This did not go without some elements of hubris and unilateralism, notably in his dealings with Moscow. But, again, it is not at all clear that the population in either West or East Germany is particularly receptive to this mood; on the contrary, available evidence points to the primacy of economic considerations and a mood of mutual distrust and irritation with the consequences for individuals, in particular for employment in the two Germanys.

Polls indicate an increased interest in the European Community, which had declined in recent years. And the Kohl government itself, in spite of the unilateralist features of his diplomatic tactics, has successfully reaffirmed Germany's commitment to the West, including Nato, and even more importantly, to progress towards a United States of Europe.

Again, all this may change. But for the time being, the only really worrying tendency in Germany is towards hostility to foreigners, particularly to migrants from the East and from the Third World. But that is a general phenomenon which is not specific to Germany and has found much more serious political expression in other Western countries.

Even in attitudes to Europe, the danger of a new emphasis on national sovereignty rather than on supranational integration as a result of German hegemony may be stronger in countries like France and Great Britain than in Germany itself. In the Soviet Union and Yugoslavia, the problem, as suggested elsewhere in this essay, lies less with the independentist nationalisms of the smaller republics than with the Russian and Serbian reactions. In Europe, it may lie less with the nationalism of the potential hegemonic power, Germany, than with its partners who used to consider themselves its equals. There seems to be no contradiction between these two judgments: in both cases, the fears of those who see their established positions threatened may lead to more irrational actions than will the aspirations of those who see the trends going their way. Conversely, it may be the former who hold the key to the solution: the best chance of preventing German nationalism from becoming imperialistic or adventurous is for the other European states to unite and create a friendly counterweight within a common framework.

This is indeed what many political leaders and movements within these countries are advocating. But the most vocal reaction represents the opposite trend. Its most spectacular and caricatural expression was the declaration of the former British Secretary for Trade and Industry, Mr Ridley, accusing the Germans of seeking to dominate Europe, and the French of acting like their poodles, and claiming that any surrender of monetary sovereignty to the European Community was equivalent to capitulation to Adolf Hitler. Without going to these extremes, it is clear that, in France, both on the Right of the political spectrum with Le Pen and to some extent, with part of the Gaullist party going back on their recent conversion to Europe, and on the Left (with the Chevènement wing of the Socialist Party and the former revolutionary writer and Mitterrand aide Régis Debray), important factions of public opinion claim that the uniting of Germany has made nonsense of the uniting of Europe, that the Community can from now on only be an instrument of German power, and that France should imitate Germany in following its own interest and in giving priority to the preservation of its national identity.

It seems that the fear of German hegemony serves as the catalyst for a variety of feelings. One is bitterness at the loss of the positions of France and Britain as great powers, a loss consummated by the Second World War and decolonization but which had been slowed down or partly masked by the Cold War and the limitations on German sovereignty. Another is perplexity at the anonymity of modern society, at the loss of control by the nation-state or by any other concrete, recognizable community. A third is the perception of a threat to national identity coming, on the one hand, from the cosmopolitanism and standardization of mass culture and consumption (often seen as 'Americanization') and, on the other hand, the influx of immigrants who, for racial or religious reasons are often seen as alien or hostile. Individual, social and national insecurity, the preoccupation with law and order, jobs and the nation are thus combined into one complex syndrome in which external threats and internal doubts are hard to disentangle.

Italy has surprised everybody, including itself, with the spectacular electoral success (in the spring of 1990) of the Northern Leagues (notably in the regions of Lombardy, Piedmont and Veneto). What is fascinating about them is that they reproduce the North–South cleavage as it is found in Yugoslavia, Europe as a whole (including Eastern Europe and the Soviet Union) and the world. The modern, industrious and efficient North refuses to pay taxes which, it says, will go to the corrupt and inefficient central bureaucracy in Rome and to the criminal mafia in the South, and more generally will subsidize the backward and lazy South. In fact, the phenomenon is as much a reaction against immigration to the North (both from the south of Italy and from Africa) as against centralization and corruption.

Overall, retrenchment, whether local, regional, national or continental, whether economic, political, religious or racial, is the great temptation. The contrast between the search for economic progress and the fear of insecurity, between the crumbling of boundaries and the nostalgia for closed and stable communities, is the greatest and most general problem.

It seems clear that, despite all their important differences, Eastern and Western Europe must both face the problem and learn to live with it.

Europe: East and West, North and South

The Cold War meant the primacy of East–West issues. With its end, they lost both their primacy and their specificity in favour of North–South relations. Not only is the situation most dramatic in the Third World, particularly in Africa, not only are the targets of racism and the candidates for immigration into Europe and the wandering homeless refugees primarily Asians and Africans, but East–West relations themselves are increasingly taking on a North–South character. Of course neither the economic backwardness nor the cultural distance from the West are the same in the Soviet Union, let alone in east Central Europe, as they are in Africa. But the primacy of social and economic divisions and conflicts over ideological and military ones is coming to Europe too. The problem of relations with Poland, as with most Third World countries, centres on debt-relief and immigration. What Mexico is to the United States and what the Maghreb is to France, the south and east of Europe (Turks and Yugoslavs yesterday, East Germans, *Aussiedler* from Russia, and Poles today) are to Germany or Austria. The tendency for rich, Western countries to close their borders as poor countries open theirs operates in the direction of the former Iron Curtain as well as the Mediterranean. The unemployment inevitably caused by economic reform in Eastern Europe will, just as inevitably, increase the search for jobs in Western Europe; hence the feeling that the population of the latter is being besieged. The racism which is spreading all over Europe, including Scandinavia, will be directed towards Poles and Russians as well as towards Arabs, and will turn, create anti-Western nationalism and resentment in the East. It will be small consolation that both sides will have a common hostility towards Gypsies and Jews.

This apocalyptic scenario is not inevitable, however. What is inevitable is the interaction between xenophobia or, simply, rejection and exclusion in the West and in the East. A vicious circle can be avoided if political action and solidarity actively try to channel and steer the inevitable conflictual communication provoked by economic and cultural interdependence in the direction of gradual integration.

The main problem of Europe is destabilization through openness: economic destabilization through trade, cultural destabilization through immigration. If handled unilaterally, these destabilizations will lead to mutual, if imperfect, closure and to mutual resentment. If handled together they may, in the long run, be to the benefit of all. This is particularly true for international institutions. The Conference on Security and Cooperation in Europe has no more important task than contributing to the multilateral management not only of territorial and minority conflicts, but also of the mutual opening of societies through communications and migrations. The Community must develop an immigration policy in close coordination with the home countries of the potential immigrants from the East and the South. Unilateral measures of closure or exclusive bilateral exceptions can only make the problem worse.

Conclusions

This survey will end with two thoughts about the future of Europe, nationalism and, above all, peace and democracy.

Peaceful coexistence is more necessary than ever. But now the problem lies not so much at the level of opposing social systems, alliances and superpowers as at the level of independent nation-states; and the peaceful coexistence of economic, social, cultural and religious communities in everyday life and at the local as well as at the national or continental levels is even more crucial.

To put it more abstractly, if one distinguishes between three levels of relations in Europe, strategic interaction, economic interdependence and social interpenetration, the chances of nationalism and the dangers to peace are to be found less on the first level than on the second and third, and particularly in their interplay. The most difficult problem is the sociocultural one, but the way economic interdependence is achieved can either exacerbate or alleviate it.

To ensure a positive outcome, the opponents of nationalism, the friends of universalism and tolerance, of peace and freedom must themselves undergo a conversion of their own. In the nineteenth century, there were three revolutionary ideologies which were sometimes allied and sometimes in conflict: liberalism, nationalism and socialism. The last two have led, through fascism and communism, through Hitler and Stalin, to such monstrous crimes and failures that they are fatally discredited, and have left the field wide open to the first. Today we are witnessing the triumph of liberalism, both in its political aspects (representative democracy) and in its economic aspects (capitalism). This is not simply a temporary fashion since it corresponds to the only system which has stood the double test of legitimacy and efficiency. But it is not a final and complete solution to the problem of peace and democracy either. We know through bitter experience that there is no substitute for freedom and that no state, system or alliance (be it as large as China or as small as Albania) can close itself off from the modern world without ultimate failure and collapse. But we also know that humanity cannot live on freedom and universality alone, that the aspirations which have led to nationalism and socialism, the search for community and identity and the search for equality and solidarity, will always reassert themselves − and are doing so now. It is to the extent that liberalism can incorporate and reconcile them with the freedom of the individual and with the interdependence of the planet that, after having won the Cold War, it will ultimately win the peace.

PART FIVE

TENSIONS

10

Beyond Nationalism and Internationalism: Monstrosity and Hope

P EACE OR WAR? Utopia or nightmare? Global solidarity or tribal conflict? Nationalism triumphant or the crisis of the nation-state? Progress on civil rights or persecution of minorities? New world order or new anarchy? There seems no end to the fundamental dilemmas and anguished questions provoked by the post-Cold-War world. One is almost tempted to turn to the language of myth and fairy tale. Perhaps we should blame the witches and bad fairies who made their wishes over the cradle of the latest born of the international systems. Perhaps the prince has been turned into a monster and will never recover his original form. Perhaps the fall of the Soviet empire has torn a hole in the heavens and in the ground underfoot, allowing us to glimpse through the ruins of the postwar structures both the shining prospect of a global community and the swarming menace of unrestrained violence.

The last image may indicate a starting point for our analysis. For, aren't aspects of the present situation so disturbing precisely because in some respects they bring us back before the nation-state and in others they project us beyond it?

From paralysis to anarchy?

Bipolarism had imposed severe limitations on the sovereignty and freedom of action enjoyed by individual states, particularly within the Soviet sphere of influence, as well as on international economic and cultural cooperation, at least behind the Iron Curtain. It was therefore to be expected that the decline and fall of the old bipolar world would provoke a renaissance of nations, opening them up to outside influences and encouraging their independence and inter-dependence. What was less sure and the subject of much debate was the form a new equilibrium among states would take, whether it would be multipolar rather than bipolar, a new bipolarity based on a North–South rather than an East–West divide, or global cooperation based on universal interdependence and solidarity. What has trans-formed the situation entirely is that, although each of these tenden-cies made some initial progress, they were disrupted and thrown off course, if not swept away entirely, in a tide of disintegration and anarchy.

First there was the break-up of the former communist multinational groupings – bloody and horrific beyond belief in Yugoslavia, peaceful and circumspect in Czechoslovakia, chaotic and occasionally violent but thus far relatively restrained in the Soviet Union. It subsequently became apparent that, within and between the newly independent nations, conflict was a more likely outcome than cooperation. The fact that they were so closely interconnected multiplied the problems of minorities and frontiers. Their interrupted historical development and long-suppressed sense of identity make them aspire to an im-possible homogeneity, one they can only begin to achieve by a process of ethnic cleansing intolerable to their minorities and to neighbouring states. Between a desired but impossible homogeneity and an inevitable but repudiated heterogeneity, the way is opened up for violence, leading to isolation and open conflict. Inevitably the violence spreads, involving the older nations and those more favour-ably placed by virtue of the war or by their geography or relative prosperity. Ethnic cleansing and war add fuel to the fires of economic inequality, or the aspiration towards an urban life style, by resurrect-ing, in scenes of dire emergency, that most devastating and appalling phenomenon of the mass exodus. But this happens at the very time when the developed nations are in the grip not only of economic crisis but also of a crisis of identity caused by the interdependence and impersonality of modern society, when they therefore tend to close themselves off, for fear of destabilization. Factional, corporate and national selfishness combine with xenophobia or racism to reinforce this exclusivism.

On the defensive, the developed democratic states don't know how to respond to the contradictory challenges from without and within, their own citizens' desire for security and community (achieved at the price of a closed society), and appeals for aid and assistance not only from new nations but above all from victims everywhere of war and oppression. As if that were not enough, their paralysis is compounded by the restraints, mostly economic, imposed on them from the outside by market forces or the law of survival of the fittest.

This dialectic between 'open' and 'closed' is taking place in a kind of chaos, in which the refugees are only one element of flux, one of many transnational forces or agencies, along with the media, financial speculators and traffickers in arms or drugs. It is a chaos that equilibrium or negotiations between states seem increasingly powerless to combat, even when the states in question are engaged in a common endeavour such as the building of Europe.

A new middle ages?

The existence of chaos nevertheless implies an aspiration to order. And it is here that we begin to see how the challenge to the sovereignty and efficacy of states relates to a supranational, if not universalist, imperative, as well as a subnational or particularist one. What is in question here is not merely the world order established at Yalta, the bipolar order, or that of Versailles, of the frontiers and states that formed part of the Ottoman and Austro-Hungarian empires, it is the order of the treaties of Westphalia, based on the territoriality and sovereignty of states. These states may have been unequal, with the great powers taking it upon themselves to decide the fate of the smaller nations, but the order they represented was nevertheless horizontal, in that it recognized no superior authority to the state as such. According to the Hobbesian definition taken up and expanded by Max Weber and Raymond Aron, the state has the monopoly of legitimate violence internally and retains for itself the right to use force externally. Today, civil wars and social violence challenge the internal monopoly, while interdependence, nuclear weapons and changing values make the legitimacy of interstate war problematic. The trends of transnational deterritorialization and ethnic reterritorialization call into question that great creation that is the modern state, the neutral authority that makes common citizenship of a territory more important than blood ties and religious divisions. The sheer diversity of types of agency, allegiance and conflict takes us back in some respects to the sixteenth century, dominated by the power of the mercantile towns and by religious wars, or even to the middle ages, with its mix of disorder and rigid hierarchy. But a middle ages without a pope or an emperor, even if the UN and United States do attempt, in a somewhat ambivalent and contradictory manner, to fulfil those roles. To put it another way, the problem we face is that of legitimacy, the need for a common spiritual authority respected by all, such as would be capable of imposing a truce or inspiring a crusade; also the need for a temporal authority capable of putting a sword into service, or accommodating under its aegis the innumerable warring factions that exist in a heterogeneous world.

The nuclear problem is a case in point. During the Cold War, the dominant issue was deterrence. The effect was to strengthen the sovereignty of the nuclear states and establish between them an equilibrium which, although intended as the means of instituting a dialogue to avoid the possibility of accident, also meant the acceptance of restrictions imposed by an autonomous entity divorced from the individual societies concerned. The idea that the two could be divorced was severely dented by the nuclear arms race of the 1980s and the Chernobyl catastrophe. But it was the dissolution of the Soviet Union that presented the major threat to the idea of US–Soviet nuclear equilibrium, as also to the French conception of a deterrence from the weak to the strong, while bringing the new issue of nuclear proliferation to the fore. This was compounded by the problem of the ex-Soviet nuclear republics, by radioactive contamination over the whole of the CIS and its neighbouring territories, the availability to other powers of its technicians and hardware, the trade in fissionable materials – and also, the fact that aspiring nuclear powers with aggressive objectives and ideologies, such as Iraq, Iran and North Korea, were within an inch of achieving their aims. Clearly, while deterrence could be treated as a matter of autonomous interstate logic, proliferation, on the contrary, threatened not only the strategic but also the political and economic domains, where it was indissociably linked with the problems of internal anarchy, economic crisis, terrorism and the arms trade. Solutions in their turn could not be derived from a diplomatic/strategic equilibrium. To be realistic, they required control to be exercised over societies and transnational movements, the logical culmination of which would be a world government, or at very least an international authority based on agreement between the great powers to control and sanction subsequent transgressors, as in the case of Iraq, hitherto unique.

That country's regime survived defeat at the hands of a US-led coalition in a war of aggression condemned by the UN. It is now subject to an embargo, obliged on pain of military reprisals to divulge and dismantle its nuclear installations, and to accept the existence on its territory of a zone where foreign powers protect a persecuted minority against its own government. Is this situation an anomaly, arising because of a unique conjunction of the economic and strategic interests of the dominant power, in this case the United States? Does it presage a move to the rule of law and the establishment of a world authority represented by the UN, or the opposite, a return to the practices of the nineteenth century and the interwar years, of which we were recently reminded by Ghassan Salamé: times of humanitarian intervention, protectorate and mandate, the equivalent of a new colonialization? Or are we for the foreseeable future committed to an era of compromise, one of 'permanent transition', where from the triple point of view of funtionality, legitimacy and power there will be coexistence, sometimes consensual sometimes conflictual, among the national, regional and universal, where morality and law, politics and the economy, humanitarian motives and military power will be as distinct in theory and as indissociable in practice as are the internal and the external, the public and private worlds?

Problems such as Cambodia, the former Yugoslavia, Somalia, indicate that the first interpretation, focusing on vested interests and power and uniquely applicable to Iraq, can only be partly true. But the second and third do not supply the whole answer either. Therefore, lest we are tempted to give up in the face of all this uncertainty, we should first try to understand a little more clearly the way the various elements of the international world fit together, as well as the disparities and disjunctions between them.

My thesis, in so far as I have one, starts with that 'gap between interdependence and control' Karl Deutsch sees as characteristic of international relations.[1] Equally, one could think in terms of a combination of interconnectedness and heterogeneity. Economic and social phenomena are dominated by transnational interaction, interdependence and interconnection, but these do not necessarily lead to equality or cooperation, at least in the short term, but quite as often to inequality and conflict between nations. The states that take the lead in such relations have less and less control over them, especially in determining the degree to which their respective societies will be open or closed. And their loss of control is not necessarily, or even usually, compensated for by other organs of regulation.

This gap between interdependence and control, in so far as it leads to greater openness, also creates instability. It is salutary for freedom of communications, but also for financial speculation or illegal trafficking. It encourages freedom of movement, but also its dysfunctioning, the tragic paradox of millions of displaced persons caught between countries of origin from which they are in flight and countries of destination from which they are barred. These phenomena in their turn produce different reactions, causing some to retreat inside their communities, others to participate in movements of transnational solidarity, admittedly often selective. These movements in their turn may provoke, overwhelm or restrict the actions of states: sometimes they may cause states to modify their ideas, perhaps lead them towards more enduring associations, regional or even global, in the service of causes extending beyond their immediate interests, anything from human rights to the fate of the planet. What they cannot do, especially where military intervention is in question, is take over their responsibilities or substitute for their plurality.

This amounts in effect to a confirmation of the Kantian contradictions. In his *Perpetual Peace*, Kant puts forward as a condition for peace the adoption by states of a republican or juridical constitution respecting the rights of man (article 1), and a cosmopolitan perspective applying to every individual, not as a citizen but as an inhabitant of the planet (article 3). And yet the central article, dealing with the relations between states, retreats in the face of the idea of a world state or even a true federation, falling back instead on the notion of a voluntary alliance of free states against war (article 2). True, the two supplements add two further dimensions that, in their different ways, transform the conditions of interstate relations. On the one hand, the guarantee of eternal peace is to be found in the role of trade and the costs of war. On the other hand, the 'secret article' requires that we leave it to the philosophers to make public the arguments for universalism.

That is very much the dialectic that seems to be operating today. In an order dominated by power struggles, the universal makes itself felt, because of material factors (economic interdependence, the communications revolution, nuclear and ecological dangers), in forms that might be summed up in the triad: *conscience* (with particular reference to abominations and injustices), *experts* (the recognition of independent authorities), and *concert* (consensus of the dominant powers as to common principles and interests). But for all that these transform the international scene, they by no means constitute a world organization capable of representing the international community and making law and solidarity prevail.

Communications and commerce

It was not by chance that the first multilateral and global international organizations, established in the nineteenth century, had to do with communications (freedom of navigation, postal and telegraphic services, railways, etc.), nor that they have been succeeded in the twentieth by organizations concerned with work (the ILO) and the coordination of international economic relations (the Bretton Woods system). It is in the latter area that international law (still centrally based on interstate relations and the mutual agreements, accords and treaties embodying them) most widely reflects the breaking down of rigid divisions between public and private, internal and external, presiding over the emergence of non-state agencies such as multinational firms and autonomous zones of 'flexible' or 'soft' law.[2] There is a sense in which the European Community and its Court of Justice represent the spearhead of a move to link interdependence and law. But, aside from this exceptional arena of peaceful and legal exchanges that constitutes relations within the developed Western world, we should not under-estimate either the dynamic of interdependence/communications/human rights in the relations with the East and the South. In the case of the Soviet Union, it was openness to the West, made inevitable by the need for aid and exchanges, and the impossibility of controlling the impact of the media, that opened up the breach into which *glasnost* and *perestroika* disappeared. From the transistor to the television, and to the fax, modern technology has opened up the possibilities of new sorts of manipulation, and at the same time imposed limitations on the dialogue between governments and their subjects. Similarly, in the West, the impact of televised horrors from Vietnam to Somalia has for the first time given some reality (albeit restricted to media coverage) to the Kantian notion that 'a violation of right on one part of the planet is being felt everywhere'; it creates, even if fleetingly, a sense of solidarity or transnational outrage that, just occasionally, has repercussions on governmental decisions on military intervention or withdrawal, although less influence on economic aid or support.

Conscience and competence

The media revolution has spectacularly reinforced a trend that began after the Second World War, as a dialectic was instituted among ethical considerations, shifts of opinion and state policy. This may be defined, at a general level, as the process of the emergence of the individual and the universal onto the international stage. Three distinct waves of activity may be identified. Immediately after the Second World War, the experience of genocide gave birth to the notion of the 'crime against humanity', and led to the Universal Declaration of Human Rights adopted by the UN in 1948. Influenced by decolonization and debates among the West, East and South on collective rights and economic and social rights, this led eventually to the various agreements of 1966. In the 1970s, the Vietnam war, the fate of the boat people, the struggle of Eastern dissidents and the nuclear threat persuaded the orphans of *Realpolitik* and revolution alike of the pressing claims of human rights, world suffering and the future of the planet.

Non-governmental movements and organizations such as Amnesty International and Médecins sans Frontières or, in the ecological sphere, Greenpeace, to a very large extent replaced political movements. But the Conference on Security and Cooperation in Europe (CSCE), particularly its third session, and the politics of President Carter, gave intergovernmental and institutional expression to their concerns at the regional level. The European Court of Human Rights, because of its right to hear cases brought by individuals, struck a body blow to government monopoly. And finally, Bernard Kouchner and Mario Bettati, as representatives of the French government, launched the campaign that culminated in an initial acceptance by the UN of the right of intervention on humanitarian grounds, bringing recognition for an idea that from the outset depended on the violation of frontiers and sovereignty.

Another aspect of the legitimacy of the non-governmental agencies in their dealings with states is the attention paid by the latter to independent technological or ethical authorities. In the same way as, in the economic sphere, reports from intergovernmental organizations such as the Organization for Economic Cooperation and Development (OECD), the Bank for International Settlements (BIS), and other expert bodies, lavish praise, blame and advice on governments, so too do the denunciations of Amnesty International or reports requested by the Secretary-General of the UN have a decisive influence on the fate of individual governments. States are not obliged to take their advice, but it is increasingly difficult for them to ignore it. The idea of inspection rights, institutionalized by the CSCE, has become accepted, and with it the idea that governments cannot use the argument of sovereignty or the dangers of interference in their internal affairs as a basis for refusing to answer to their peers or to world opinion as to the manner in which they treat their citizens.

Is it possible to go beyond expressions of outrage or solidarity, beyond such declarations of principle and demands for explanation? That is the question posed by the third period of these developments, in the post-Cold-War 1990s. The inherent logic of bipolarity was that expressed by Khrushchev in his confrontation with the UN Secretary-General Dag Hammarskjöld: 'There are neutral countries, there are no neutral men.' While neutral countries had acquired the status of covetable objects, international organizations and humanitarian actions, campaigns for the rights of man or for peace, ran a permanent risk of serving as the tool of one or other camp, or at least being seen as doing so by the other power. Once the confrontation between the two was ended by the defeat of totalitarianism, it was clear that would prove an embarrassment for the non-aligned countries, but it was also possible to hope for a golden age, in which the United Nations, humanitarianism, human rights, solidarity and ecology would replace the arms race and the indirect confrontation of the two superpowers. Some of these things have come to pass. The UN has indeed returned to occupy centre stage. But the collapse of a number of states and the upsurge of ethnic conflicts has created emergency situations which, in making the need for help and arbitration even more pressing, have also made the whole exercise more difficult. Certain institutions such as the CSCE, which was supposed to foster cooperative notions of security and implement peaceful settlements of conflict, have in the event been rapidly reduced to impotence. The same is true of the efforts at mediation made by the CSCE, the UN or ad hoc institutions like the commission of arbitration proposed by France in the case of the former Yugoslavia. In the phrase of Jean-François Deniau, 'We wanted the rule of law without the use of force, we got the use of force without the rule of law.'

Concert and constraints

It is precisely this relationship between rule of law and use of force, between legitimacy and power, that lies at the heart of current difficulties. Whether we are dealing with collective security or humanitarian aid, it is the question of intervention, and specifically military intervention, that has become central. Remarkably, it is no longer rejected so much in principle, in the name of sovereignty or non-interference in the internal affairs of states. In the preceding decades, it seemed that the sole acceptable justification for military intervention was defensive, with the exception of wars of liberation or independence, even to the point where interventions like that of Vietnam against Pol Pot or of Tanzania against Idi Amin were represented by their instigators as responses to aggression. Today on the other hand there is a continuity in UN resolutions allowing free access to victims (43,131, 8 December 1988), humanitarian corridors (45,100), resolution 678 of 29 November 1990, authorizing the use of force against Iraq as aggressor against Kuwait, 688, concerning the protection of the Kurds in Iraq, 706, enjoining Iraq to sell its oil in order to give humanitarian aid to its population, and finally 794, of 3 December 1992, authorizing measures of a military nature 'to establish as soon as possible the necessary conditions for the delivery of humanitarian assistance wherever needed in Somalia'.

What matters today is the identity and legitimacy of the authority determining the intervention, the means it uses and results it achieves, and above all, the structure of the international order it presupposes or promotes.

The new turn of events that makes an appeal to the UN an effective proposition is the unblocking of the situation in the Security Council, by reason of the non-use of the Soviet and Chinese vetoes, the fact that between the permanent members of the Security Council, from the most powerful down, and the Secretary-General of the UN, a minimal consensus exists that makes multilateral action possible.

Does that mean, then, that in Korea, the Gulf or Somalia, we were looking at UN operations as such? In the last case, yes, as the initiative came from the Secretary-General, but the first two are better described as operations determined on and conducted by the United States, with the authorization and multilateral legitimization of the Security Council. But in what sense can that body be said to represent either the law or the international community? That in a nutshell is the problem of the representativeness of an organism based on states not peoples and, among those states, on a hierarchy dating back to 1945 and including no permanent members from Germany, Japan or the Third World.

It is clear that, before one could begin to talk of an international community making or applying the law, there would need to be a fundamental reform of the UN, covering the composition and powers of the Security Council and the powers of the Secretary-General, together with the establishment of a permanent or ad hoc supra-national military force, charged, as Boutros Boutros-Ghali has asked, on the one hand with preventive action, and on the other with imposing peace, as opposed to keeping a peace that has already been achieved. Above all it would need to be given the resources and personnel appropriate to its enlarged role. Today its various operations founder because of lack of resources or lack of freedom of action, and the states that most pride themselves on its existence, like the United States, are by no means the first to pay up when it comes to financing the organization.

True, there are already hints of this new preventive role, for example in sending the blue berets to Macedonia. True also that temporary UN trusteeship would seem the only solution for certain countries or territories in the grip of anarchy or war, such as Nagorno-Karabakh, Bosnia-Herzegovina or Somalia. True, in 1992 as in 1960, it only needed a Secretary-General willing to assert himself for the states – on whom in the last analysis he depends – to be obliged to take account of his views and accord him a sort of vague representativeness in his own right. But the fact remains that the reality of the world order, in so far as such a thing exists, is less like a global judicial community and more like the nineteenth-century concert of Europe, if not actually the Holy Alliance itself. It is an agreement of the great powers (within the framework of the Security Council or G7) to avoid conflicts among themselves, to limit the spread of other types of confrontation, to try to manage the death throes or convalescence of the 'sick men' of Europe (in the same way as the Ottoman Empire was the 'sick man' of the nineteenth century), and generally to try to keep anarchy within bounds in the environment.

The paradox is that, once again, the demands emanating from this environment far exceed the protection or control that is on offer, let alone conquest or domination by hegemonic powers.

The United States, Western Europe and Japan have in a sense become masters of the world by default, because their adversaries collapsed and because, having eliminated war from their own relationship, however much their interests may diverge, whatever the sometimes ruthless competition that exists between them, they are united by the bonds of liberal ideology and the capitalist economy. But they have neither the doctrine nor the psychological inclination or desire, nor probably the resources, that would make them want to govern the rest of the world, especially if that implied policies of genuine openness and active, lasting intervention.

How then is it possible to create a new world order? At the Congress of Vienna in 1815, dynastic legitimacy was the solution Metternich had to offer. In Versailles in 1918, Wilson had another answer, the right of peoples to self-determination, or the nationality principle. Both these men had the power to redraw the map. Today it is the Western countries, whose victory in the Cold War has given them no such powers, that must ask all the questions. What is a nation? Who has the right to a state? How to arbitrate among historical legitimacy, self-determination, economic viability and acceptance by other powers in the region? How to choose between two evils, moving frontiers or moving populations? The new concert has no coherent answers to offer because there are none, because for the most part they could not in any case be imposed from outside, but also because liberal ideology can offer no more than frequently self-contradictory universal principles, a preference for negotiation and multilateralism, and a dislike for the use of force. This ideology risks leaving the world without defence against those who worship at the shrine of the passions of fear, hate or glory, not the values of pluralism and compromise.

The Western democracies are the more disinclined to revive the old imperial scenario, as it goes against the whole tenor of the development of their way of life and historical consciousness. The emphasis on the individual, the respect for human life and dislike of risk that characterize democratic societies, as well as the bad conscience and bitter taste left by the colonial past and adventures such as the Vietnam war, encourage them rather to retreat from the prospect of military action. That is clearly true of Europe, the various French military expeditions and Great Britain's intervention in the Falklands notwithstanding. But nor is the United States any less constrained by these considerations, even though it is the only nation capable of intervening on a world scale and more inclined than any other to do so. Whenever that country makes an intervention, its excessive deployment of human and technological resources is primarily explicable by the concern to keep loss of life to a minimum.

More generally, the ambiguous or contradictory nature of the relationship between the military and the humanitarian is to be explained by the fact that the latter is not only a moral imperative, it is also an ideology, one of the few, along with nationalism, that can still attract popular support, helped by the sensitizing effect of the media. A humanitarian effort on the ground, when halted by tyranny or anarchy, must in practice make appeal to the political and hence eventually to the military. In its turn it may be used as a hostage by these tyrannical or anarchical forces, and in this way become an obstacle to the intervention it both longs for and dreads. It may then be used as an alibi for the political or military inaction of governments: that at least is the reproach levelled at the French style of humanitarian state aid. Conversely, it may also be used as an alibi for action or intervention. The various US expeditions are only justifiable in the eyes of the public when they are undertaken in the name of what is right and for humanitarian reasons, not to serve national or geopolitical interests. In the case of Somalia, what is at stake is to feed the starving, even if it is clear that humanitarian or military intervention has no value unless it is prompt, unless it leads on to local projects of long-term protection and reconstruction (which today could only be multilateral) and unless also it is accompanied by a willingness on the part of the home country or countries to receive and support those under their protection, their persons, customs and the products of their labour.

There can be no intervention without integration. That is the twofold duty of which empires acquitted themselves rather admirably, a task rejected however by the democratic societies and nation-states in crisis, which tend to retreat into their shells. That is true of the United States which, despite more open immigration policies, nevertheless sends refugees from Haiti back to sea. It is even more true of the European Community, whose member countries cannot so much as contemplate the possibility of a common approach to the problem of immigrants, including former detainees from the Yugoslav camps, the responsibility for whom they are content to leave to more immediate neighbours like Germany (where as we know reactions of xenophobia have been the result, and which in its turn has unloaded the problem onto even more vulnerable countries such as Poland, Hungary or Croatia).

Selections and limitations

Does that mean to say that the centre can and should retreat into its fortress or shelter behind its doors and, as some have suggested, simply let the 'new barbarians' get on with it?[3] It is tempting to do so, but clearly it is neither an acceptable option morally nor realistic politically, ecomomically or strategically. The West cannot send back all immigrants − and indeed in the long term it needs them − nor can it censor the media which brings horrors into every home, nor can it escape the transnational influences by which it is linked to the periphery, even if these take the form of drugs, pollution or nuclear proliferation. But the action it takes will always be selective and limited, and therefore relative and disputable. Contrary to the views of those who see humanitarian action as being something only for doctors, political or miltary intervention as being justified only as a function of tangible economic or geopolitical interests, and for whom international law is something that happens only in the Court of Justice at The Hague, there is in fact a vast grey area, whose ambiguities should not serve as a pretext for inaction. In the case of Hitler or Pol Pot, can we ever decide if the intervention that deprived them of further victims was humanitarian or political, if it was more because of the need to save lives or to deter other would-be ethnic cleansers?

There are three types of case in which intervention has to be regarded as an option: aggression by one recognized state against another; the massacre by a totalitarian state of its own citizens, whether for ideological or ethnic reasons; the collapse of the apparatus of state in a country descending into anarchy. Iraq, Cambodia and Somalia are examples of each of these cases, while former Yugoslavia in a sense is a combination of all three.

Obviously the concert, if it exists, cannot intervene in all civil wars or wars of aggression, or against every tyranny, any more than it can put a stop to all famines or natural disasters or integrate all the nations on the periphery. Choices always have to be made, and these choices, as well as corresponding to a calculation of interests, costs and risks, always involve some quite arbitrary factor. That relativism, however, is tempered by the two following considerations. First, there are cases where calculation concerns only the means to be employed, action being an absolute requirement: few would deny that Hitler's genocide was such a case. And there are also means that would have the effect of destroying the whole object of the exercise, whatever that may be: once again, few would deny that, whatever the horrors of the Gulag, it would have been indefensible to blow up the planet or annihilate the Soviet population in order to eliminate Stalin. Between these two extreme positions, however, there exists a broad band of cases in which unconsidered action is as much to be condemned as inaction. That the United States may intervene in Somalia because it does not involve any risk but cannot in Bosnia because that would cause loss of life, that is an idea that could equally well have been applied to intervention against Germany in the 1930s. To say that one cannot act everywhere is not the same as saying one cannot act anywhere, or that any case ought to be judged in isolation from its particular context. The exemplary and deterrent effect of action (suggesting, in the absence of evidence to the contrary, that a reaction of a similar order would be likely in comparable circumstances) assumes an even greater importance.

Yet that only underlines, in taking the most striking example, the inevitably fragmented and often contradictory nature of any world order imaginable today. The contradiction manifests itself on three levels.

First, problems (and in the area of ecology for example, solutions as well) are becoming more and more global in nature, but power continues and will for the foreseeable future continue to belong to states or particular non-state actors.

Second, the situation and its problems are becoming increasingly complex and multidimensional, but the international organizations and world authorities able to deal with them are and will go on being limited in scope and usually single-issue-based. One can just about imagine an international authority entrusted with managing nuclear affairs operating under the aegis of the UN, but it could not begin to match up to the complex and diffuse nature of the problem of proliferation, which extends to every level of transnational society.

And finally, whereas during the Cold War particular conflicts tended to be interpreted from the perspective of the central conflict, today there is a much more universal consensus as to the principles by which these should be viewed, although the reality of the individual conflicts themselves has become infinitely more particular and more fragmented. There is a growing divergence between understanding and reality, so that law and humanitarian concern are on the defensive in an era characterized by suspicion. But have we not in fact always lived in such a condition? And how could international politics be exempt from the division and tension between the universal and the particular, the absolute and the relative, that is the most enduring feature of human life?

11

Towards a Pluralist Universalism?

Philosophy between tribalism and nomadism

THIS MAY appear to be a rather abstract topic compared with other much more specific and detailed studies of tribalism and nomadism.[1] However, that impression may be dispelled at once by asking if it isn't possible to regard the philosopher as the nomad par excellence, whose innate wanderlust takes him beyond the certainties and shared beliefs of the tribe. Consider Rousseau's note X in his *Discourse on the Origin of Inequality*, where he asks:

> Will we never see the return of those happy times when peoples did not make it their business to philosophize, but the Platos, the Thales and the Pythagorases, with their burning desire for knowledge, embarked on the most ambitious voyages purely for their own education, travelling far and wide to cast off the yoke of national prejudices, to learn to know men by the similarities and differences between them, and to acquire that universal knowledge that does not belong exclusively to a particular century or country but, being of all times and all places, is as it were the common knowledge of the wise?

Here Rousseau arrives at the Platonic ideal of the *Laws*, according to which all journeys are normally forbidden to ordinary citizens, but Plato's spokesman is called the 'stranger'. Each city has its own beliefs and laws, which are accepted as corresponding to the natural order; it is the philosopher who, by travelling and comparison, draws the distinction between nature, which is one, and customs, which are many. But this distinction is potentially explosive for social order: hence the need for the cave and the 'noble lie' by which, in *The*

Republic, the citizens are made to believe their community and hierarchy are natural rather than mere conventions.

Out of this distinction between nature and custom emerges a dialectic of diversity and universality, which we may represent in the form of a typology of possible positions.

According to the first, which is the naive or unreflecting position, it is our own society that is in conformity with nature and others that are based on custom.

According to the second, which corresponds to the discovery of exoticism in the sixteenth and especially the eighteenth centuries, it is our customs that have moved away from nature, while 'they', living elsewhere or in the past, are in conformity with nature. This is the myth of the noble savage.

It is then but a step to the third position, which states that all orders that claim to be natural are in fact based on custom. This is cultural relativism, summed up in the phrase: 'What is true this side of the Pyrenees, is untrue on the other.' Montaigne, particularly in his essay 'On Cannibals', alternates between the second and third of these positions.

Fourth, one may seek to rediscover nature by means of subtraction. Starting with all the different customs, nature will be either what is left, the element all customs have in common, which is the underlying logic of Kantian formalism, or else it will be what was there at the beginning but has been obscured by different customs over the course of history: that is the position adopted by Fichte, who bases the spiritual superiority of the German people and language on their original character.

It is also possible, and this is the fifth and last position, to try to arrive at nature by means of addition or combination. In the Hegelian philosophy of history, there is a progression, and nature is what is revealed at the end. Radical historicism thinks rather in terms of a juxtaposition, so that according to the great German historian Ranke, 'each nation relates immediately to God'. One might call this latter position 'absolutist relativism'. But if each nation or culture arrives in its own way at absolute truth, or a unique relationship with the universal, what then is the nature of the dialogue between cultures? Is the truth of each incommunicable to the rest, or does there exist a common code, which would then be the true universal?

We come back to our original question, concerning the possibility of a pluralist universalism. Is this a total universalism, subsuming within it the plurality of particularisms? And if it is, can these latter accept one another as such? Or is this a plurality of particularisms that are mutually exclusive, each claiming to have sole access to the universal and disputing the rival claims of the rest? We have come full circle, for this is the phenomenon we have previously described as universalist nationalism, which claims the prerogative of a superior position and universal vocation for its own nation or its own culture.

The problem in the history of ideas

The history of ideas may be seen as a succession of these positions. Writers from Meinecke to Todorov have retraced the passage from the French eighteenth century to the German ninetenth century, from classical reason to exoticism and the noble savage, then from the universality of the French Enlightenment to German romanticism and nationalism. Louis Dumont makes particular play of the contrast.[2] But no matter whether it be Rousseau or Herder, the great philosophers of German idealism or Nietzsche, each one attempts either to articulate or transcend the opposition of particular and universal, rather than allow himself to be trapped within one or other. Joël Roman has demonstrated this with reference to two theorists who are paradigmatic for their nations, Fichte and Renan.[3] I shall not repeat his exposition, but I would like to show that same tension, that same endlessly repeated but never quite successful endeavour, at work in twentieth-century writers who speak to us more directly. The two pairs who suggest themselves for the purpose are Max Weber and Eric Weil, and Hannah Arendt and Jürgen Habermas.

Max Weber is the sociologist who has provided the best description of the movement towards universalization, as the process of 'routinization', of rationalization in every sphere (religion, music, law, administration, economics, politics) culminating in the triumph of formal, instrumental and bureaucratic rationality. But he also foresaw the spiritual vacuum this rationalization would produce and called for the emergence of new prophets or a return to old ones. And above all, while insisting on the primacy of rationality with respect to sociological method and social development, he also insisted it could supply no answers to the ultimate questions, whether metaphysical, ethical or aesthetic, where we would find ourselves at grips with a plurality of values, irreducible and ultimately contradictory. Each of us would simply have to take a gamble as we chose the banner under which to fight this 'war of the gods'.

In Eric Weil's *Philosophie politique*,[4] we find the same duality of the universal and the particular, but in a less dramatic and polarized form. For him too, modern society is in principle universal, dominated by technology, bureaucracy and economics, while at the same time modern man is essentially unsatisfied; it is within particular communities that he finds what is sacred to him, the sense of a common existence, which cannot dispense with the nation, or at any rate the state.

Weil is a rationalist, occupying a position between Hegel and Kant. He enlists their distinction between formal *rationality* and the *reasonable* existence, as lived in a community, as an element of his own approach to political dialogue and theoretical truth.

For Hannah Arendt, politics is action.[5] She is critical of abstract universalism, to the point that she rejects the label of philosopher. She mounts a spirited attack on the attitude of philosophers, whose belief in the primacy of theory and the contemplative life causes them to scorn the active life that is particular and conflictual. But the latter is increasingly at risk. Arendt's thinking is pessimistic: collective life appears to contain perfect moments (revolution, the establishment of a 'public space') but is always destined to slip back into routine, a mechanical life in which the ability to act and the faculty of inter-action are drowned or swallowed up by the pre-eminent modern notion of process, whether that of totalitarian violence or the daily round of eating, working and sleeping.

Habermas too explores the duality of a technological world that is governed by instrumental action, that is universal and tends to dominate our lives, and a world of interaction, of symbols and communication, that is in large measure denied to us today.[6] But he criticizes Hannah Arendt for separating communication and interaction from reason, and he puts forward his own idea of an ethics of reciprocity and dialogue based on 'communication without domination', clearly inspired by Kant's 'kingdom of ends', or in other words the republic of rational citizens.

Thus we see the tension inherent in the paradoxical notion of 'pluralist universalism', with writers whose positions are very close distinguished by the emphasis they place on universality or on plurality, or on the contrasts or similarities between them.

Which universalism? A philosophical problem

Clearly the debate would be made clearer if we could agree on the nature or definition of the universal. But any such definition is bound to be influenced by the route by which it was arrived at. The various possible routes may be described in terms of a spatial metaphor, identifying positions corresponding more or less to those we discovered for the similar problem of nature and custom.

The search for the universal may be expressed in terms of length, breadth, height or depth.

We may identify it with humanity, like Auguste Comte, or with Hegel's *Weltgeist*, the spirit that has emerged in the course of history.

We may define it as a geographical rather than a historical global condition, identifying it with the fate of the planet, or with a universal culture consisting in the synthesis of particular cultures.

We may consider that the one true universal is to be found nowhere but in the transcendental dimension, of God or Being, the foundation of all things. Or we may follow St Augustine's injunction: *In te redi; in interiore homine habitat veritas*, and seek the key to the universal in the internal life of each individual.

Perhaps the real debate lies here, between the dimension of externality, or historic action, and that of interiority, or spiritual quest, as defined by Jean Grenier. Where André Malraux made a character in *L'Espoir* reply to the question, 'What do you do with your soul if there is no God and no Christ?', with 'Transform the greatest possible breadth of experience into consciousness', the author of *Entretiens sur le bon usage de la liberté* turned the sentence round to read instead, 'Transform the greatest possible depth of consciousness into experience.'

This is a debate we ought not to cut short, because it is about nothing less than answering the question of the meaning of human life. On the other hand, while sticking to our chosen plan of a comparison of the various theoretical positions, at one remove as it were, we cannot ignore the question in our title, concerning the possibility of a pluralist universalism. Henceforward our guiding principle, the opposition in terms of which we need to orient ourselves, must be to distinguish between theories where the tension of the terms universal and plural is capable of resolution and those where that contradiction is more to be relished or endured than overcome.

A tension capable of resolution?

There are two possible means of avoiding or transcending the tension of universality and plurality: religion and dialectic. In monotheistical religions, the contradiction is resolved on two counts. For one thing, God is both universal and personal. For another, each individual or person is both unique and infinitely to be valued, because made in God's image. In the philosophical domain, dialectic prides itself on performing the same miracle. Sartre defines dialectic as 'the universal singularized': by using its 'totalizing' approach he claims, for example, to rediscover an intimate unity worthy of Flaubert, as opposed to standing at the crossroads of a number of general determinations. Hegel had already made reference to a 'concrete universal'. But the question we must ask is whether these formulations do not promise more than they can deliver, whether they are not essentially semantic or at the very least conceptual resolutions of the problem, that fail to take account either of the rigour of the abstract universal or, as Kierkegaard insisted with some force, the uniqueness of the individual.

But no doubt the most decisive criticism of Hegelian or Sartrean endeavours was provided long ago by the inventor of 'transcendental dialectic' himself, Emmanuel Kant. There are two sorts of philosophical mind: the Hegelians and the Kantians. For the former, the concept progresses; and in so doing it subsumes and transcends the fixed oppositions, which are experienced as unsurmountable obstacles by the understanding (*Verstand*) and the 'unhappy consciousness' (*unglückliches Bewusstsein*). For the Kantians, it is in recognizing the partial and paradoxical nature of our knowledge and the radical opposition between the *a priori* and the empirical, or between theory and practice, that we have a chance, without betraying either, of building bridges across the chasms that separate them.

A tension preserved?

With Kant, the notion of respect that obliges us to treat other reasonable beings 'never as a means only but always also as an end' is one of these bridges. But it does not eliminate the tension between the priority accorded to respect for universal law and that accorded to respect for individuals which, depending on the interpretation, puts the emphasis more on the universal or more on the plurality. In the same way, in the *Critique of Judgment* and the shorter works on the philosophy of history, a link is established between pure and practical reason; a certain indirect apprehension of the universal operates through a plurality of particular experiences, that of the beautiful and the sublime in nature and art, or the enthusiasm aroused by an event such as the French revolution.

The essential distinction is that between determinant judgment, which proceeds from the universal to the particular, and reflective judgment, which proceeds from the particular to the universal. The latter, as it applies to questions of taste, operates by appeal rather than demonstration. Kant's famous definition of aesthetic experience ('beauty is what is universally pleasing without a concept' – or 'generally' rather than 'universally' if we adopt the translation of *allgemein* preferred by Hannah Arendt) appeals to a principle of 'universal validity': I feel that my particular experience does not just apply to me, I make the gamble that other people have a corresponding experience, that there is a 'common sense' of the beautiful and the sublime which, although we cannot demonstrate it, we must nevertheless postulate, if we are not to be untrue to the quality of our own experience.

From Hannah Arendt onwards, Kant's recent interpreters have emphasized the political relevance of these ideas of a 'common sense', 'universal validity' and 'reflective judgment'. This has provided a new answer to the classic question of the historical and cultural universality or relativity of human rights, namely that they are, if not universal, then at least universalizable, in other words that it is not a question of imposing from outside a definition that is universally valid but rather of seeking a universal dimension in the unique experiences of different cultures.

That is very much the spirit in which authors closer to us, such as Michael Walzer and Paul Ricœur, are conducting their researches.

The former, in a text called 'The two universalisms',[7] uses the Bible as his source for drawing a distinction between what he calls 'covering-law universalism' and 'reiterative universalism'. The first corresponds approximately to the Kantian 'determinant judgment', and is a unique law with universal validity that is revealed exclusively to Israel, 'the light of the nations'. The second, which corresponds to Kant's 'reflective judgment' is, to use Walzer's own phrase, in a 'particularist perspective' and manifests 'pluralizing tendencies'. He bases most of his arguments on an extract from the Book of Amos, in which God asks: 'Are you not as children of the Ethiopians unto me, O children of Israel? . . . Have not I brought up Israel out of the land of Egypt? and the Philistines from Caphtor, and the Syrians from Kir?'[8] According to Walzer's interpretation of this excerpt, liberation is a particular experience that is repeated for each oppressed people. Each people has its own liberation, but it is achieved in each case through the same unique God, who regards oppression as universally to be detested.

True, Walzer does not avoid the inevitable ambiguities. He prefers to put the emphasis on the plurality of cultures and types of experience, but does not really address the question of the dialogue between them, or the definition of a common code that would make such a dialogue possible. In extreme cases such as genocide, he accepts the possibility of a transcultural judgment, but he insists principally on the idea that each culture will live through the fundamental universal experiences (like those of oppression or human dignity) according to its own particular code.

This whole area is analysed with a characteristic blend of lucidity and modesty by Paul Ricœur. In his work *Soi-même comme un autre*,[9] he advances the idea of an 'inchoative' or 'contextual' universal. We cannot abstract ourselves from what we are, but nor can we eradicate thoughts of the universal. Ricœur insists, like Habermas, on dialogue and reciprocity, but unlike him, he chooses to preserve an area that is free of the opposition of subjective and objective, arbitrary and rational, namely that of conviction. He then sets up a dialectic between conviction and debate: our convictions represent our being, our culture and our faith, but they should also be submitted to a process of argument, even though we know the discussion will at best lead to a definition of common ground, never its identification.

This may seem faintly reminiscent of Weber, but instead of the tragic and irreducible character of the 'war of the gods' there is hope, perhaps religious in origin, of reconciliation and unity, destined to remain always inaccessible but without the prospect of which the dialogue would make no sense.

From philosophical problem to the real world

In conclusion, I should like to refer to a few examples showing the relevance of the concepts and doctrines we have explored to the problems that concern us today, where I believe we find exactly the same tensions and difficulties at work.

The most striking example is that of the relationship between human rights and culture. It seems to be very much in the spirit of the times that all of us are instinctively universalist from the point of view of ethics and relativist where culture is concerned. On the one hand, the idea of human rights, compassion, the battle against torture and famine wherever they are to be found, have all made great strides. We no longer hesitate to condemn attacks on human dignity under any regime or in any land. But we are on the other hand very wary of Western cultural arrogance, we are very sensitive to the charge that belief in the superiority or uniqueness of our culture is a reflection of white male supremacy, and we refuse to accept a hierarchy as between 'high' and 'low' culture. The multiculturalist movement in the United States, dubbed political correctness by its opponents, is the most obvious example. Allan Bloom in *The Closing of the American Mind*[10] pokes fun at this combination of moral universalism and cultural relativism. And yet it is nothing new: just such a combination featured in the writings of Kant, whose formalist universalism did not prevent him stressing the diversity of peoples. No one has succeeded in overcoming this tension in a satisfactory way. Cultural anthropologists in particular have a natural tendency towards cultural relativism. That is why, for Lévi-Strauss, our horror of anthropophagy is neither any more nor any less legitimate than the comparable horror among cannibal peoples for the institution of prison among 'civilized' peoples. Respect for cultural diversity must inevitably conflict with respect for human dignity in cases like, for example, female circumcision. Hence too the double danger that exists within racism (and that also applies, as P.-A. Taguieff emphasizes,[11] to unreflecting antiracism) of eliminating universality in favour of difference, or difference in favour of universality.

The obvious solution would be the mutual influence and mutual respect of cultures. That is what Lévi-Strauss anticipated at his famous conference held in 1951 on the subject of race and history. Twenty years later, however, in *Race et culture*,[12] he was to place the emphasis firmly on the dangers of syncretism, and the need for different cultures to maintain a degree of isolation, even a certain antagonism between them, if they were not to lose their identity.

This question of collective identities is at the heart of the second and more political example, the debate on liberalism and culture and on individualism and community.

For the past twenty or so years, the debate in political philosophy has been dominated by a liberal and individualist approach that is also universalist, consisting as it does in the reinterpretation and formalization of theories of social contract which base society and its legitimacy on the consent of individuals. I am thinking in particular of the works of Rawls, Dworkin and Nozick.[13] This approach has been subject to the criticisms of the 'communitarians' of Left and Right alike, for whom the individual in the abstract does not exist, since it is impossible to arrive at the nature of a political subject by making an abstraction of the concrete determinations, social and above all cultural, that are vested in him by a particular tradition and a particular community. This is the criticsm voiced by such writers as Sandel, Taylor or McIntyre.[14]

The liberal response would be that the particularity of our age is to have brought to light a universal phenomenon, namely, that identity is not given once and for all, but constructed or chosen by a conscious or unconscious process of identification. More specifically, it would make the point that the distinctive feature of our societies is the plurality of allegiances and influences, and that it is in the choice of his priorities, and the roles and strategies that flow from them, that the freedom − the universal freedom − of the individual resides. To which the 'communitarians' in their turn would reply, echoing Rousseau, that it is precisely that multiplicity of contradictory allegiances and identifications that introduces division into the human soul and into the cities, causing distress and schizophrenia and a yearning for security and unity that can be provided only by tradition and community. But, the liberals will say, in wanting to impose these on emancipated modern individuals, do we not run the risk of totalitarianism, of social discrimination and chauvinism?

How to escape from this circular argument? One of the leading experts on nationalism, Ernest Gellner, suggests a combination of cultural plurality and political unity.[15] He wants the great political groupings (like the defunct Soviet Union) to be preserved, as the only viable remedy against anarchy, but he also wants the preservation and flowering of the multiple cultural identities of the peoples of which they are composed. In the same way, Jean-Marc Ferry, with reference to the construction of a united Europe, wants the different nations to retain their own cultural identities, but for there to be a single identity, a single postnational European citizenship, that is purely political and procedural, and that acts as the umbrella, or context, for all the various cultural identities.[16]

Anyone of a pessimistic cast of mind would be inclined to fear the opposite, that national cultures would increasingly lose their specificity under the influence of modern society and transnational mass culture. And the more individual peoples lost their identity, the more they would feel the temptation to reconstruct one artificially. The closer they were to their neighbours culturally speaking, the more they would be tempted to oppose them politically, or by the use of violence, purely in order to convince themselves of their own identity and recreate the difference between 'them' and 'us' that belongs to the essence of politics.

To decide between these two points of view, we would probably need to proceed to a more detailed analysis, distinguishing between all the various levels and dimensions of culture and politics. Somewhere between traditional culture, the influence of the mass media and the quest for personal development, in the domain of philosophy and art, through culture in the sense of *Bildung*, it might just be posssible to construct a route leading from the particular to the universal. Similarly, in the area between politics defined as the cement of the social fabric, and politics defined as the search for salvation through a broader community, and politics as competition and the cut and thrust of conflicting interests, there is perhaps a place for partial communities, existing within the context of liberal society, but looking beyond it. There is no culture and no politics that can boast of a direct route to universality, but all bear the mark of their inspiration by and aspiration towards the universal, without which (as totalitarianism and twentieth-century wars have shown only too well) culture and politics alike run the risk of straying off course, with appalling consequences. But like the God of the Jansenists, it is a 'hidden universal'. Let us therefore conclude with two of Pascal's aphorisms: 'We have an idea of the truth that is resistant to all Pyrrhonism. We have an inability to prove it that is resistant to all dogmatism', and 'You would not seek me if you had not found me.'

CONCLUSION

12

War and Peace in the Twentieth Century

The following is based on the text of an interview conducted by Marcel Gauchet, Pierre Manent and Pierre Rosanvallon and edited by Agnès Antoine.

Do you think the fall of the Berlin Wall marks the end of the twentieth century?[1]

Certainly it is the end of a century marked by its two world wars and its two great totalitarian regimes, marked therefore by confrontation on a world scale, a century in which there has been not merely ideological conflict but actual conflict between warring ideologies. In 1914, we left behind a world of diplomacy and warfare that was relatively well mapped and existed within defined limits. Then, through what Raymond Aron has called the 'technological surprise', we were plunged suddenly not only into total warfare but also totalitarianism. And, from the first Sarajevo to the Berlin Wall, relations between the great world forces always had that dual character, universalist in respect of ideas, and potentially global in respect of their sphere of operations, even though the confrontation was expressed in many different configurations, sometimes all-out war and sometimes Cold War, sometimes involving three protagonists and sometimes bipolar. States were well aware that classical diplomacy had ceased to apply, that the fate of governments and of humanity itself hung in the balance, and, conversely, that internal policies everywhere would hinge on this confrontation on the world stage.

After the fall of the Berlin Wall, all the questions that it had been possible to place on hold throughout the twentieth century once again came to the fore. Are we, for example, thanks to economics and trade, moving towards a world at peace, in which war has become redundant, or are we returning instead to a state of permanent conflict between nations? In the eighteenth and nineteenth centuries, it was after all prophesied that trade, and subsequently the industrial and scientific society (or in the Marxist vision, revolution), would make war redundant. Yet at the other extreme there was Nietzsche proclaiming that the twentieth century would be the century of wars for world domination, conducted in the name of philosophical principles.

In the first scenario, it was argued right up to the eve of 1914 that war could no longer happen, because it would be irrational in a world where territory was no longer an essential component of wealth – see Norman Angell's well-known argument in *The Great Illusion* – and because the world had become interdependent. So the English writer H.N. Brailsford could express the view, in July 1914, that 'in Europe the era of conquest is over, with the possible exception of the Balkans and maybe the fringes of the Austrian and Russian empires; it is as certain as anything in politics can be that the frontiers of national states have finally been stabilized. It is my belief that there will be no more wars among the six great powers.' Following the 'surprise' of 1914–18, a new period of euphoria set in with the creation of the League of Nations, and this lasted a few years before it was terminated by Germany's ascension and wars in Ethiopia, Spain, etc. After the Second World War, there was a yet briefer window of optimism, in 1945–7, with the foundation of the United Nations Organization, the alliance between America and Russia and the fruition of Roosevelt's visionary policies, but the Second World War was soon to be followed by the Cold War, ushering in the bizarre phenomenon one historian, John Lewis Gaddis, has dubbed 'the long peace'. At Versailles, he believed, the states had tried to establish a 'just' peace, based on the notion of self-determination, and this had proved a disaster. The Second World War, on the other hand, was immediately followed by partition and conflict, and this 'unjust' peace, leaving Germany and Berlin divided, acknowledging totalitarianism, seemed to him much more stable than the peace of Versailles. However, his analysis was made on the eve of the collapse of this world order, and so was very much the counterpart of those doomed prophecies of 1914.

The fact remains that today we are in a situation much like that of 1815, after the French Revolution, or 1918, after the First World War, although with the difference that we come to the table empty-handed. Metternich for example believed in a principle of dynastic legitimacy, and had a programme for its restoration, Wilson believed in a principle of self-determination. We on the other hand know only too well that neither of these two principles has proved effective, but we do not know what to put in their place. We can no longer use the methods of implementing a new order that were available to Metternich or Wilson, of dividing up states and distributing them among the rest.

What strikes me particularly, however, about the last three or four years, is the way we have, I think, as far as the subject of war and peace is concerned, recapitulated the whole cycle of the twentieth century, or at least of the interwar years. We have had a period of euphoria, coinciding with the idea of collective security, the new role of the UN, agreement between the great powers to enforce order in the Gulf War; first the concept of the end of history, as announced by Fukuyama,[1] then that of the new world order a year or two later. Now, with Yugoslavia, that phase is already over and the fear has returned that outbreaks of hostilities between nations are destined to remain regular occurrences.

This may have been the century of confrontation directed at the achievement of world domination, yet one has the impression of living now in a world that is both more universal and also more fragmented. Although it is true that the great ideologies have disappeared, with the exception of Islamic fundamentalism, which probably should not be accorded quite the metaphysical and onto-logical significance some have been inclined to ascribe to it,[2] never-theless, with computers, faxes, television, all the different means of communicating in real time, people are living more than ever before in a global environment. There is also a sort of hypocritical consensus as to liberal democracy. And certainly there is an 'end of history' in one sense, if one may so describe the fact that no great new principles appear to be on the horizon.

Yet on the other hand, we also live in a world that is much more fragmented. During the Cold War there was a universal key to the understanding of all conflicts, whereas today, where everything is interdependent, we have one part of the world where war is not even a distant prospect, another where a sort of general anarchy seems to prevail, with tribes and groups bearing arms against each other, and yet another, Asia for example, where we see a re-emergence of the classic pattern of countries rising in power and influence, with attendant arms races. We find ourselves living in a world that to a greater extent than ever before is the same for all of us, and a world where a number of very different rationales exist in close proximity, although we no longer possess the global keys necessary to understand them. In that sense we may certainly say that the twentieth century is over.

But when did the twentieth century begin? Are there not in fact two beginnings to the twentieth century: either the war of 1914–18 or the war of 1939–45, and the ideology-based bipolar world it gave birth to? Also, does not the war of 1914–18 belong fundamentally to the nineteenth century?

On this point I would tend to follow Raymond Aron's line in *The Century of Total War*: everything changed in the course of the 1914-18 war. It started as the result of a failure of the nineteenth-century system of diplomacy and led via an unpredictable series of events to the 'technological surprise', which caused the establishment of a war economy and the organization of states on a military footing. Some of these states collapsed; this was followed by the revolution of 1917, and the totalitarian regimes that resulted from it, with the ideological passions they nourished. There was a sort of dialectic of military, social and ideological factors, with the effect that, in August 1914 we were in the nineteenth century and from 1917 onwards we were in the twentieth.

What would the twentieth century have been like if the events of 1917 had not taken place?

It would certainly have been fundamentally different without communism, but I don't think we should see the role of Germany and Hitlerism between the two wars as any less crucial. The world did not become bipolar in 1917, contrary to the opinion of historians such as Arno Mayer, who look at all these things purely from the point of view of the question of the struggle for social justice.

Furthermore, what in my view is absolutely fundamental is that in this century we have discovered the fragility of humanity, in both senses of the term: on the one hand the fact that humanity could be destroyed by nuclear weapons, on the other that its conventions and moral codes could be blown apart by violence. After 1914, faith in the linear progress of democracy, prosperity and peace was severely shaken, and it became apparent that history could take many very different courses. For Kojève, and for certain contemporary writers such as Baechler or Fukuyama, this was no more than a hiatus, or 'parenthesis', in the evolution of the world towards one 'universal and homogenous state' according to the former, or towards liberal democracy and economic liberalism according to the other two, exactly as was predicted in the nineteenth century. It seems to me personally that what the twentieth century has demonstrated is that nothing could be less sure. True there is a sort of inevitability about the market and democratic values, because no possible traditional reference point has survived of an organic or cosmological model, but at the same time human and social factors are potentially much more explosive. Are not democracy and the market, like the European Community, merely fair-weather friends, institutions whose existence is threatened the moment there is an economic, social, political or military crisis of sufficient gravity? Are they not mere islands in a world where it is predominantly chaos and the will to power that prevail? Which is the mainstream and which the incidental? Which is central and which parenthetical?

As there was following 1815, and again following 1918, there is agreement today on legitimacy, specifically democratic legitimacy. But that agreement does not encompass a political world order, for it provides equal justification for the violent struggles of those at the periphery and for our peaceful European organization at the centre. We no longer have the idea of a political form possessed of authority and legitimacy, as well as a territorial, institutional organization. Is not the crisis we are experiencing a crisis of political form, more specifically the form of the nation? On the one hand, we renounce this form as we move towards a more or less supranational Europe, with a sort of territorial blindness that means we speak always of 'Europe', whether it be of the six, the twelve or more, as if it made no difference. On the other hand, on the periphery, space becomes an object of frenzied desire, there is if you like a condition of territorial hypersensitivity. Haven't we become incapable of considering the political problem of territory, the problem of the 'terrestrial order' to adopt the language of Carl Schmitt?

Those who today are rediscovering the state, sovereignty and the ideas of Carl Schmitt seem to me to be in the same category as Dante with the empire, or the owl of Minerva, which wakes only at dusk.

But in the case of Dante, if the form of the empire was disappearing, at least the form of the nation was emerging, whereas today, there seems to be no form succeeding that of the nation.

Absolutely. Some describe the current situation as a whole that is made up of a number of interlocking strata. They stress the diversity of types of actors and, taking as their model periods of transition such as the fifteenth and sixteenth centuries, with the mercantile towns and the Hanseatic League, regard the situation as holding out the prospect of greater openness, flexibility and tolerance. But one can also see in it the seeds of the exact opposite, all the reasons why it was necessary to invent the modern state in the first place, to combat religious wars, pillaging bands, anarchy, insecurity, superstition, etc. Perhaps we are in a 'new middle ages', but as I have suggested elsewhere,[3] it is a middle ages without a pope and without an emperor. The UN tries its best to be a pope, the United States makes an effort to act as the emperor, but they are poorly equipped for the task. We are in a period of flux where it is not enough to brandish the words 'state', or 'sovereignty', or 'politics' in order to bring these things into being. Yet there is no other principle we can substitute. Who knows, perhaps it is necessary to have periods of out-and-out anarchy or civil war in order to gestate something new, much as Hans Magnus Enzensberger predicted with his references to a civil war both 'global and molecular', a widespread pattern of uncontrolled violence extending from suburbs to states. Once again we are experiencing the polarity of *Gemeinschaft* and *Gesellschaft*. And the great institutions that were supposed to act as the mediators, to combine bureaucratic rationality with an affective bond, are in crisis, whether they are nation-states or supranational communities.

There are two distinct and fundamental problems. On the one hand, the problem of the nationalist aspirations uncovered and indeed encouraged by the fall of empires (first the Ottoman and Austro-Hungarian and later the Soviet empire). And on the other hand, the fate of the nation-state itself. As to the first, it may be argued that the upheavals that made a bloodbath of the former Yugoslavia and the Caucasus are merely repetitions of what happened in the past to all the West and Central European states where today there are established nations and stable frontiers. If that were the case, one would be obliged to predict long periods of fratricidal struggle and conquest and population displacement before it was possible for the nation-state to take hold on a permanent basis. All one could hope is that it would take less time and spill less blood than in the nineteenth and twentieth centuries. But where would it end (are the Abkhazians a nation? what about the Gagauzians?), and is it conceivable that all this would take place without external interference?

But the second problem remains, one that is common to all regions of the world, those that are split over territories and those that are not. This is the desire to cling to what is closest, to create an instant community in which populations feel at home, like a sort of extended family, and it is a phenomenon that occurs precisely because people feel invaded on all sides. The simultaneous nature of communications is a form of openness that leads to destabilization. The more inexorable the presence of the outside world, the more there is a search for identity and for community, in a dialectical process that was already described by Raymond Aron. Can the nation-state still respond to this aspiration? And conversely, can there exist in the nation-state a non-territorial principle that is also an effective principle of order and of politics? Will there be a reaffirmation of territoriality or will this widespread pattern of violence lead to the rise of new Caesars or new prophets?

I don't know. The one thing I am convinced is true is that the division between 'us' and the 'rest' (and not necessarily the 'friend–enemy' division of Carl Schmitt) is fundamental to human experience. But is that 'us' the nation, is it the territory or is it some other category or grouping? I don't know. We all of us are selective in our allegiances, for as Rousseau said, humanity's friend is nobody's friend. I personally am more particularly sensitive to the problem of refugees, because I was one myself. I am also more moved by conflicts in the East, which is close, than by wars in more distant Somalia, and I cannot say that for me, with my cosmopolitan history, it is national solidarity that counts the most; but that is clearly not true of the majority of people. It remains an open question which comes first, civic or ethnic nationality. A conflict of loyalties exists, and at the same time a desire for a single identity that renders all others superfluous. But in the West, and in countries that were formerly part of empires, the nature of identity is not obvious: it is for example unclear which takes precedence, Iraqi, Arab or Islamic identity.

If the millennium-old form of the nation is indeed running out of steam, that is an event that touches the history of the world. To what extent would it then cause us to reinterpret the past? Is this the end of the nation or merely the end of a particular modality of the nation?

The latter question is highly pertinent. Are we talking about the disappearance of the nation-state, that is to say, adopting Gellner's definition, the union of a government and a bureaucracy in a territory where a certain congruence exists between cultural and political identity? In this respect it seems that a certain divergence has occurred. European federalism has shown us (even though no such thing as a European 'federation' actually exists) that, in both the ideal and the reality, considerable variation will occur depending on the sector involved. Thus, depending on whether it is a matter of agriculture or defence, one will be for example more Catalan or more Spanish, more European or more North Atlantic. But does this new state of affairs mean the end of the nation? And is it the civic or the ethnic nation that is in crisis? Is a 'marginalized' nation, forming just one level among many, still a nation? That is the question.

Is it not the classical definition of the nation that is changing, or in other words the anatomy of national identity, as between its political form and its cultural form? The history of the nation was the history of the process of achieving a congruence between political sovereignty on the one hand and the population and economic organization on the other. Today, only a negative definition of the nation exists. People no longer have any sense of what they are building together but only of what they unite in detesting absolutely. Thus, in Yugoslavia, the inhabitants have passed from a weak principle of combination to a strong principle of separation, but there is no symmetry between the two acts.

I agree completely with that analysis. As to cultural/political identity, there are a number of writers – Jean-Marc Ferry or Jürgen Habermas, also Ernest Gellner – who believe what is needed today is to preserve individual cultural identities but at the same time to have a broad political grouping. When I hear this said, I always think of the famous story of Isadora Duncan, who wrote to Bernard Shaw suggesting that for the good of humanity they should have a child, which would have the beauty of the one and the brains of the other. Bernard Shaw replied: 'But what would happen if it had my beauty and your brains?' I am very much afraid that all these famous cultural identities are in process of being eradicated by modernization, by Americanization, by television, by a whole process of homogenization of different ways of life, but that at the same time, at the heart of this uniformity, the need to be separate will become even more pronounced. It used to be said that the Fifth Republic was all about becoming Americanized while retaining the appearance of anti-Americanism. Today, as we are in the process of being Americanized, we invent an exaggerated cultural identity to mark us off from the rest. It was a nineteenth-century Englishman who described the nation as a group of people united in a common lie as to their origins and a common hostility to outsiders. In our time, it is the hostility that comes first, only then do we look to our origins.

Returning to the question of war as the key to an understanding of the twentieth century, does the notion of 'parenthesis' adequately describe the years of the 'nuclear peace'?

Raymond Aron said of this period 'peace impossible, war unlikely'. In his book on Clausewitz he nevertheless attaches less significance to the nuclear factor, maintaining that even if the bomb had never existed there would not have been a Third World War, as the experience of two world wars, changing values and an underlying shift in moral consciousness would have prevented it. And the fact is, extraordinary though it seems when one thinks of it, no one in the developed West for one instant imagines war will break out between France and

Germany over Alsace-Lorraine, or that Sweden will retake Norway and Denmark. Is this the result of democracy, bourgeoisification, the devaluation of the territorial principle, modern individualism? Whatever the answer, in this respect, the eighteenth- and nineteenth-century thinkers were clearly right. The prestige attached to military uniform and the flag has disappeared, and along with it that of territory: one has only to look at the lack of enthusiasm with which the Hungarians regard Transylvania or the West Germans East Germany.

But that phenomenon, extraordinary and fundamental though it may be, does not represent the situation fully. Reverting to the idea of 'peace impossible, war unlikely', I personally think that peace has become a little less impossible, because there is no longer any great bipolar ideological confrontation, and war a little less unlikely, because the world has reverted to a sort of anarchy and unpredictability in which, although nuclear apocalypse in which the whole planet blows up may be even more improbable, quite major wars remain a possibility, including perhaps nuclear wars occurring as a result of the escalation of local wars. I believe the Cold War period, the period of bipolarity, did indeed impose a sort of extended freeze or hiatus, some vast 'parenthesis'. In the developed world, we had abandoned Clausewitz's idea of war as a political instrument, there was an entirely abstract upper stratum of deterrence based on nuclear equilibrium, the idea of non-war, and then at the other extreme, at the lowest level, there was widespread background terrorism, manipulation, wars pursued by indirect means. Classical diplomacy and the great wars that typified the history of Europe, whether they were limited, national or world wars, those indeed were put on hold, or placed if you like 'in parenthesis'.

It is this that is beginning to change, although one may wonder if the world will revert to the great interstate wars of the past or whether there will be instead an effect of erosion or dispersal, setting up a widespread pattern of generalized violence. Whether or not we have entered the postnuclear age is the main question that preoccupies the specialists of today. It seems to me, on the one hand, that nuclear weapons will continue to exist and to be very important. On the other hand, the brand of nuclear logic espoused and taken to extremes by France (namely, deterrence as non-war), arms control, peaceful dialogue (which has not been without influence politically as it produced detente – and here I cannot help thinking of Kant: 'An agreement which has been extracted pathologically for the purpose of establishing a society can be converted into a moral whole'!), that whole system explored in the theories of Thomas Schelling and non-zero-sum games, based on a mixture of collaboration and conflict, all that has been blown apart since the collapse of the Soviet Union. Today, nuclear logic is no more, there are no rules by which to play the game. The nuclear question is inseparable from many others, from the problem of the proliferation of conventional missiles, the problem of civil wars, what becomes of the Russian scientists, and the nuclear arms races between India and Pakistan or between Israel and the Arab countries. It is possible to create islands in which a certain equilibrium and rationality prevail, but scenarios of nuclear terrorism are once again in prospect – you may remember how the Chechen president attempted to blackmail Boris Yeltsin? The characteristic of the world today is that everything that is rational represents only one part of the truth, and even that is questioned on all sides. In the past, the doctrine of deterrence matched the civil character of our societies: an invisible hand, or abstract mechanism, took charge of our security, and we did not have to bother our heads with it. But today the nuclear issue can no longer be considered in isolation, it is inextricably mixed up with everything else.

Is there not a sort of optical illusion in operation when we consider this nuclear 'parenthesis'? For, throughout the period of deterrence, there were colonial wars and conflicts such as that between India and Pakistan. What for us is new is the importation into Europe of forms of conflict that never stopped in the regions of the world that did not form part of our bipolar system. So, we ought not have too much of a Western bias in our history of the twentieth century. Perhaps what we see happening today marks not only the end of the hiatus but also some sort of process of de-Westernization at work in the world?

I have been thinking that for a long time. Despite the theory of the 'long peace' brought about by the division of Europe and the balance of terror, I have always maintained that this bipolar peace did not apply to the Third World, and also, that even for Europe itself it was no more than one dimension of the reality. Which is not the same as saying that peace in Europe depended on war raging on other continents. At one time, the idea did the rounds that, since the great powers could no longer confront one another directly, they did so by proxy in the Third World. I have always thought this theory over-stated and inadequate. But in Europe itself, the balance of terror in fact masked a widespread social unrest that in the end boiled over. And my specific area of interest has for some twenty years now been the exploration of the underlying (or sometimes, as in 1968 or 1981, sudden) transformation of societies in Europe, in comparison with the rigidity of the bipolar system.

Today, the waters have swept away the dykes that shored up that system. And there are now two forms of de-Westernization or de-Europeanization at work in the world. The first is represented by the new eminence of Asia, in the economic sphere, or so at least the Americans believe, but also in the military sphere, with the rearmament of Japan and of China, at the very moment when the latter is no longer threatened by the Russians; this is happening within the context of a thrust for regional hegemony comparable with that enjoyed by Europe in the classical era. The second is, as we have said, the return of a certain type of conflict to Europe, one that had been thought to have vanished once and for all. It is perhaps for that reason I was very interventionist over Yugoslavia, as the conflict seemed to me a test of the rules of the game for Europe: if Europe allowed Milosevic what it denied Saddam Hussein, what rule was being applied?

Have we undergone a fundamental transformation in our societies, a 'historical miracle', which means that war has become unthinkable, and we can no longer envisage mobilizing our forces for Sarajevo because we can no longer mobilize our forces for anything at all, or is this simply a transitory phase, will Europe react with aggressive xenophobia as it responds to a flood of refugees? Personally I tend to think that violence could break out, because I believe in the scapegoat mechanism described by René Girard, yet at the same time I am convinced that the particular form of violence consisting in interstate war between Western neighbours is dead and gone for the foreseeable future.

I think what has changed radically today in our attitude to war is not only the fact that our societies have ceased to worship heroes and warfare, and have moved on instead to a cult of private happiness that precludes individual commitment to outside causes, but also that the consequences of war are far more visible than they used to be. There is television.

There was a moment when the discovery of the Serb camps aroused a wave of solidarity in France – it was the abhorrence at seeing the suffering of one's fellow men that Rousseau has described. But after a short while, people wearied of it: instead of trying to change the situation, they changed the channel.

Perhaps the media have a desensitizing effect. The violence that is always present in television series, the news that provides us with a daily quota of disasters, and even scenes of death, leads to a lack of sensitivity, a hardening. Yet at the same time, in the United States, the fact that ten American soldiers died in a car accident in Kuwait is experienced as a tragedy that places a question mark over the whole US presence in that country.

253

The Americans do indeed have a quite extraordinary sensitivity about 'American losses'. Stanley Hoffmann had a good way of expressing it: he said we should no longer talk in terms of immunity for non-combatants but immunity for American combatants. Today, we only go to war if we are absolutely sure no soldiers are going to die.

If in the long run it proves to be the case that we have no more wars among ourselves, and no war with others, and if as a result our armies have a military budget barely sufficient to tick over in peacetime, and if at the same time, all around us, the symptoms of international delinquency are on the increase, how long will we be able to go on avoiding the consequences of violence at the periphery? And if we are forced to confront it, how do we adapt ourselves to the changed situation? If the international situation becomes threatening, will not the 'fair-weather' elements of our democracies have to be modified?

I can see reasons for being very concerned indeed. The scenario whereby a conflict such as the Yugoslav conflict leads us into world war, or even a general European war, seems to me unlikely. However, I think human nature has potentialities which in private man, or economic man, remain dormant, but which always threaten to be reactivated, though doubtless in some form other than interstate war. Today for example a consensus exists over closed frontiers, as in the Schengen Accords, over sending the boat people back to sea, over the Albanians, and especially over the Arabs, but given the degree of interpenetration that already exists, can such policies be implemented without a hardening of attitudes within our societies? During the Cold War, the fear existed on the Left, and was also expressed by some Americans, that the big military budgets involved in maintaining an opposition to Soviet totalitarianism would make us lose our sense of our reason for living, that we would become in effect 'garrison states'. In fact, what seems to me most striking is the amount the Western states have spent in this area, while remaining civil societies, with very little feeling of war-mongering, and anticommunism restricted to being virtually an internal phenomenon, as for example with McCarthyism. If we take measures to protect ourselves against migrations from the East and South, will we be capable of the same restraint? One might suspect not, for, to paraphrase the gospel, there will always be strangers among us.

Another subject for concern is nuclear proliferation and nuclear anarchy, which represent grave threats to world peace.

I would see the threat arising more from internal causes, a certain disintegration of the social order leading to an appeal to a strong man, to a myth, to some alliance of primitive feelings with modern technologies, I don't know what. From the point of view of pure *Realpolitik*, there seem to me intimations that what is beginning to happen, outside the Western sphere, is that the world is being carved up by regional leaders, who the liberal democracies leave in power as long as they maintain order, as in Syria, Lebanon, Russia and Georgia, and even Serbia in respect of the Yugoslav republics. This up to a point is the view held by François Mitterand. Can such a model work today, of a world carved up into little regional entities, each with a strong man at the helm, of peace maintained by force? Will there be no conflict between these powers, between Japanese and Chinese for instance? Will we not be led to intervene? Can we have our island of bourgeois prosperity protected by police or tariff barriers, avert our eyes from the planet's woes on our television screens, send back the refugees and let the rest of the world massacre themselves all around us? Such a view seems to me unacceptable but at the same time I have no way of explaining how we can progress from our current non-involvement towards a sort of 'contamination' that would gradually restore us to a sense of our responsibilities towards the world.

If Russia rebuilds its empire, with our blessing, is not Europe once again exposed, within a relatively short time frame, to the problems of balance of power and defence against this new threat, or renewal of an old threat?

It is a classic problem in the theory of international relations. Would the Russia of the Tsars have been as much of a threat to Europe as was communist Russia? Baechler's thesis at a certain point was that if 1917 had not happened, Russia would have rapidly become very powerful and very soon constituted a threat to Europe. I rather think the opposite. It seems to me that it was possible to live with that great power, and that the underlying reason why it was necessary to oppose communism, which in the end collapsed by itself, was that it contained a universal potential that threatened us, not only from without but from within, via the Communist Party and the fifth column.

As for the Russia of today, no longer communist, if it were to be purely military or reactionary, does it constitute a threat? Can the West continue to live in prosperous isolation while surrounded by several more warlike empires? I believe there are broad world trends like consumerism that have reached even the Russians, which certainly offer no inducement to wage foreign wars. Or is the reverse true? Does appetite revive the more you eat, will these countries not be content with the limited ambition of being regional empires, something the West after all would be quite willing to accept? Will they inevitably resurrect their global ambitions, so that the whole process will start again from scratch? No one knows the answer.

Historically, each nation has interpreted itself as one version of the universal, and preferably the best version, including Russia, whose universalism was communism, and the United States, which found its universal principle in democracy. Is it possible that in some way, and somewhat paradoxically, the collapse of the idea of nationhood has also brought about the disappearance of the idea of a universal that offers a guiding principle for the world? True there is a homogeneity about the world, in the sense that we now have the so-called global village, yet at the same time we begin to feel the lack of a universal image, for the only legitimacy is purely individualistic and purely economic. Do you see any new universals emerging?

There are trends in the West, like ecology, which claim to be substitutes for politics (see *Das Prinzip Verantwortung* by Hans Jonas), the point being to leave the planet habitable for future generations. There is also humanitarianism, *sans-frontiérisme*, which cuts across ideologies and emphasizes direct intervention wherever there is suffering in the world. But there are no true universals in prospect. It is here that the problem of 'nation Europe' comes to the fore, and I have myself developed somewhat different views on this topic. When the idea of Europe took shape after the war, the nation–state seemed both too close and too distant, so that the founders of European reconstruction, like Monnet, thought it better for the political organization to function on a number of different levels, with a regional level below the new state level and a supranational level above it. It was an approach focusing on the state rather than the nation, in its relation to the universal. Today there can be no doubt that the nation is ailing, but that Europe is in an even worse case, and that the European Community has succeeded neither in achieving closeness with its citizens nor in creating a new universal.

Political philosophy has always focused on problems of peace, justice and legitimacy within political bodies. Equally it has always had the greatest difficulty in considering relations between nations. Does the end of the twentieth century not also mark the end of that dichotomy, and are we not entering a world where external problems will become internal ones, and vice versa?

Yes, but this dichotomy will not disappear so much or indeed solely because, as liberals from Kant to Monnet would have wished, international relations have become law-abiding, peaceful and governed by economics, like the internal affairs of states. Rather it will do so at least as much because the opposite is happening, because that internal order itself is crumbling, and it is those internal relationships that are now subject to violence and dependent on fragile and precarious equlibriums, just like international relations. I do indeed believe the dichotomy that has prevailed until now represents a blind spot in political thinking.[4]

Philosophies of history cover the field of international relations, offering at least in very broad terms a general view of the subject: we have Hegel finally setting out the constitution of the nation-state on the basis of the principles of the French Revolution, or Kant proclaiming his cosmopolitan law. Events up to a certain point in time tended to lend support to the ideas of both Kant and Hegel, sometimes more one, sometimes more the other. Does the current situation appear to justify Hegel and Kant, as Fukuyama claims, or does the new anarchy challenge what was the implicit philosophy of history of our societies?

Personally I would not claim to have a philosophy of history, I merely observe and describe events, and I can see that the optimistic philosophies of history of the eighteenth and nineteenth centuries appeared old-fashioned in the light of two world wars and two totalitarian regimes, whereas now, with economic principles and a certain spirit of pacifism prevailing in our societies, and the downfall of absolutist ideologies, they have taken on a new life, Kant with Doyle and Hegel with Fukuyama. Since the events in Yugoslavia, I myself am less interested in Kant and Hegel, human rights and the legal constitution of the state than in the political passions, hence more in Rousseau and Nietzsche, where the tension lies between compassion and the desire for power, or in Machiavelli, Hobbes and Locke, and notions of glory, security and prosperity.

I could describe the way my own ideas have developed in terms of the classification adopted by the American political theorist Kenneth Waltz,[5] in his perspective on the various political philosophies and their approaches to the problem of war and peace. As you know, he distinguished three tendencies, or 'images': human nature, the nature of certain political regimes and the structure of the international system.

I myself have travelled that route in reverse: in the 1960s my interests were concentrated on strategy, diplomacy and arms control; after 1968 and the Prague Spring, I realized there were upheavals taking place in society that I had not in the least expected, and I became more interested in the evolution of Western and communist societies, as well as the international ramifications of that evolution;

and now, faced with the war in Yugoslavia, it is more the anthro-pological question, the question of human passions, *l'histoire du sujet*, to adopt the term used by Marcel Gauchet, that concerns me. What interests me above all is to find out the underlying cause of all the changes that seem to have come about in the human personality, notably the weakening of *thymos* and the increased self-interest that is typical of modern man. Today, in other words, I am going back to that 'first image', the fundamental question remaining of course that of the interplay of the individual, society and the international system. Having started life as a philosopher and then moved into international politics, I am in a sense coming full circle as I revert to philosophy and the order of the soul.

Notes

Introduction

1 Cf. the opening sections of 'Communist Totalitarianism: The Transatlantic Vagaries of a Concept' (chapter 6) and 'An Elusive but Essential Notion' (chapter 7).

2 *History of Political Philosophy*, ed. Leo Strauss and Joseph Cropsey (Chicago, Rand McNally, 1963).

3 See below, p. 86.

4 *Change and Security in Europe*, Adelphi Papers, 45 and 48 (London, Institute for Strategic Studies, 1968).

5 See my article 'Le retour du pacifisme en Europe', *Le Débat*, December 1981; and below, 'Ethical Issues in Nuclear Deterrence' (chapter 5).

6 P. Grémion and P. Hassner, *Vents d'Est: vers l'Europe des etats de droit?* (Paris, Presses Universitaires de France, 1990).

7 See *Vukovar–Sarajevo: la guerre en ex-Yougoslavie*, ed. V. Nahoum-Grappe (Paris, Editions Esprit, 1993), to which I contributed the chapter 'Les impuissances de la communauté internationale' (pp. 83–118).

8 Hence my loyalty also to the tradition of Raymond Aron, the friendship of Jean-Claude Casanova and the periodical *Commentaire*.

9 'Communisme impossible, démocratie improbable', *Esprit*, February 1990.

10 'Modelling while Rome burns', typescript, January 1990.

11 *The National Interest*, summer 1989.

12 *Foreign Affairs*, 72: 3 (summer 1993).

13 See J.-C. Rufin, *L'Empire et les nouveaux barbares* (Paris, J.C. Lattès, 1991).

14 H.M. Enzensberger, *Aussichten auf den Bürgerkrieg*. Cf. Yves Michaud, 'Les violences de l'histoire', *Esprit*, October 1994.

15 R. Kaplan, 'The coming anarchy', *The Atlantic Monthly*, February 1994.

16 Cf. T. Schrecker, 'The borderless world and the walled city', report to the XVI Congress of the International Association of Political Science, Berlin, August 1994 (mimeograph).

17 Gareth Evans, 'Cooperative security and intra-state conflict', *Foreign Policy*, 96 (autumn 1994), p. 3.

18 Ibid., p. 12.

19 I discussed this latter topic in two articles in the *Revue française de science politique*, 'On ne badine pas avec la force' (March 1971) and 'On ne badine pas avec la paix' (March 1973), omitted from this volume for reasons of space.

20 Some initial thoughts on the collapse of the totalitarian regimes may be found in my article 'Les révolutions ne sont plus ce qu'elles étaient', in *Quand les dictatures se fissurent*, ed. J. Semelin (Paris, Desclée de Brouwer, 1995).

21 K. Minogue and B. Williams, 'Ethnic conflict in the Soviet Union: the revenge of particularism', in *Thinking Theoretically about Soviet Nationalities*, ed. A. Motyl (New York, 1992), p. 233.

22 For a development of this idea, see my article 'Beyond nationalism and internationalism: ethnicity and world order', *Survival*, summer 1993.

1 *Beyond the Three Traditions: The Philosophy of War and Peace in Historical Perspective*

1 Martin Wight, *International Theory: The Three Traditions*, ed. Gabriele Wight and Brian Porter (Leicester and London: Leicester University Press for the Royal Institute of International Affairs, 1991; paperback edn, April 1994). This chapter is an edited text of the nineteenth Martin Wight memorial lecture given at the Royal Institute of International Affairs on 17 March 1994.

2 Raymond Aron, *Le Grand Schisme* (Paris, Gallimard, 1948) and *Les Dernières Années du siècle* (Paris, Julliard, 1984).

3 Francis Fukuyama, *The End of History and the Last Man* (London, Hamish Hamilton, 1992).

4 Samuel P. Huntington, 'The clash of civilizations?', *Foreign Affairs*, 72:3 (summer 1993).

5 Max Singer and Aaron Wildavsky, *The Real World Order: Zones of Peace/Zones of Turmoil* (Chatham, NJ, Chatham House Publishers, 1993).

6 Hans Magnus Enzensberger, *Aussichten auf den Bürgerkrieg* (Frankfurt, Suhrkamp, 1993).

7 Kenneth Waltz, *Man, the State and War: A Theoretical Analysis* (New York, Columbia University Press, 1965).

8 Jean-Jacques Rousseau, 'The state of war (1756)', in Stanley Hoffmann and David Fidler, eds, *Rousseau on International Relations* (Oxford, Clarendon Press, 1991). p. 44.

9 Ibid., p. 43.

10 G.W.F. Hegel, *Principles of the Philosophy of Right*, trans. F.W. Knox (Oxford, Clarendon Press, 1942), para. 330, p. 212.

11 I. Kant, *Ideas for a Universal History with Cosmopolitan Intent* (1784), fourth and seventh propositions. See *The Philosophy of Kant: Immanuel Kant's Moral and Philosophical Writings*, ed. Carl Friedrich (New York, The Modern Library, 1949), pp. 21, 127.

12 I. Kant, *Conjectures on the Beginnings of Human History* (1786). See *Kleine Schriften für Geschichtsphilosophie* (Hamburg, Felix Meiner Verlag, 1973), p. 62, final remark.

13 I. Kant, *Doctrine of Law* (1797), conclusion. See *Metaphysik der Sitten* (Meiner, Philosophische Bibliothek, 1945). p. 208.

14 I. Kant, *Perpetual Peace* (1795), section 2, in *The Philosophy of Kant*, ed. Friedrich, pp. 437–46.

15 I. Kant, *Ideas for a Universal History*, fourth proposition, ibid., p. 120.

16 Hegel, *Principles of the Philosophy of Right*, paras 333, 334, pp. 213–14.

17 G.W.F. Hegel, *System of Ethical Life*, III, s. 1. See *System der Sittlichkeit* (Meiner, Philosophische Bibliothek, 1967).

18 Raymond Aron, 'L'aube de l'histoire universelle', in *Dimensions de la conscience historique* (Paris, Plon, 1961), *The Dawn of Universal History* (London, Weidenfeld & Nicolson, 1961), p. 270.

19 Raymond Aron, *War and Industrial Society* (London, Oxford University Press, 1958).

20 Aron, *Dimensions*, p. 270.

21 Ibid., p. 284.

22 Friedrich Nietzsche, *Thus spake Zarathustra: A Book for All and None*, prologue, s. 5 (London, Allen & Unwin, 1967).

23 Ernst Nolte, *Three Faces of Fascism*, part 5 (London, Weidenfeld & Nicolson, 1965).

24 Michael Doyle, 'Kant, liberal legacies and foreign affairs', *Philosophy and Public Affairs*, 12:3–4 (1983).

25 Francis Fukuyama, *The End of History*.

26 Ole Wæver, 'International society: theoretical promises unfulfilled', *Cooperation and Conflict*, 26:4 (1991).

27 Michael Ignatieff, *Blood and Belonging: Journey into the New Rationalism* (London, BBC and Chatto & Windus, 1993).

2 Force and Politics Today

1 See his *Paix et guerre entre les nations* (Paris, Calmann-Lévy, 1962).

2 According to David Wood, *Conflict in the Twentieth Century*, Adelphi Papers, no. 48 (June 1968), out of 84 conflicts between 1939 and 1968, only 28 took the form of wars between states. According to Istwan Kende, 'Twenty-five years of local wars', *Journal of Peace Research*, 1 (1971), the figure is 15 wars out of 97, since 1945.

3 *Violence, Rationality and Unpredictability: Apocalyptic and Pacific Tendencies in Studies of International Conflict*

1 For a summary, assessment and authoritative critiques of this approach, see Jessie Bernard, F.H. Pear, R. Aron and R. Angell, *The Nature of Conflict: Studies on the Sociological Aspects of International Tensions* (Paris, Unesco, 1957). For a more recent evaluation, see too the incisive critique by C. Œconomo, 'Guerres et sociologues', *Revue française de sociologie*, 2:2 (1961), pp. 22–37. For a recent account by one of the most senior and experienced exponents of the

Unesco method, see O. Klineberg, *The Human Dimension in International Relations* (New York, Holt, Rinehart & Winston, 1964), vol. 8

2 She refers briefly to a third, the study of semantic confusions, but dismisses it, like the tensions approach, as denying the importance of conflicts of interest and value.

3 *Journal of Conflict Resolution*, 6:1 (1962), p. 94.

4 R. Mack and R. Snyder, 'The analysis of social conflict: towards an overview and synthesis', *Journal of Conflict Resolution*, 1:2 (1957), p. 213.

5 See J. Freymond, *Le Conflit sarrois (1945–1955)* (Brussels, Editions de l'Institut Solvay, 1959), pp. 15–21.

6 Karl Deutsch, 'Mass communications and the loss of freedom in national decision-making: a possible research approach to interstate conflicts', *Journal of Conflict Resolution*, 1:2 (1957), p. 200.

7 T. Schelling, *The Strategy of Conflict* (New York, Galaxy Books, 1963), p. 15.

8 T. Schelling, 'War without pain, and other models', *World Politics*, 15:3 (April, 1963), p. 467.

9 K. Boulding, *Conflict and Defense: A General Theory* (New York, Harper Torchbooks, 1963), pp. vii–viii.

10 *Journal of Conflict Resolution*, 1:1 (1957), p. 1.

11 For an account of the project, see 'The Conflict Study Project at Stanford', *Journal of Conflict Resolution*, 4:2, p. 243. The conceptual framework is described in R. North, H. Koch, D. Zinnes, 'The integrative functions of conflicts', ibid., 4:3, p. 355. For an example of the method and its results, see R. North, H. Koch, D. Zinnes, 'Capability, threat and the outbreak of war', in *International Politics and Foreign Policy*, ed. J. Rosenan (New York, Free Press of Glencoe, 1961), pp. 469–83. A related and to date more satisfying investigation is the comparative study of acute international crises (focusing on the examples of Suez, Berlin, Quemoy and Cuba) by C. McClelland, 'The acute international crisis', *World Politics*, 14:1 (October 1961), pp. 182–204.

12 A. Rapaport, *Fights, Games and Debate* (Ann Arbor, University of Michigan Press, 1960).

13 Ibid.; and A. Rapoport, 'Formal games as probing tools for investigating behavior motivated by trust and suspicion', *Journal of Conflict Resolution*, 7:3 (1963), pp. 570–9.

14 See the article cited in the previous note and, in particular, 'The armers and disarmers: is debate useful?', *The Nation*, 2 March 1963, which represents one of the great comic moments in the contemporary social sciences. Rapoport, whose entire theory consists in demonstrating the need for moving from hostility to discussion, putting oneself in the place of one's adversary in order to understand the element of truth contained in his position, how yours appears to him, etc., baldly states he has nothing to say to his colleagues who favour deterrence or even arms control because he regards them as enemies lacking all humanity!

15 'Managing the arms race', in *National Security*, ed. D. Abshire and R. Allen (New York, Praeger, 1963), pp. 643–8.

16 See A. Rapoport, 'Lewis Richardson's mathematical theory of war', *Journal of*

Conflict Resolution, 1:3 (1957), pp. 249–99; Boulding, *Conflict and Defense*, ch. 2: 'The dynamics of conflict: Richardson process models', pp. 19–91.

17 K. Boulding, 'The prevention of World War III', in *Legal and Political Problems of World Order*, ed. S. Mendlovitz (New York, The Fund for Education concerning World Peace through World Law, 1962), p. 18.

18 See the excellent book by Fred C. Iklé, *How Nations Negotiate* (New York, Harper, 1964).

19 See the virtuoso display by Zbigniew Brzezinski, 'How to control a deviation', *Encounter*, September 1964, pp. 77–89, and 'The problematics of Sino-Soviet bargaining', in *Unity and Contradiction*, ed. K. London (New York, Praeger, 1962), pp. 302–409.

20 John C. Harsanyi, 'On the rationality postulates underlying the theory of cooperative games', *Journal of Conflict Resolution*, 5:2 (1961), pp. 179–96.

21 See Pierre Hassner, 'Entre la stratégie et le désarmement: l'arms control', *Revue française de science politique*, 14:4 (December 1963), pp. 1019–49.

22 Stanley Hoffmann, 'Terreur et terrier', *Revue française de science politique*, 11:4 (December 1961), p. 956.

23 See P. Green, 'Method and substance in the arms debate', *World Politics*, 16:4 (July 1964), pp. 642–67. The author discusses a selection of articles on this theme published in the *Journal of Conflict Resolution*.

24 'Le marchandage tacite et la solution des conflits', *Revue française de science politique*, 14:40 (August 1964), p. 749.

25 A. Wiener and H. Kahn, eds, *Crises and Arms Control* (Harmon-on-Hudson, NY, Hudson Institute, 1962), p. 19.

26 'Comment', in *Limited Strategic War*, ed. K. Knorr and T. Read (New York, Praeger, 1962), pp. 253–6.

27 Schelling, 'War without pain', pp. 483–7.

28 See C.H. Cooley, *Human Nature and the Social Order* (New York, 1902), quoted by Q. Wright, 'International conflict and the UN', *World Politics*, 10:1 (1957), p. 38; K. Boulding, 'National images and international systems', *Journal of Conflict Resolution*, 3:2 (1959), p. 120; O. Holsti, 'The belief system and national images', ibid., 6:3 (1962), p. 244; U. Broffenbrenner, 'The mirror-image in Soviet-American relations', *Journal of Social Issues*, 17 (1961), pp. 45–6; C.E. Osgood, *Alternative to War or Surrender* (Urbana, University of Illinois Press, 1962).

29 Morton Deutsch, 'Trust and suspicion', *Journal of Conflict Resolution*, 2:4 (1958), p. 265; J.D. Singer, 'Threat perception and the armament dilemma', ibid., p. 90; D. Zinnes, 'Hostility in international decision-making', ibid., 6:3 (1962), pp. 236–43.

30 Rapoport, 'Formal games', 'Step-wise disarmament and sudden destruction in a 2 person game', *Journal of Conflict Resolution*, 8:1 (1964); J. Shellenberg, 'Distributive justice and collaboration in non zero-sum games', *Journal of Conflict Resolution*, 8:2 (1964), pp. 147–51.

31 Schelling, *The Strategy of Conflict*, p. 20.

32 J.-B. Duroselle, 'La stratégie des conflits internationaux', *Revue française de science politique*, 10:2 (June 1960), pp. 287–309; 'La nature des conflits

internationaux', ibid., 13:2 (April 1964), pp. 294–308; 'Le marchandage tacite et la solution des conflits', ibid., 14:4 (August 1964), pp. 738–54.

33 J. Vernant, 'Le jeu diplomatique à l'âge nucléaire', *Revue de défense nationale*, May 1963, pp. 862–8; 'La théorie des relations internationales à l'âge nucléaire', ibid., December 1963, pp. 1914–21; 'Chypre: réflexions sur un conflit', ibid., October 1964, pp. 1632–8.

34 A. Joxe, 'La crise de Cuba: entraînement contrôlé vers la dissuasion réciproque', *Stratégie*, 1 (summer 1964), pp. 60–88.

35 In *Revue de défense nationale*, May 1963, p. 863.

36 In *National Security*, ed. D. Abshire and R. Allen, p. 641. See also the comments by O. Morgenstern.

37 H. Kahn, 'L'avenir de la stratégie atomique américaine', *Bulletin SEDEIS*, *Futuribles* supplement, 82 (1 October 1964), p. 36.

38 Schelling, *The Strategy of Conflict*, pp. 54, 58, 99.

39 Ibid., pp. 15, 21.

40 Ibid., p. 43.

41 Ibid., p. 16.

42 Ibid., p. 199.

43 '. . . to exploit the risk of general war and learn to acknowledge that brinkmanship is a style of contest that may have to go on between us and the Soviets for quite some time': in *National Security*, ed. Abshire and Allen, p. 645.

44 Ibid., p. 648. My italics.

45 'La crise de Cuba', p. 80.

46 See note 32.

47 See my interpretation in 'Entre la stratégie', pp. 1044–5; also comments on the conclusions of a committee of inquiry of the US Senate, in Klaus Knorr, 'Failures in national intelligence estimates. The case of the Cuban missiles', *World Politics*, 16:3 (April 1964), pp. 455–67.

48 According to US witnesses, the precipitate Soviet withdrawal also came as a great surprise to the United States. I am convinced that was the case, although this third point is open to interpretation. My thanks to the Rockefeller Foundation, who made it possible for me to talk to witnesses during a trip to the USA in 1963.

49 *The Strategy of Conflict*, p. 169.

50 In *National Security*, ed. Abshire and Allen, p. 604.

51 See R. Löwenthal, 'After Cuba, Berlin?', *Encounter*, December 1962, pp. 48–56. For an excellent discussion of possible Soviet intentions, which also concludes by supporting the hypothesis of a political manoeuvre focused indirectly on Berlin, see A. Horelick, *The Cuban Missile Crisis: An Analysis of Soviet Calculations and Behavior*, memorandum RM3779PR (Santa Monica, Rand Corporation, 1963) and *World Politics*, 16:3 (April 1964), pp. 363–90.

52 See R. Hilsman, 'The Cuban crisis: how close we were to war', *Look*, 25 August 1964, p. 20. This article, like Joxe's study, gives striking examples of the entirely unpredicted nature of communications between the two sides during the crisis. But he also insists, like all the US sources, on the atmosphere of uncertainty as to Soviet intentions that pervaded White House decisions.

53 See the special issue of the *Journal of Conflict Resolution*, 6:1 (1962), devoted to games and bargaining theory; notably F. Iklé and N. Leites, 'Political negotiation as a process of modifying utilities', p. 20; H. Kuhn, 'Game theory and models of negotiation', p. 81; and especially J. Harsanyi, 'Bargaining in ignorance of the opponent's utility function', p. 29, where the author, having rebuked Schelling for abandoning mathematical rigour, ends up drawing a distinction between heterogeneous and homogeneous value systems, which hardly lend themselves to exact calculation.

54 See Bertrand de Jouvenel, *L'Art de la conjecture* (Paris, Editions du Rocher, 1964), pp. 163–80.

55 In fact, all indications point, at least in the East, to a 'great debate' on Cuba that took place after the crisis rather than before. If there was a 'highly educational demonstration', its failure – leading to Khrushchev's indictment – is more apparent than the motives for it.

56 G.W.F. Hegel, *Phenomenology of Spirit* (Oxford, Oxford University Press, 1977), p. 10.

4 The Nation-State in the Nuclear Age

1 H. Mendershausen, *Trans-national Society, Sovereignty and Leadership: The Environment of Foreign Policy* (Santa Monica, Rand Corporation, August 1967).

2 This distinction is close both to Hoffmann's three notions of national situation, national consciousness and nationalist ideology (see his 'Obstinate or Obsolete? The fate of the nation-state and the case of Western Europe', *Daedalus*, summer 1965), and to Rosecrance's distinction of resources, control and direction in *Action and Reaction in World Politics: International Systems in Perspective* (Boston, Little, Brown, 1963), p. 279.

3 John Herz, *International Politics in the Atomic Age* (New York, 1959); K. Boulding, *Conflict and Defense: A General Theory* (New York, Harper Torchbooks, 1963).

4 G. Modelski, 'The international system', *World Politics*, October 1961, pp. 133, 143.

5 P. Gallois, *The Balance of Terror* (New York, 1961); J. Burton, *International Relations* (Cambridge, Cambridge University Press, 1965).

6 'Défense dirigée ou défense tous azimuths?' *Revue de défense nationale*, December 1967.

7 See his *System and Process in International Politics* (New York, 1957).

8 See the seminal article by A.L. Burns, 'From balance to deterrence: a theoretical analysis', *World Politics*, 1957, ix.

9 P. Gallois, *Les Paradoxes de la paix* (Paris, 1967), pp. 184–9, 275.

10 G. Snyder, *Deterrence and Defense* (Princeton, NJ, Princeton University Press, 1961), p. 14.

11 A. Wohlstetter, 'Illusions of distance', *Foreign Affairs*, January 1968.

12 See T. Schelling, *Arms and Influence* (New Haven, Conn., Yale University Press, 1966), pp. 69–71.

13 See R. Aron, *Paix et guerre entre les nations* (Paris, 1962), p. 368; K. Knorr, *On*

the Use of Military Power in the Nuclear Age (Princeton, NJ, Princeton University Press, 1966), pp. 17–80; K. Deutsch, 'The future of world politics', *Political Quarterly*, January 1966.

14 K. Waltz, 'International structure, national force and the balance of world power', *Journal of International Affairs*, 2 (1967) pp. 215–32.

15 In *Survival*, November 1967, p. 374.

16 See Z. Brzezinski, 'The American decade', *Foreign Service Journal*, January 1967, and 'The implications of change for U.S. policy', *Department of State Bulletin*, 3 July 1967.

17 See K.F. von Weizsäcker, 'Uber Weltpolitische Prognosen', *Europa-Archiv*, 1966.

18 W. Hanrieder, 'The international system – bipolar or multibloc?' *Journal of Conflict Resolution*, 9: 3 (1965), pp. 299–308.

19 See, E. Haas, *Beyond the Nation-State* (Stanford, Stanford University Press, 1964), pp. 68–76.

20 For comparisons between the balance of terror and the balance of power, see in particular A.L. Burns 'From balance to deterrence'; Snyder, *Deterrence and Defence*; and R. Aron, *Le Grand Débat: initiation à la stratégie atomique* (Paris, Calmann-Lévy, 1963), ch. 6; C.E. Zoppo, 'Nuclear technology, multipolarity and international stability', *World Politics*, July 1966; R. Osgood and R.C. Tucker, *Force, Order and Justice* (Baltimore, 1967), ch. 2.

21 Zoppo, 'Nuclear technology', p. 201. See also the remarks of Erasmus on 'Polycentrism and proliferation' and of C. Gasteyger on 'Nuclear prospects and foreign policy' in *Survey*, January 1966.

22 In *Change and Security in Europe*, Adelphi Papers, 45 and 48 (London, Institute for Strategic Studies, 1968). I owe the formulation in terms of 'mirages' to Miss Joan Pearce, of the Institute for Strategic Studies. For a sophisticated analysis of the problem of guarantees, see Stanley Hoffmann's contribution to A. Buchan, ed., *A World of Nuclear Powers?* (New York, Columbia University Press, 1966), pp. 89–123.

5 *Ethical Issues in Nuclear Deterrence: Four National Debates in Perspective (France, Great Britain, the United States and West Germany)*

1 Aristotle, *Rhetoric*, 1, 2, 1357a–b; quoted by B. Manin, 'Volonté générale ou délibération? Esquisse d'une théorie de la délibération politique', *Le Débat*, January 1985.

2 M. McGwire, 'The dilemmas and delusions of deterrence', ch. 6 in *The Nuclear Crisis Reader*, ed. Gwin Prins (New York, Vintage 1984), p. 93.

3 R. Jervis, *The Illogic of American Nuclear Strategy* (Ithaca, NY, Cornell University Press, 1984), p. 168.

4 See R. Levine, *The Arms Debate* (Cambridge, Mass., Harvard University Press, 1963), in particular chs 2 and 3.

5 In *Nukleare Abschreckung*, ed. Uwe Nerlich and Trutz Rendtorff (Baden-Baden, Nomos, 1989), ch. 16, pp. 537–58.

6 On apocalyptic ethics, see W.B. Gallie, 'Three main fallacies in the discussion

of nuclear weapons', in *Dangers of Deterrence*, ed. N. Blake and K. Pole (London, 1983), pp. 158–66. Günther Anders at one extreme, André Glucksmann at the other, are the best current examples of the apocalyptic attitude. The sceptical philosopher Odo Marquand has aptly characterized this attitude as the 'Romantik der abnormalen Situation' and the 'Versuchung des Krisisstolzes'. See his interview with *Süddeutschezeitung*, 19–20 September 1987.

7 This would seem to be the prescription of A. Wohlstetter, among the strategists, and of H. Lübbe, among the moral philosophers.

8 See my 'Arms control and morality', in *Ethics, Deterrence and National Security*, Foreign Policy Report (Oxford, Pergamon-Brassey, June 1985), pp. 31–49.

9 See his prewar article, 'Totaler Staat, totaler Feind, totaler Krieg' (1937) and his *Nomos der Erde im Volkerrecht des 'Jus Publicum Europaeum'* (Cologne, 1950).

10 See A. Glucksman, in *La Force du Vertige* (Paris, 1983).

11 See my 'Peut-il y avoir une interprétation culturaliste de la stratégie nucléaire?, *Annuaire ARES*, 1981.

12 See his articles 'Der Spring' [1958] and 'Uber Verantwortung heute' [1959], in *Die Atomare Drohung* (Munich, 1986).

13 See my 'On ne badine pas avec la paix', *Revue française de science politique*, December 1973.

14 See Freeman Dyson, *Weapons and Hope* (New York, Harper, 1984).

15 G.H. Keyworth, 'Ballistic missile defense: an option for a world disarmed', *Issues in Science and Technology*, Fall 1984.

16 Robert W. Tucker, *The Nuclear Debate* (New York, Holmes & Meier, 1985).

17 Paul Bracken, *The Command and Control of Nuclear Forces* (New Haven, Yale University Press, 1983), p. 2.

18 *Commentaire*, 32 (spring 1984), and 33 (winter 1985).

19 F. Iklé, 'Nuclear strategy: can there be a happy end?', *Foreign Affairs*, spring 1985, pp. 810–26.

20 In *Nukleare Abschreckung*.

21 L. Wieseltier, 'When deterrence fails', *Foreign Affairs*, spring 1985, pp. 827–48.

22 See their 'Ten-fold reductions in the superpower nuclear arsenals', *Bulletin of the Atomic Scientists*, 41 (August 1985).

23 'Buy like a madman, use like a nut', *Philosophy and Public Policy*, 6:2 (spring 1986).

24 'No first use and no cities; why do people disagree?', in *Nuclear Deterrence: New Risk, New Opportunities*, articles by Catherine McArdie Kelleher, Frank J. Kerr and Georg H. Quester (Oxford, Pergamon-Brassey, 1985), pp. 158–78.

25 'Conflicting conceptions of deterrence', in *Nuclear Rights/Nuclear Wrongs*, ed. E. Frankel Paul et al. (Oxford, 1986), pp. 43–73.

26 'No first use and no cities', pp. 174–5.

27 See my 'Superpower ethics: Western European dilemmas', *Ethics and International Affairs*, I (1987), pp. 23–37.

28 R. Hardin and J. Mearsheimer, 'Introduction', *Ethics*, 95:3 (April 1985), p. 415.

29 Ibid., p. 412.

30 See R. Dahl, *Controlling Nuclear Weapons: Democracy versus Guardianship*

(Syracuse, NY, Syracuse University Press, 1985), and the debate in *Dissent* (spring and summer 1986) on the articles by G. Kateb on 'Nuclear weapons and individual rights'. For a summary of the discussion, see J. Stegenga, 'Nuclearism and democracy', a paper presented at the annual meeting of the North American Society for Social Philosophy, Chicago, September 1987.

31 Octavio Paz, *One Earth, Four or Five Worlds*, trans. Helen Lane (New York, Harcourt Brace Jovanovich, 1985).
32 E. Tügendhat, 'Rationalität und Irrationalität der Friedensbewegung und ihrer Gegner', in *Nachdenken über die Atomkriegsgefahr und warum man sie nicht sieht* (Berlin, 1986).
33 See J. Delbrück, 'Die Auseinandersetzungen in den Vereinigten Staaten und der Bundesrepublik', in *Abschreckung und Entspannung*, Institut für Internationales Recht, 76 (Berlin, Duncker und Humboldt, 1977).
34 Jonathan Schell, *The Fate of the Earth* London, 1982.
35 See for example *Gottes Frieden des Völkern* and *Frieden politisch Fördern: Richtungsimpulse* (1986).
36 See Manfred Hättich, *Weltfrieden durch Friedfertigkeit?* (Munich, 1985).
37 *Dangers of Deterrence* Routledge & Kegan Paul, 1983; *Objections to Nuclear Defense* (Leiden, 1985).
38 A. Kenny, *The Logic of Deterrence* (London, Firethorn Press, 1985).
39 D. Fisher, *Morality and the Bomb* (London, Croom Helm, 1985).
40 'Moral risks and value-balancing', *The Month*, April 1986, pp. 113–19.
41 See my 'La France, l'atome et l'Europe, ou le réalisme de l'irréalisme', *Revue internationale de défense*, February 1984.
42 *Friedensinitiative Philodophie: um Kopf under Kriege*, ed. Christian Schulte (Frankfurt, Luchterhand, 1987).
43 P. Sloterdijk, *Kritik der Zynischen Vernunft* (Frankfurt, Suhrkamp, 1983).
44 Octavio Paz, *One Earth*.

6 *Communist Totalitarianism: The Transatlantic Vagaries of a Concept*

1 C. Friedrich and Z. Brzezinski, *Totalitarian Dictatorship and Autocracy* (New York, Harper, 1956).
2 A. Besançon, *Court traité de soviétologie à l'usage des autorités civiles, militaires et religieuses* (Paris, Hatchette, 1976).
3 E. Voegelin, *The New Science of Politics* (Chicago, University of Chicago Press, 1952).
4 G. Breslauer, *Five Images of the Soviet Future: A Critical Review and Synthesis* (Berkeley, University of California Press, 1978).
5 'Conservateur de quoi?', *Commentaire*, autumn 1978, pp. 357–9; and *Anatomie d'un spectre: l'économie politique du socialisme réel* (Paris, Calmann-Lévy, 1981), pp. 28–38.
6 S. Bialer, *Stalin's Successors* (Cambridge, Cambridge University Press, 1980).
7 See A. Inkeles and R. Bauer, *The Soviet Citizen: Daily Life in a Totalitarian Society* (Cambridge, Mass., Harvard University Press, 1959).
8 K. Deutsch, 'Cracks in the monolith: possibilities and patterns of disintegration

in totalitarian systems', in *Totalitarianism* (Cambridge, Mass., Harvard University Press, 1959).

9 P. Wiles, 'Comment on Tucker's movement-regimes', *American Political Science Review*, 55 (1961), pp. 290–3; P. Hollander, 'Observations on bureaucracy, totalitarianism and the comparative study of communism', *Slavic Review*, 26:2 (June 1967), pp. 302–7; W. Odom, 'A dissenting view on the group approach to Soviet politics', *World Politics*, July 1976, pp. 542–67.

10 In *L'Italie et le fascisme* (1926), p. 221.

11 E. Halévy, *L'Ere des tyrannies* (Paris, Gallimard, 1938).

12 W. Gurian, *Der Bolschewismus* (Freiburg, 1931); E. Voegelin, *Politische Religionen* (Vienna, 1938).

13 M. Curtis, 'Retreat from totalitarianism', in C. Friedrich, M. Curtis and B. Barber, *Totalitarianism in Perspective: Three Views* (New York: Praeger, 1969), pp. 153–80.

14 Z. Brzezinski, 'Totalitarianism and rationality', *American Political Science Review*, 50 (1956), pp. 751–63.

15 R. Löwenthal, 'Totalitäire und demokratishe Revolution' [1960], reprinted in B. Seidel and S. Jenkner, *Wege der Totalitarismus-Forschung* (Darmstadt, 1968), pp. 359–82.

16 R. Tucker, 'The dictator and totalitarianism', *World Politics*, 17 (1965), pp. 555–84.

17 R. Tucker, 'Does Big Brother really exist?', in *1984 Revisited: Totalitarianism in Our Century*, ed. Irving Howe, (New York, Harper, 1983), ch. 6, pp. 89–112.

18 P. Wiles, 'Comment', pp. 290–3; J. Azrael, 'Varieties of de-stalinization', in *Change in Communist Systems*, ed. Chalmers Johnson (Stanford, Stanford University Press, 1970), pp. 135–52.

19 A. Meyer, *The Soviet Political System* (New York, 1965).

20 G. Skilling, 'Soviet and communist politics; a comparative approach', *Journal of Politics*, 22:2 (May 1960), pp. 300–13.

21 J. Hough, 'The Soviet system: petrification or pluralism?, in *Dilemmas of Soviet Politics*, ed. Z. Brzezinski (1969).

22 F. Castles, 'Interest articulation: a totalitarian paradox', *Survey*, autumn 1969, pp. 116–33.

23 Odom, 'A dissenting view', pp. 542–67.

24 Susan G. Solomon, ed., *Pluralism in the Soviet Union: Essays in Honour of Gordon Skilling* (London, Macmillan, 1983).

25 J. Hough, 'Pluralism, corporatism and the Soviet Union', ibid., p. 58.

26 W. Taubman, 'The change to change in communist systems: modernization post-modernization, and Soviet politics', in *Soviet Politics and Society in the 1970s*, ed. H. Morton and N. Tokes (New York, Free Press, 1974).

27 J. Kirkpatrick, *Dictatorship and Double Standards* (Washington, DC, American Enterprise Institute, 1982).

28 Michael Walzer, 'Failed totalitarianism', in *1984 Revisited*, ed. Howe, ch. 7, pp. 103–21.

29 See the contributions of A. Smolar, J.-L. Domenach and J. Rupnik to

Notes

Totalitarismes, ed. G. Hermet, P. Hassner and J. Rupnik (Paris, Economica, 1984).
30 A. Zinoviev, *Homo sovieticus* (Paris, Julliard, 1983).
31 M. Djilas, 'The disintegration of communist totalitarianism', in *1984 Revisited*, ed. Howe, ch. 9, pp. 136–48.
32 W. Odom, 'Choice and change in Soviet politics', *Problems of Communism*, May–June 1983, pp. 3–22.
33 M. Friedberg, 'Cultural and intellectual life', in Robert S. Byrnes (ed.), *After Brezhnev: Sources of Soviet Conduct in the* 1980s (Bloomington, Indiana University Press, 1983).
34 K. Papaïoannou, *L'Idéologie froide* (Paris, Pauvert, 1967).
35 L. Kolakowski, 'Totalitarianism and the lie', in Howe, ed., *1984 Revisited*.
36 Claude Lefort, *L'Invention démocratique: les limites de la domination totalitaire* (Paris, Fayard, 1981).

7 An Elusive but Essential Notion

1 See chapter 6 above.
2 Ch. 2 in *Totalitarismes*, ed. Guy Hermet, Pierre Hassner and J. Rupnik (Paris, Economica, 1984).
3 M. Hybler, 'Le système Gorbatchev', *L'Autre Europe*, 15–16, (1988).

8 Nationalism and International Relations

1 E.H. Carr, *Nationalism and After* (London, Macmillan, 1945), pp. 51–2.
2 E. Haas, 'International integration: the European and the universal process', in *International Stability*, ed. D. Hekhuis, J. McClintock and A.L. Burns (New York, Wiley, 1964), p. 229. The article was originally published in 1961.
3 Compare the following two texts.

To counter the national ideal, the international ideal was born. And we need to realize, throughout the latter years of the century there was hardly one leading thinker who did not believe it obvious that the Internationale was going to rule the world, that we had gone from provinces to kingdoms, and we would go from nations to the Internationale. Victor Hugo thought so, Jaurès thought so. And what do we see today? What we see, on a map or globe where once there were so few nations, we see nothing but emergent nations. It is not Marx, with the ideas of the Internationale, who has triumphed today, it is Nietzsche, who said 'The twentieth century will be the century of national wars'. And the twentieth century has had just such wars. And when we turn to Africa, a myriad of nations is there. When we turn to Asia, where the idea of nations was probably never even conceived of, it is now the land of the Indian nation and the Chinese nation. And when we think of the last adherent of what was the Internationale, that is, Stalin, we remember that, watching the falling snow that once buried the

Teutonic knights and the Grande Armée, the Georgian Stalin said, 'I made Russia'. The world in which we live is a world of nations, and all political thinking that does not first recognize the world for what it is, is in vain.

> (André Malraux, 'Une présence humaine et généreuse',
> *Nouvelle frontière*, 5 [January 1964], pp. 2–3)

The time approaches when we must fight to achieve world domination, and this fight will be conducted in the name of *philosophical principles*. Now the forces are gathering, we are training ourselves in the great principle of the kinship of race and blood. 'Nationality' is a far more subtle concept than that of race: it is fundamentally a scientific discovery that we presently incorporate into our feelings; wars have the function of teaching us these ideas, and they will acquit themselves of this task. Then will come social wars which will incorporate other concepts. Until finally the concepts do not serve merely as pretexts or names, etc., for national movements and *the most powerful concept* imposes itself of pure necessity . . . I am excluding all those national wars, those new 'Empires' and everything that clutters the foreground. What matters to me – for it is what I see slowly and almost hesitantly preparing itself – is a united Europe. For all the mighty and profound minds of the century, the task to which they bent their minds was to make ready this new synthesis and anticipate, on a trial basis, the 'European' of the future. Only in the hours of weakness or when they grow old do they fall back into the narrow perspectives of their 'homelands' – and then they bcame patriots . . . But what stirs in such minds as these, what is expressed as the need for a new unity, is accompanied by a great economic event that explains it: the small European states, by which I mean all our present states and Empires, will become economically untenable, given the sovereign requirements of large-scale international relations and the large-scale commerce which demand the supreme extension of universal exchanges, world trade. (Money alone will sooner or later force Europe to aggregate in a single mass.) But if it wants to be in good condition to enter the first for world domination, – it is obvious against whom it will be directed — Europe will doubtless need to reach an 'accomodation' with England.

> (F. Nietzsche, *The Will to Power*, vol. 2, book 4, ch. 2: 'The twentieth
> century', fragments 70 and 71, pp. 244–5, in the French translation
> by G. Bianquis (Paris, Gallimard).

4 'The planned direction of the national economy is one of the fundamental, essential and inalienable attributes of the sovereignty of the socialist state . . . The sovereignty of the socialist state implies that the latter possesses wholly and in practice the means of translating these attributions into action by retaining control of all the levers of power controlling economic and social life. Transferring these levers of power to the domain of supranational bodies, or outside the state, would make sovereignty an idea devoid of content . . . State planning is unique and indivisible, there can be no question of taking parts or sections away and transferring them outside the state.' Extract from

the declaration of the Central Committee of the POR, April 1964. Quoted, in English translation, from 'L'Economie roumaine', *La Documentation française*, 2 January 1965, no. 315, annex, pp. 46–7.

5 Hence the contradiction which we sometimes find lucidly analysed, sometimes employed unconsciously by the subtlest and most profound advocates of European nationalism. At one moment all but one of the Europeans are being reproached for their submissiveness and torpor, at the next, it is suggested that one represents all the rest, so that in the end its decisions and beliefs are attributed to Europeans who repudiate them, or to Europe as a whole, whose political non-existence and internal contradictions have only just been exposed. Cf. Stanley Hoffmann, 'Discord in community', in F. Wilcox and H.F. Haviland, *The Atlantic Community* (New York, Praeger, 1963), pp. 13, 28; and 'Silence de l'Europe', *Esprit*, November–December 1964. The only way of avoiding the contradiction would be to distinguish between Europe and the Europeans, as Giraudoux or Bernanos distinguish between France and the French. But would not such a distinction, already debatable in the case of an existing nation, be based on a purely arbitrary decision in the case of a political entity whose existence, orientation and purpose is precisely the subject under discussion?

6 The following two comments are relevant: one by A. Wolfers, to the effect that the insularity of the Anglo-Saxon powers, in leaving them a greater freedom of choice, has helped them adopt a philosophy of foreign policy that is more idealistic or more moral as compared with the continentals, coping with power struggles and the demands of *raison d'état*; the other, by E.H. Carr, to the effect that the use of economic rather than military power is the sign not of morality but of a superior degree of power. There could not be a greater contrast in beliefs and style than between the Anglo-Saxon leader of a coalition and the leader of an average continental power.

7 S. Schram, *Mao Tse-tung* (Paris, Armand Colin, 1964).

8 Hoffmann, 'Discord in community', p. 19.

9 Philip Windsor in a book review published in *Survival*, January–February 1965, p. 46. See also, for the distinction between patriotic and ideological nationalism, and the parallels between Russian and American nationalism, John Lukács, *A History of the Cold War* (New York, Anchor Books, Doubleday, 1962), p. 304. The author points out the combined sense of universalism and particularity that from the outset have characterized the two national views, explaining the ambiguous nature of both forms of nationalism. To be a citizen of the United States or the Soviet Union means subscribing to a political principle as well as belonging to a nationality. Hence the implied global significance, the absence of fixed limits imposed by history or territory, which may lead to idealism, imperialism or a mixture of the two.

10 Kostas Papaïoannou, 'Marx et l'état moderne', *Le Contrat social*, July 1960, p. 218.

11 See J.-L. Talmon, *Political Messianism: The Romantic Phase* (London, Secker & Warburg, 1961), part V, '1848, the trial and the debacle', in particular section 4, 'The failure of the international revolution', pp. 472–87, and the conclusion, p. 513. Also, M. Collinet, *La Tragédie du marxisme* (Paris,

Calmann-Lévy, 1948), part III, 'La nation', in particular section 3, 'L'avènement des nationalismes', pp. 185–95.

12 Cf. Malraux, *Nouvelle frontière*, p. 2: 'General de Gaulle said to me one day that he wondered whether Napoleon's tragedy had not been that he provoked nationhood outside France, and whether the greatest captain of modern times had been defeated not in the military sphere but on the day when, instead of sending a national army to fight royalist forces, he found himself facing nations called Spain, Austria, Prussia and Russia.'

13 This brief history is based on the account given, in the context of a comparison of international systems, by R. Rosecrance, *Action and Reaction in World Politics: International Systems in Perspective* (Boston, Little, Brown, 1963).

14 Cf. Franz Borkenau quoted in Carr, *Nationalism and After*, pp. 19–20; also Carr's own analysis, ibid.; R. Aron, *Les Guerres en chaîne* (Paris, Gallimard, 1951), ch. 15, 'Les socialismes nationaux', pp. 334–56; Lukács, *History of the Cold War*, pp. 326–9; J. Kautsky, *Political Change in Underdeveloped Countries: Nationalism and Communism* (New York, John Wiley, 1962), pp. 78–89.

15 Hannah Arendt, *The Origins of Totalitarianism*, 2nd edn (London, Allen & Unwin, 1961), pp. 222–67.

16 R. Pipes, 'The forces of nationalism', *Problems of Communism*, January–February 1964, pp. 1–7.

17 'The dynamo of nations', *The Economist*, 11 July 1964, p. 130.

18 In *Communism and Revolution*, ed. C.E. Black and T. Thornton (Princeton, NJ, Princeton University Press, 1964). See the analysis by S. Schram in 'D'une doctrine unitaire à une réalité différenciée: à propos de l'évolution du communisme mondial', *Revue française de science politique*, 15:1 (February 1965), p. 133.

19 See J.F. Brown, 'A patchwork quilt in Eastern Europe', in *Talking to Eastern Europe*, ed. G.R. Urban (London, Eyre & Spottiswoode, 1964), pp. 97–8.

20 R. Aron, *Paix et guerre entre les nations* (Paris, Calmann-Lévy, 1962), p. 398.

21 Rupert Emerson, *From Empire to Nation: The Rise to Self-assertion of Asian and African Peoples* (Boston, Beacon Press, 1962), pp. 378–97.

22 G. Barraclough, 'Problems of nationality', *New Statesman and Nation*, 15 May 1964, p. 770.

23 Malraux, *Nouvelle frontière*, p. 4.

24 Ibid.

25 Ibid.

26 Anouar Abdel-Malek, *Egypte, société militaire* (Paris, Seuil, 1962), p. 9.

27 H. Morgenthau, *Politics among Nations* (New York, A. Knopf, 1952), p. 268.

28 Kautsky, *Political Change*.

29 Cf. the exposition by Renouvin, in P. Renouvin and J.-B. Duroselle, *Introduction a l'histoire des relations internationales* (Paris, A. Colin, 1964), pp. 189–204.

30 John Bowle, *World Order or Catastrophe?* (London, Ampersand, 1963), ch. 2. 'The nationalist idea', pp. 43–141.

31 Lewis Namier, *Avenues of History* (London, Hamish Hamilton, 1952), p. 25.

32 B. Akzin, *State and Nation* (London, Hutchinson, 1964), p. 199.

33 C.M. Woodhouse, *The New Concert of Nations* (London, Bodley Head, 1964), p. 71.
34 *Le Figaro*, 10 March 1964.
35 Rosecrance, *Action and Reaction*, p. 194.
36 Walter Sulzbach, 'Fürstentum und Nationalstaat', *Zeitschrift für die Gesamte Staatswissenschaft*, August 1963, pp. 405–39.
37 G. Liska, *Nations in Alliance: The Limits of Interdependence* (Baltimore, The Johns Hopkins Press, 1962).
38 See A. Wolfers, *Discord and Collaboration* (Baltimore, The Johns Hopkins Press, 1962).
39 See the work of Haas and Lindberg in the United States, Kitzinger in Great Britain, G. Zellentin in Germany, and A. Marchal in France.
40 See E. Haas, *Beyond the Nation State: Functionalism and International Organization* (Stanford, Stanford University Press, 1964), p. 47 and *passim*; and the discussion among Haas, 'Technocracy, pluralism and the New Europe', in *A New Europe*, ed. S. Grauhard (Boston, Houghton Mifflin, 1964), p. 674; Hoffmann, 'Discord in community', *passim*, and 'European process at Atlantic cross purposes', *Journal of Common Market Studies*, 3:2, p. 92; and L. Lindberg, 'Decision making and integration in the European Community', *International Organization*, 19:1 (1965), pp. 56–80.
41 This article was based on research on the development of the international system undertaken in 1963, courtesy of the Rockefeller Foundation.

9 Cultural Identity and Civil Society: The New Nationalist Challenge

1 R. Dahrendorf, *Reflections on the Revolution in Europe* (London, Chatto & Windus, 1990), pp. 92–3.
2 C.P. Snow, *The Two Cultures and the Scientific Revolution* (Cambridge, Cambridge University Press, 1962).
3 R.W. Leonhardt, 'Nur die Region ist eine Heimat', *Die Zeit*, 12 October 1990.
4 M. Kundera, 'Un Occident, Kidnappé – ou la stratégie de l'Europe centrale', *Le Débat*, November 1983, pp. 3–22. Also published as 'The tragedy of Central Europe', *New York Review of Books*, 26 April 1984.
5 E. Todd, *The Explanation of Ideology: Family, Structures and Social Systems* (Oxford, Blackwell, 1985), p. 230.
6 'Huddled masses, on the move', *The Economist*, 13 October 1990, pp. 25–6.
7 J. Plamenatz, 'Two types of nationalism', in *Nationalism: the Nature and Evolution of an Idea*, ed. S. Kamenka (London, Arnold, 1976).
8 I. Bibó, *Misère des petits Etats d'Europe de l'Est*, (Paris, L'Harmattan, 1986), p. 462 (translated from the Hungarian).
9 See K. Deutsch et al., *Political Community in the North Atlantic Area* (Princeton, NJ, Princeton University Press, 1957), *passim*.
10 J. Habermas, 'Der D.M. Nationalismus', *Die Zeit*, 30 March 1990.

Notes

10 Beyond Nationalism and Internationalism: Monstrosity and Hope

1 *The Analysis of International Relations* (Englewood Cliffs, NJ, Prentice Hall, 1988).
2 See *Ramsès 1993* (Paris, Dunod, 1992).
3 J.-C. Rufin, *L'Empire et les nouveaux barbares* (Paris, Lattès, 1991).

11 Towards a Pluralist Universalism?

1 A reference to the conference 'Tribalisme et nomadisme' held in Orléans, 3–4 September 1992, organized by the Délégation au développement et aux formations (DDF) of the Ministère de la culture et de la francophonie.
2 L. Dumont, *Homo Aequalis*, vols 1 and 2 (Paris, Gallimard, 1985 and 1991).
3 See J. Roman, Preface to Ernest Renan, *Qu'est-ce qu'une nation?* (Paris, Presse Pocket, 1992).
4 E. Weil, *Philosophie politique* (Paris, Vrin, 1984).
5 See H. Arendt, *The Human Condition* (Chicago, University of Chicago Press, 1958).
6 See J. Habermas, *The Theory of Communicative Action*, vols 1 and 2, trans. Thomas McCarthy (Boston, Beacon Press, 1984 and 1987).
7 M. Walzer, 'Les deux universalismes', *Esprit*, December 1992.
8 Amos, 4–7, quoted ibid.
9 P. Ricœur, *Soi-même comme un autre* (Paris, Seuil, 1990).
10 A. Bloom, *The Closing of the American Mind* (New York, Simon & Schuster, 1987).
11 In *La Force du préjugé* (Paris, Gallimard, col. 'Tel', 1990).
12 C. Lévi-Strauss, *Race et histoire* (Paris, 10–18, 1967).
13 See John Rawls, *A Theory of Justice* (Cambridge, Mass., Harvard University Press, 1971); Ronald Dworkin, *Taking Rights Seriously* (Cambridge, Mass., Harvard University Press, 1977); and Robert Nozick, *Anarchy, State and Utopia* (New York, Basic Books, 1974).
14 See Michael Sandel, *Liberalism and the Limits of Justice* (Cambridge, Cambridge University Press, 1982); Charles Taylor, *Sources of the Self* (Cambridge, Mass., Harvard University Press, 1989), *The Malaise of Modernity* (Concord, Ontario, Anansi, 1991), *Multiculturalism* (Princeton, Conn., Princeton University Press); and Alasdair McIntyre *After Virtue* (Notre Dame, Ind., University of Notre Dame Press, 1984).
15 E. Gellner, *Nations and Nationalism* (Oxford, Blackwell, 1983).
16 J.-M. Ferry, *Les Puissances de l'expérience* (Paris, Le Cerf, 1991).

12 War and Peace in the Twentieth Century

1 F. Fukuyama, 'The end of history', *The National Interest*, summer 1989; and *The End of History and the Last Man* (New York, Avon Books, 1993).
2 Samuel Huntington, 'The clash of civilizations', *Foreign Affairs*, 72:3 (summer

1993). For this writer, the nineteenth century represents the war of nations and the twentieth the war of ideologies, while the twenty-first will be the war of civilizations. He broadly sketches a sort of universal history in the manner of Spengler or Toynbee, with the emphasis on problems of religious allegiance. Over and above his sometimes debatable theories, his article and the reactions it has aroused raise the interesting question, whether it is civilizations that are the agents of international politics or the states which capitalize on them.

3 See above, p. 217.
4 See above, p. 17.
5 Kenneth Waltz, *Man, the State and War: A Theoretical Analysis* (New York, Columbia University Press, 1959). See above, p. 16.

Index

Index

Index

Index